High School Achievement

HIGH SCHOOL ACHIEVEMENT

Public, Catholic, and Private Schools Compared

JAMES S. COLEMAN
THOMAS HOFFER
SALLY KILGORE

Basic Books, Inc., Publishers   *New York*

The information in this report results from research sponsored by the National Center for Education Statistics, U.S. Department of Education, Contract No. OE–300–78–0208. Contractors undertaking such projects are encouraged to express freely their professional judgment. This report, therefore, does not necessarily represent positions on policy of the Government, and no official endorsement should be inferred.

Library of Congress Cataloging in Publication Data

Coleman, James Samuel, 1926–
   High school achievement.

   References: p. 278
   Includes index.
   1. High school students—United States—Statistics.
2. Academic achievement. I. Hoffer, Thomas. II. Kilgore,
Sally. III. Title.
LA222.C54   373.18'0973   81–68411
ISBN 0–465–02956–6   AACR2

CONTENTS

v

Contents

LIST OF FIGURES

LIST OF TABLES

List of Tables

List of Tables

List of Tables

List of Tables

PREFACE

THE data and analyses presented in this book are from the first (1980) wave of the National Center for Education Statistics (NCES) study, High School and Beyond, a longitudinal survey of U.S. high school seniors and sophomores. This survey was conducted for NCES by the National Opinion Research Center (NORC) at the University of Chicago.

The report upon which this book is based is one of a set of four that constitutes baseline descriptions and initial analyses of a very rich data set. The study was designed to be relevant both to many policy issues and to many fundamental questions concerning youth development and educational institutions. It is intended to be analyzed by a wide range of users, from those with immediate policy concerns to those with interests in more fundamental or long-range questions.

There are 1,015 high schools in the sample, which is described in greater detail in chapter 1. Several special strata were included in the sample with probabilities higher than their occurrence in the population, to allow for special study of certain types of schools or students. These included:

- Hispanic strata, with probabilities of selection to ensure sufficient numbers of Cuban, Puerto Rican, and Mexican students for separate analysis
- A stratum of Catholic schools with high proportions of black students
- A stratum of non-Catholic private schools, oversampled to ensure enough schools for analysis
- A stratum of public alternative schools
- A stratum of private schools with high-achieving students

For analyses that do not separate out these strata, the strata are downweighted to their proper population weights, so that the weighted sample is representative of high school seniors and high school sophomores in the United States and in each of the nine census regions (subject to the points mentioned previously, substitution of schools, and completion rates).

Information from several sources was obtained in the survey. Students completed questionnaires regarding their school experiences and coursework, the post-high school plans, and general family background. They also completed a battery of tests covering general, as well as specific, areas of achievement. School officials completed questionnaires covering items of information about the schools. Finally, teachers completed checklists concerning students in the sample whom they had had in class in order to provide information beyond the students' own reports about themselves.

As succeeding waves of data on a subsample of these students become available (at approximately two-year intervals), the richness of the data set, and the scope of questions that can be studied by the use of it, will expand. The data are available at a nominal fee from the National Center for Education Statistics. In addition, use of the data in conjunction with NCES's study of the cohort of 1972 seniors (available from NCES), for which data at five time points are now available, will enrich the set of questions that can be studied.

The main body of this book (chapters 1 through 6 and appendix) is based on a draft report, *Public and Private Schools*, released by NCES on April 7, 1981. Extensive controversy following the report's release led to further analyses reported here (mostly in the addendum) and were incorporated as well in the final report delivered to NCES on December 3, 1981. The book contains in addition a prologue and epilogue, which locate this research within a larger body of research on high schools and in which some of its implications for the organization of American high schools are discussed.

ACKNOWLEDGMENTS

THE initial design of High School and Beyond was created by the Longitudinal Studies Branch of NCES. Edith Huddleston, NCES project officer for High School and Beyond, and William Fetters, mathematical statistician, have guided this project since its inception and have been responsible for many aspects of the research design. The design of High School and Beyond by NCES and its modifications by NORC were greatly aided by consultations with many groups interested in American education and by continuing guidance from the project's National Planning Committee.

A study of this scope and magnitude would not have been possible without the active cooperation of many persons at various levels of educational administration: Chief state school officers, Catholic archdioceses and other private school organizations, principals and teachers in the schools, and of course, the students and their parents. The expertise, support, and persuasiveness of numerous study coordinators at participating schools was especially valuable to the successful conduct of the study.

We owe a great debt to all those people on the field and project staffs of High School and Beyond whose efforts brought into being the data that will make possible further study of issues involving young people and their schools, data on which the present report is based.

We are grateful to Martin Kessler for his initiative in undertaking to publish this book at a time when the report on which it was based was highly controversial. And finally, to those reviewers and critics whose comments (in most cases made without rancor) forced us to pursue some of these issues more intensively than we originally had, we owe a debt of gratitude. We would like to mention especially panels convened by the Committee on National Statistics of the National Research Council and by the National Institute of Education; and reviewers in the November 1981 issue of *Harvard Educational Review* and the April 1982 issue of *Sociology of Education*.

Acknowledgments

Our colleagues at NORC and the University of Chicago not only provided valuable criticisms and suggestions, but also assisted in many of the dreary, but essential, tasks associated with putting a report of this nature together. In particular, we would like to thank Peter Mueser who read and commented on the entire report and Jim Wolf who cheerfully provided assistance in preparing the report. Of the support services at NORC that, by efforts beyond the call of duty, made possible the completion of this report at this time two deserve special mention: Data Processing and Word Processing, both of which have our deep gratitude.

PROLOGUE

NOT so many years ago, educators measured the "quality" of a school by the resources which went into the school, not by the quality of the students who came out of it. The most ambitious attempt to do this systematically was that of Paul Mort (1946), who established a set of criteria of a good school, most of which were indicated by the resources that could be provided by outlays from the board of education. They included such things as increased school library facilities, smaller pupil-teacher ratios, and nonteaching professional support staffs.

In the 1960s, with the initiation of large-scale surveys of students in national samples of schools (especially in Project Talent and the Equal Educational Opportunity Survey), attention began to shift from resource inputs to the outcomes of education, and in particular to achievement in basic verbal and mathematical skills. Although these cognitive skills constitute only one type of educational outcome, it is one on which there is little disagreement and one which is relevant to both elementary and secondary education. Although these basic cognitive skills are more nearly the responsibility of elementary schools, it is regarded as the high school's responsibility to carry students forward from the level reached in elementary school.

This focus on the outcome of schooling received its greatest impetus from the initiation, as part of the War on Poverty in the middle 1960s, of federally financed educational programs which had as explicit goals[1] the growth of basic cognitive skills. What was obvious for these programs— that the character of the program should depend on its measured effectiveness—gradually became evident for schooling generally. Thus the idea that the effects of the various components of schooling should be systematically assessed came into being.

But this shift of attention to the outcomes of education did not bring

[1] Head Start was the largest of these programs, but a considerable amount of funding was also provided to experimental programs such as Follow Though and Experimental Schools.

with it an avalanche of new information about the ways in which schools bring about achievement in cognitive skills. Instead, the most striking result was that variations in schools made considerably less difference in a child's achievement than did variations in that child's family background.[2] An almost equally significant result was that in general, those resources that had been regarded as measures of a school's quality showed little or no detectable relation to achievement, thus raising doubts about the assumptions that had been held concerning a school's quality.[3]

These results have discouraged those who view schooling as a powerful equalizer of opportunity. They even cast doubt on the belief that schools are effective institutions of learning. For while the studies have not shown that schooling per se has little effect, neither have they shown positive evidence of strong effects. Some might attribute these results to a methodological problem. Since schooling is universal in the United States (and in developed countries in general), there is no adequate comparison group available to contrast with those who are in school.[4] But others, with equal justification, might reply that the lack of evidence of strong effects is due to the real absence of strong effects—that is, schooling does not make a difference.

More optimistic results have been noted in several recent studies. Heyns (1977) compares learning during the school year to that over the summer and finds that the effects of schooling appear strong; Murnane (1975), examining only disadvantaged children, also finds greater learning while school is in session than while school is out. The IEA studies (See Coleman, 1975) show substantial intercountry differences in achievement, suggesting that intercountry variations in schools, possibly greater than the variations within a country, lead to sharply different levels of achievement.

Yet despite this evidence that schools *do* make a difference, not much is known about what characteristics of schools affect achievement. Far more is known about those characterstics of schools that make little or no differ-

[2] Various studies indicate that variation in school characteristics can account for only 10 to 25 percent of the variance in student achievement. Even this fraction of the variance is in part accounted for by differences in average family backgrounds in different schools. In contrast, measured differences in family background among students ordinarily account for 20 percent or more of the total variance; this constitutes something like a lower bound to the total effect of all measured and unmeasured background characteristics. The total between-family variance is usually found to be greater than .5. (See studies reported in Taubman, 1977.)

[3] One of the latest of these is Eric A. Hanushek's "Throwing Money at Schools" (1981). Hanushek examines the results of 130 studies and finds that while some characteristics of a school influence achievement, the general level of resources, as measured by per pupil expenditure, shows no consistent relation to achievement.

[4] Even early dropouts from school cannot be used for this purpose, because being self-selected, they are not a group comparable to those still in school.

ence.[5] The task of gaining some idea of factors affecting achievement and of the effects of their variations on American education is not a simple one; but large-scale surveys of students involving national samples of schools provide one approach to this task. Their principal virtue is coverage of a large enough set of schools to preclude finding fortuitous differences between schools having high and low achievement, and attributing causal significance to these fortuitous differences.[6] Their principal deficiency is superficiality of measurement, leading either to measurement errors or to failure to measure the right characteristics of schools. Despite the latter difficulty, large-scale surveys constitute one of the most important means for discovering what it is about schools that makes them more or less effective in accomplishing their goals.

Surveys of this sort are expensive and are undertaken irregularly and infrequently. Project Talent in the early 1960s was the earliest; the Equal Educational Opportunity Survey (1966) was another, the National Longitudinal Survey of High School Seniors of 1972 was another; and the current survey of 1980 sophomores and seniors, High School and Beyond, is another. National Assessment of Educational Progress is a continuing survey with some of this potential, but it has been used only in descriptive ways and at the level of students rather than schools.[7]

A particularly valuable aspect of High School and Beyond for the study of school differences and their impact on achievement is the inclusion of more than 120 high schools from the private sector. The value of their inclusion is that private high schools tend to differ from schools in the public sector in a number of ways. They operate in a different relation to parents, who have spent money to enroll their child in the school and thus

---

[5] There is also some evidence that internal variations in the treatment that different children in the same school get (such as having different teachers) also make a difference. See Hanushek, 1971.

[6] For example, a study like that of Rutter, et al. (Rutter, 1979) attempts to find differences between schools that affect achievement, using a set of twelve schools to do so. The Rutter study is a good one within this genre. Yet while such a study can gather rich data on this small set of schools, the variations among schools are so numerous that it is not possible to offer more than suggestions about the factors that may be responsible for achievement differences among the schools.

[7] The initiation of National Assessment exemplifies well one of the difficulties that has plagued the study of factors affecting achievement in schools. When National Assessment was begun, there was sufficient fear that this was the first step toward a national curriculum, that the survey was designed in ways that would not facilitate interschool comparisons and the study of school effects. As a consequence, National Assessment, while valuable for charting changes in achievement over the years, has not been very useful in the study of sources of these changes or of achievement differences at a point in time.

More generally, there is a widespread tendency in educational evaluation to understate any differences in effectiveness among schools or among different educational programs. The analysis of the Follow Through planned variations probably exemplifies this best. (Some of these analyses are presented in Rivlin and Timpane, 1975; see also Elmore, 1976.)

can be expected to be more involved with the school and to reinforce the school's demands. They operate in a different relation to their students, who know the school is not required to keep them. They generally impose greater academic demands and maintain stronger standards of discipline. They are usually smaller, and most of them operate on less money per pupil than does the average public school, though some have expenditures considerably higher than public schools.

These and other differences make the inclusion of private schools in a national survey especially useful for the study of factors affecting academic achievement. It makes it possible to raise the question of whether the broad differences between public and private schools do affect achievement—though self-selection into the private sector increases the difficulty of answering the question. Comparing the outcomes in private and public sectors will suggest differences to look for among schools, whether in the public sector or the private sector, in the search for factors affecting achievement.

There is a second area of knowledge about education quite apart from that affecting school achievement which private-public comparisons can illuminate. This has to do with different modes of organizing education. Setting aside for a moment the fact that some schools are supported by the state and some by parents, high schools in America represent several different patterns of organization. One, the most common, is organization around a geographic area, with the school district a locality, and attendance at a particular school within the district determined by residence. Another is specialization around a particular kind of training, for example technical high schools, vocational schools, and high schools of performing arts. Some schools are organized around certain interests, such as health sciences or languages. Still another mode is organization not by residential area, but by religious identity, such as Catholic schools, Lutheran schools, Jewish schools, and the recently growing number of conservative Christian schools. Organization around a particular philosophy of education, as exemplified by alternative schools, traditional preparatory schools, or military academies is yet one more type. There are overlaps between some of these categories, since schools of a given religious group often adhere to a distinctive educational philosophy (for example, Catholic schools and Friends schools). Nevertheless, the distinction remains.

From the beginning of American public education, it has been assumed that the appropriate mode of organization in a democracy is around a residential community. But there have recently arisen a number of challenges to this assumption. The most familiar is assignment according to race rather than residence, in order to accomplish more racial integration.

Another which is sometimes used in large cities (ordinarily subject to some kind of racial criterion) is open choice among schools within the district, sometimes subject to an admissions examination. Since the major portion of educational expenditures come from state rather than local taxes, it has been increasingly suggested that there be open choice of a school by parents and students, regardless of the school district in which the student lives. The use of vouchers or entitlements which allow a parent to choose among schools, whether public or private, has been proposed in several states in recent years.

While this book cannot provide information about the differential functioning of schools organized under all these varying principles, it can provide some information on the different modes of organization reflected in the public-private dichotomy, particularly the two principles of organization around residence (the principal mode in the public sector) and organization around a religious identity (the principal mode in the private sector). The importance of such a comparison lies precisely in the questions increasingly raised about the appropriateness and even the continued viability of assignment to school by place of residence. Indeed, it should be recalled that this ideal of the common school based on a residential community, as propounded by Horace Mann and others, arose not only at a time when most people resided in small, well-defined communities, but also at a time when the "school" in question was elementary school, not high school. That principle, in early days, was not regarded as incompatible with specialized public high schools among which parents and students could choose.

This book, comparing public and private schools, is based on a report from High School and Beyond, a longitudinal study of sophomores and seniors in American high schools. The survey, designed by the National Center for Education Statistics and carried out by the National Opinion Research Center was designed for a variety of research purposes, and the comparison of public and private schools was not among the principal purposes. For this reason, the sample design and the survey instruments are not optimum for this purpose. Nevertheless, the survey provides the most complete information available to date for the comparison of public and private schools.

This book includes descriptions of the size distribution and geographic distribution of public and private schools (in chapter 2), descriptions of the basic resources found in public and private schools (in chapter 4), and descriptions of the ways the schools function (in chapter 5). It compares the student composition of public and private schools and attempts to answer the question of the overall impact of the private sector on segregation by race and ethnicity, by income, and by religion (in chapter 3). Finally, in chapter 6, it examines achievement in public and private schools and attempts to answer the question of whether attendance in the private sector has an impact on a child's achievement. As part of this examination, it looks also at differences among schools within the public sector which parallel the public-private differences, in order to examine the effect of these differences in school functioning on achievement (in chapter 6, pages 159 to 175).

The genre of research in which this book falls is social policy research, that is, research directed toward issues of public policy. Consequently, organization of this book is around those research questions that can inform policy toward private education. As with social policy research generally, however, the greater long-range contribution is likely to be on the more general question of what characteristics of schools affect achievement, and the question of what is the appropriate way of organizing education. The epilogue discusses some of these more general implications of the results for secondary education.

High School Achievement

1

Introduction

AMERICAN elementary and secondary education has been generally education in public schools, supported by taxes and governed by local school boards. There have recently been changes in the structure of support and control, with state and federal governments playing increasingly important roles in both respects. But the public-school character of elementary and secondary education has remained largely unchanged. Currently and for many years, the percentage of American children in private schools has been about 10 percent.

However, the role of private schools in American education has emerged as an important policy question in recent years. Although any answer to this question depends in part on values, it also depends on facts—facts that address such questions as: How well do public and private schools work for children? Do they work better for some types of children than they do for others? Are private schools divisive, and, if so, in what ways? Are private schools more efficiently managed than public schools, and, if so, why?

Recent policy discussions concerning private schools in the United States have included proposals that would increase their role in American education and proposals that would decrease their role. On the increase side, there have been proposals for tuition tax credits for private schools (a bill to provide such credits was narrowly defeated in Congress). At the state level, proposals for educational vouchers have been discussed, and in

California a recent attempt was made to get such a proposal on the ballot for referendum. On the decrease side, the Internal Revenue Service proposed in 1979 that a racial composition requirement, more restrictive than that imposed on most public schools, be a criterion for maintaining tax-exempt status. This was one of a series of attempted policy interventions to constrain the use of private schools by whites seeking to escape a mandatory integration program in the public schools.

These conflicting policy efforts are all based on certain assumptions about the role of private and public schools in the United States. Examining these assumptions, and showing the falsity of those that are not correct, will not in itself resolve the policy questions concerning the roles of public and private education in America. Those policy questions include certain value premises as well, such as the relative roles of the state and the family in controlling a child's education. Examining them will, however, strengthen the factual base on which the policy conflicts take place. To aid in doing this is the aim of this report.

Policy Premises and the Research Agenda

It is useful to begin the process by reviewing some of the most widely held premises underlying policy proposals that would affect the role of private education in the United States. It is these premises, not the policy proposals, for which research such as this provides information.

Premises underlying policies that would increase the role of private schools:

1. Private schools produce better cognitive outcomes than do public schools with comparable students.
2. Private schools provide better character and personality development than do public schools.
3. Private schools provide a safer, more disciplined, and more ordered environment than do public schools.[1]
4. Private schools are more successful in creating an interest in learning than are public schools.
5. Private schools encourage interest in higher education and lead more of their students to attend college than do public schools with comparable students.

[1] Some authors go so far as to argue that private schools reduce crime through reducing either in-school crime (a significant portion of teenage crime) or out-of-school crime (see West 1980 and Lott and Fremling 1980).

6. Private schools are smaller and thus bring about greater degrees of participation in sports and other activities than do public schools.
7. Private schools have smaller class sizes and thus allow teachers and students to have greater contact.
8. Private schools are more efficient than public schools, accomplishing their educational task at lower cost.

Premises underlying policies that would decrease the role of private schools:

1. Private schools are socially divisive along income lines, skimming off the students from higher income backgrounds and segregating them in elite schools.
2. Private schools are divisive along religious lines, segregating religious groups in separate schools.
3. Private schools are divisive along racial lines, in two ways: they contain few blacks or other minorities and thus segregate whites in private schools from blacks in public schools; and the private sector itself is more racially segregated than the public sector.
4. Private schools do not provide the educational range that public schools do, especially in vocational and other nontraditional courses or programs.
5. Private schools have a narrower range of extracurricular activities and thus deprive their students of participation in school activities outside the classroom.
6. Private schools are unhealthily competitive, and thus public schools provide a healthier affective development.
7. Facilitating the use of private schools would aid whites more than blacks and those better off financially at the expense of those worse off; in addition, it would increase racial and economic segregation.

Some of these premises underlying school policies are held by policy makers whose decisions affect the relative roles of private and public schools in America, and some are held by parents who choose between private and public schools for their children. Thus, information on the correctness of these premises is useful not only for educational policy making in a nation, state, or city, but also for parental choice. Parents have a good deal of direct information on some of the questions implicit in these premises (such as the level of discipline imposed in the public and private schools in their locale), but almost no information on others.

The current study, at its present stage, can provide better information on some of these questions than on others, because different questions require information about different aspects of schools. Some of the questions concern the effects of schools on students within them. Premises 1, 2, 4, and 5 from the first list and number 6 from the second list raise questions of this sort. These questions are the most difficult to answer, because the experimental design implicit in most of these questions (the same child in a public school or a private school would develop differently) is not possible in practice. Consequently, statistical analyses must be substituted for an experimental design, and such analyses are always subject to problems of inference. If data from more than one point in a child's school career are available, the statistical analysis is more powerful, and some of the problems of inference are eliminated. Such data do not now exist in this study, although they will be available on the sophomores in late 1982. For the present, substitute statistical techniques are used, some of which make use of the fact that information is available on two cohorts. These statistical techniques will be discussed at appropriate points.

A second set of the questions requires information on the distribution of students among schools. Premises 1, 2, and 3 from the second list are of this sort. Obtaining such information is much less problematic than obtaining information on effects of schools. It is directly available for the sample of schools and sample of students in the study. The only inferential problem is estimation of the characteristics of all U.S. schools from those of the sample. Because these samples were drawn with known probabilities from the universe of U.S. schools of different types, this estimation can be carried out without difficulty (see, however, the discussion of sampling at the end of this chapter).

There is, however, sometimes a question of another type lurking behind those of simple student distribution: What effect would a policy that increased or decreased the number of students in private schools have on the distribution of students? For example, the question might be raised: What would be the effect of tuition tax credits on racial segregation in the schools? Premise number 7 in the second list raises a question of this sort.

The answers to this kind of underlying question are not so directly accessible as the answer to the simple question of the current distribution of students. There are additional problems of inference involved, which means that these questions can be answered with less certainty than the questions about current distribution.[2]

A third type of question involves comparing characteristics of the public and private schools themselves. These characteristics include both the resources of public and private schools and what goes on in the schools. Premises 3, 6, 7, and 8 from the first list and 4 and 5 from the second are related to such questions. Information about school resources and about

---

[2] An illustration of the difficulty of answering such questions conclusively is provided by recent and continuing conflicts over the anticipated effect of particular types of court desegregation decisions on white flight, and thus on the resulting degree of racial segregation in the schools.

what goes on in the schools was reported at various points in the school and student questionnaires and, like the information on distribution of students among the schools, is inferred for U.S. schools as a whole simply by the inference from sample to universe.

These distinct sets of questions lend themselves nicely to structuring a study designed to provide a broad overview of public and private schools. Answers to these questions can be grouped into four major divisions: the student composition of public and private schools, the resources that go into public and private schools, the functioning of public and private schools, and the outcomes of public and private schooling. Or, put more simply, Who is in the schools? What resources go into them? What goes on? and What comes out? These four divisions, prefaced by a chapter on the geographic and size distribution of public and private schools, constitute the four analytic chapters of this report. A concluding chapter examines the premises outlined here in light of the findings of the analyses. An epilogue examines implications of these results for high school education in America. Finally, an addendum addresses various questions raised in the controversies surrounding the report on which this book is based.

The Distinction Between Research Results and Policy Consequences

Although the questions examined in this report are designed to be relevant to policy, it is important to recognize that research results do not translate directly into predictions about policy consequences. For policies with complex and indirect consequences, such as those involving private schools, this point is especially important. There are a number of illustrations in this report. One has to do with differential effectiveness of public and private schools toward particular outcomes for comparable students. Consider the outcome of achievement in basic cognitive skills of reading, vocabulary, and mathematics, covered in chapter 6. Suppose the research result is that the average Catholic school (a category that is useful for illustration, since it is the only homogeneous group of schools in the private sector that is large enough to be treated separately in the analysis) is more effective for the student from an average background than is the average public school. Let us assume that the problems of differential selection into the Catholic schools that make such an inference hard to establish have been overcome. Then what are the discontinuities between

7

the research result and any action? Several different levels of action may be imagined, and several different sources of discontinuity:

A Parent, Deciding Whether to Send a Child to Catholic or Public School. First, such a decision is ordinarily based on a rather broad range of outcomes of schooling, and we have examined only a subset of them. But even if the parent were interested only in these consequences examined here, there is another problem. The parent is not interested in the average Catholic school as compared to the average public school, but the particular Catholic school and public school which are the concrete alternatives. And the parent is not interested in how the schools function for the *average* student, but for a particular student, a given son or daughter.

Clearly for such action, the illustrative result is not of great value. What would be of greater value is a result of much more complexity, a kind of three-dimensional matrix, showing how outcomes in particular kinds of Catholic schools compare to those in particular kinds of public schools for particular kinds of students.

A Legislature, Deciding Whether to Provide Educational Vouchers Usable for Public or Private Schools. Again, there are many different outcomes of such a policy that may be relevant to the decisions beyond the narrow cognitive skills referred to in this illustrative result. Apart from this, however, there are several other serious discontinuities. First, the greater effectiveness of the Catholic schools for a given student may not be directly due to school policies, but instead to the reinforcement provided by a particular student body composition. If this were so, then the introduction of a new set of students would dilute or eliminate the source of the effects.

Second, the greater effectiveness may be due to characteristics of the school staff which are in limited supply, and not to be found in the new schools that open to serve the expanded demand for Catholic schools. If this were so, there would be no increased achievement as a result of the policy.

Third, the greater effectiveness might be due to the greater commitment on the part of student or parent or both when the parent is paying tuition for the child to attend school. If this were so, then the introduction of vouchers, which eliminated payment even by those who currently use the Catholic school, would not only fail to bring about an increase in achievement of the new entrants, but would eliminate the source of the greater achievement for existing students in these schools.

Fourth, the new policy might be accompanied by greater federal intervention in and regulation of schools in the private sector, introducing the same constraints on their authority that currently exist for public schools.

If the new policy brought such regulation, and if the greater effectiveness were due to the lesser constraints on authority enjoyed by schools in the private sector, then the new policy would eliminate the source of that greater effectiveness.

There are, of course, processes through which the greater effectiveness might occur which would be unaffected by the policy, such as greater commitment to a school attended by choice, or a distinctive educational philosophy of the Catholic schools which would be found in the new school as well. What is important to recognize, however, is that a new policy does not merely extend the educational programs already in existence to a larger group. It changes a number of conditions, and some of those conditions might be important to any differential effectiveness of the programs. Research may be able to discover something about the mechanisms through which this differential effectiveness occurs, and if so, it can be more informative about the possible effects of a new policy. But what is important to recognize is that the matter is not so simple as extrapolating a given effect to a broader set of students through introduction of a new policy.

A word is necessary on the classification of schools used in the report. For much of the analysis, schools are classified not into two sectors, but into three—public, Catholic, and other private schools. This is done because Catholic schools constitute by far the largest single group of private schools and constitute a less diverse array of schools than all private schools taken together. It would be useful to make various subdivisions among the other private schools, separating out the different religious subgroups and distinguishing the nonreligious schools according to some criterion, but that is outside the scope of this report. In further work with these data, carried out either by us or by other analysts, some such distinctions will be possible, in part because two special samples of schools were drawn: Catholic schools that had high proportions (30 percent or more) of black students in them, selected in addition to the representative sample of Catholic schools; and a special sample of "high-performance" private schools—the eleven private schools with the highest proportions of their graduating student bodies listed as semifinalists in the 1978 National Merit Scholarship competition.[3]

In chapter 3 and parts of chapter 6, only the three sectors, public, Cath-

---

[3] A second criterion in selecting these schools was that no two schools would be drawn from the same state. Only one school was eliminated by this criterion. There is a submerged stratification in this mode of selection, since different norms for the National Merit Scholarship tests are used in different states. The eleven schools selected by this procedure do show broad geographic distribution. One of the eleven schools is Catholic, the other ten are non-Catholic.

olic, and other private, are compared. However, in chapters 4, 5, and 6 (pages 72 to 178), two additional sets of schools are included in the comparison. These are the eleven high-performance private schools mentioned previously, and a set of twelve high-performance public schools.[4] These schools are included to provide extremes that can better illuminate some of the research questions posed in the report. Because of the way they were drawn, these schools do not represent any other than themselves; thus they are not "sectors" like the public, Catholic, and other private sectors.[5] Further, the results reported for these high-performance private and public schools cannot be generalized to a larger population of schools or students, but they do suggest something about the character of schools that produce high-achieving students.[6]

The Sample of Schools and References to a Broader Population of Schools.[7]

The schools sampled for this study were drawn from what is perhaps the most complete listing of American public and private high schools in existence. (This listing will be described at the beginning of the next chap-

[4] The twelve high-performance public schools were selected in exactly the same way as the eleven high-performance private schools, except that they were chosen from the sample of 894 public schools after the sample was drawn and data collected. Because they were not drawn from the total population of U.S. public schools, whereas the high-performance private schools were drawn from the more than 6,000 private schools in the country, the high-performance public schools are a somewhat less select set.

[5] When the high-performance private schools are separated out from the two major private sectors, the results for those sectors, which are always reported in weighted form, are hardly affected by the loss, since the weights of the high-performance private schools, when part of the private school sample, are very small. Throughout this report, the tabulations and analyses for the Catholic and other private sectors do not include the specially sampled high-performance private schools, which, as explained, affects the results for those sectors very little. (An exception to this exclusion is chapter 3, where the high-performance private schools are included in the "other private" category.) The high-performance public schools are, however, included as part of the public sector in all tabulations and analyses, since they were drawn in the sample to represent particular strata including other high schools. To be consistent, the private school sectors should have included the high-performance private schools; and the separate tabulations for the high-performance public schools should not include in their weights any weight for schools other than themselves. As pointed out, however, that would hardly affect results obtained in this report.

[6] This probably constitutes a deficiency in the sample design in selection of the high-performance private schools. If the sample were being drawn again, we would prefer to see two subgroups like these, but representative of some identifiable segments of American private and public schools.

[7] A sample design report for the High School and Beyond Study as a whole can be obtained from the National Center for Education Statistics.

ter). Even that listing, however, is incomplete, especially for the heterogeneous category of private, non-Catholic schools. New schools in this sector come into existence with some frequency; and there are existing schools too small to be located or too independent to be willing to be included on any listing, even nongovernmental. Thus, it is necessary to realize that this category of schools is not closed and well defined, but is both heterogeneous and amorphous, ranging from large, well-endowed preparatory schools to a long tail which includes free schools with a few students in casual attendance. There are schools in this long tail which were not included in the list from which the sample was drawn; and even if they had been, the heterogeneity and amorphousness of the category makes it difficult to gain a sense of the population of other private schools for which the sample as drawn was representative.

In this study, as with all surveys, the sample available for analysis is not the same as the one that was drawn. In part, this is because listings are inaccurate, a fact which is discovered only at the time the data are to be collected. In the sample for this study, there were some listings which were in error; for example a school might no longer be in existence or not properly a high school within the definition of the population of schools. These errors were replaced by resampling within the stratum for which a sample allocation had been made.

In addition to replacement due to inaccurate listing, there are refusals to participate. In this study, refusals could occur at the school level (due to a refusal of either the school district or the school), or the student level. Substitution of a school within the same substratum was carried out for schools which refused; but no substitution was made for student refusals or student unavailability due to continued absence. The sample of schools, and students, distinguished according to public, Catholic, and other private sectors (each of which constituted strata for which sample allocations were made in the sample design), is given in table 1–1. Overall, 71 percent of the schools initially drawn which were eligible participated in the survey. But this rate changed from a high of 79 percent in the Catholic schools to a low of 50 percent in other private schools. The final realized sample size was 91 percent of the size of final list of eligible schools, as shown in row 7 of table 1–1, but this includes some schools that are substitutes.

Within the schools, the student response rate for the questionnaire overall was 84 percent, a rate which ranged from a high of 93 percent for the Catholic sector to a low of 83 percent for the public sector. Most of the student nonresponse, 72 percent out of the total non-response of 11,432, was due to continued absence, with only 3 percent due to refusals.

TABLE 1-1

Sample of Schools as Drawn Corrected Through Replacement, and as Realized, and Sample of Students as Drawn and as Realized

Item	Total	Public	Catholic	Other Private	H.P.
1. Total numbers of schools represented by sample	20,316	15,766	1,571	26,966	12
2. Initial sample size	1,122	984	88	38	12
3. Number of eligible schools	1,019	893	86	28	12
4. Number of eligibles after replacing ineligibles	1,118	982	88	36	12
5. Final realized sample size	1,015	893	84	27	11
School Response Rates					
6. Among initial eligible schools (row 3)	.71	.70	.79	.50	.75
7. Final rate neglecting substitution (row 5/row 4)	.91	.91	.95	.75	.92
Number of Students					
8. Total eligible students	70,170	62,027	5,965	1,387	791
9. Sophomores eligible in final school sample	35,338	31,241	2,975	727	395
10. Seniors eligible in final school sample	34,832	30,786	2,990	660	396
11. Sophomores in final sample	30,280	26,448	2,831	631	370
12. Seniors in final sample	28,450	24,891	2,697	551	311
Student Response Rates					
13. Sophomores (row 11/row 9)	.86	.85	.95	.87	.94
14. Seniors (row 12/row 10)	.82	.81	.90	.83	.79

In the analysis throughout chapters 3 to 6, the results reported describe exactly the sample of schools and students (albeit weighted according to their frequency in the population). It is in the generalization from this sample to the population of students (or schools) in a given sector that problems of imprecision or bias arise. Generalization to the sector as a whole, of course, is where the interest lies, rather than in the sample per se.

All of the changes in the sample between initial design and final realized sample, with the exception of replacements due to incorrect listing, are potential sources of bias in the representativeness of the sample. Without information on the schools and students who were in the intended sample but not in the realized sample, the effect of this potential bias is unknown.

The sampling problems for the other private schools are particularly severe. For two reasons the generalizations from the other private sample can only be made with considerable uncertainty. The first is sample size: The number of schools in the sample is only 27, and the number of students in the sample is only 631 sophomores and 551 seniors, by far the

dents in the sample is only 631 sophomores and 551 seniors, by far the smallest numbers of schools and students in any of the three sectors. The consequences of this small sample size for sampling errors, and thus for generalizations about the other private schools, can be estimated, and we will turn to that in the heading "Sampling Error."

The other source of problems with the other private school sample is that the potential bias is greatest there. The fraction of original schools participating (before substitution) was smaller than in any other sector. Of the twenty-eight eligible schools in the original sample only fourteen participated, giving a 50 percent rate, while the next lowest was 70 percent in the public sector.

Because of the potential bias, and to a lesser extent because of the small sample size (lesser because the effect of sample size is simply in variability of estimates, and that effect can be estimated, while the effect of potential bias is unknown), generalizations about the non-Catholic private sector as a whole from the other private schools in the sample should be quite tentative. Comparisons between the Catholic sector and the public sector are on much stronger ground because sampling variability is less, and potential bias due to nonresponse of schools is less in both these sectors.

We have attempted to exercise special caution in making generalizations about other private schools throughout these chapters. However, the reader should keep in mind the present discussion at each point in the analysis.

The sample size deficiencies in the private sector are due to the design of High School and Beyond as a multipurpose study. The non-response deficiencies are largely due to the extreme heterogeneity of schools in this sector, which in any case reduces the meaningfulness of any generalizations about "non-Catholic private schools" as a whole.

SAMPLING ERRORS

The descriptive statistics in chapters 4 and 5, and in parts of chapters 3 and 6, ordinarily consist of comparisons of percentages in a given response category in each sector. Standard errors of these percentages, indicating the precision of the reported percentage as an estimate of the percentage in the sector as a whole, are not given. Instead, approximate standard errors that can be applied to these tables are shown in the appendix table A–2. That table shows, for example, that if the reported percentage for sophomores is around 50 percent in a given sector, the standard error for that percentage is about 0.5 percent in the public sector, 1.8 percent in the Catholic sector, 5.2 percent in the other private sector, 4.2 percent in the high performance public sector, and 6.2 percent in the high-performance private sector. The large standard errors in some sectors are due to the smaller sample sizes, and in the case of the other private sector, the heterogeneity of the sector.[8]

Because of the disparities in standard errors in the three major sectors, a rough rule of thumb may be used for standard errors of differences between sectors: the standard error of the difference is approximately the size of the larger standard error of the two sectors being compared. The much higher standard error for the other private sector shows the imprecision of the estimates in that sector, as estimates of the percentage in the population of students in that sector. This is one source of uncertainty about generalizations to the population of students in non-Catholic private schools. The other, of course, is potential bias, referred to earlier.

Most of chapter 6 consists of analytical questions concerning the differential effects of schooling in the three sectors. The comparisons in these cases are based on numbers derived from complex statistics, such as regression coefficients or some transformation of them. Standard errors have been calculated and are reported for these numbers, because table A–2 cannot be used in these cases, and because causal inferences depend on the comparisons made in these sections.[9] In the case of one especially important comparison, table 6–7, a standard error estimate was empirically obtained, using Balanced Repeated Replications (BRR) (Kish and Frankel, 1974).

[8] The effects of heterogeneity of the other private sector also shown in the standard error estimates for the high-performance private sector, since the "sample design effect" correction factors had been calculated for the other private sector are used for the high-performance private sector. If a separate correction factor had been calculated for the latter sector, it would probably have been much smaller. Thus the standard error estimates for that sector are probably somewhat high.

[9] Sample design effect correction factors discussed in the preceding footnote have not been incorporated into these standard errors because of previous work indicating that for complex statistics such as multiple regression coefficients, the design effect is close to 1.0 (Kish and Frankel, 1974).

2

The Size and Geographical Distributions of Public and Private Secondary Schools

THIS CHAPTER provides an overview of the distribution of public and private education in the United States, emphasizing, along with a few general characteristics of interest, how private education is distributed geographically. These tabulations, unlike those in the remaining chapters of the report, are based on data for all schools in the United States. The data are from the National Opinion Research Center (NORC) 1978 school universe tape, which was developed and compiled from several different sources.[1]

[1] The NORC school universe file was created from the following sources:
A. A school universe file for fall 1978, prepared by the Curriculum Information Center, Denver, Colorado, a private organization
B. A public school universe file for Fall 1978 constructed by the National Center for Education Statistics (NCES) from the Fall 1978 Survey of Public Schools
C. A private school universe file for fall 1978 prepared under contract to the National Center for Education Statistics
D. A supplementary U.S. Civil Rights Commission file of a large sample of public schools in the United States, fall 1976
Because file A was the most complete file, grade spans and enrollments were used from that file if the school was on that file. Files B, C, and D were used to augment this file.
Because of the different source material, total numbers of schools and total enrollment

As observers have often noted, the diversity within the domain of private education is in many respects greater than the differences between public and private education in general. This diversity should not be lost sight of, but neither should it obscure the fact that for some purposes it is necessary to consider the private sector of American secondary education as a whole.

To provide a general understanding of private schools while retaining a part of the diversity that is present among them, most of the analyses in this report treat private education in two broad sectors—Catholic and non-Catholic (or "other private," as the latter are termed). (These two are augmented by a third set, a group of specially selected high-performance schools referred to in chapter 1.) In this chapter, however, there is an effort to present some of the diversity that is lost with this dichotomization of private schools. In the next section, the classification of school types is expanded to include a breakdown of the "other private" category into "religious-affiliated" and "nonreligious-affiliated" for comparison of public and private schools along geographic and enrollment lines. Then, in the second part of this chapter, where the focus shifts to selected characteristics of private secondary schools, additional distinctions within the religious-affiliated category are introduced to indicate some of the variability to be found there.

Enrollment and Geographic Comparisons of Public and Private Secondary Education

Table 2–1 shows the number of schools and estimated[2] student enrollments at the secondary level for public schools and various kinds of pri-

---

differ slightly from those published in the 1978 Fall Enrollment Survey for public schools, and from the NCES Bulletin 80-BO1 for private schools. No correction has been made for the change in cohort size between 1978 and 1979.

The Curriculum Information Center file contained no information on type of private school beyond the Catholic versus non-Catholic classification. Consequently, in some tables of this chapter, a "private, non-Catholic" unclassified category will be shown, consisting of the non-Catholic schools that did not appear in the NCES private school universe file.

[2]Since enrollment figures for the schools are only available for all grades in the school, the figures given here (and in the rest of this section) for grades 9 through 12 are estimates that may be subject to some error. The enrollment figures are computed by, first, obtaining the average number of students per grade (each school's total enrollment divided by the total number of grades in the school) and, second, multiplying this average by the number of high-school-level grades that the particular school has. For schools that have only high-school grades, this of course equals the total enrollment.

TABLE 2-1

National Figures for Number of Schools and Estimated Enrollments in Grades 9-12 in Public and Private Education: 1978-79 School Year[a]

	U.S. Total	Public	Private				
			Total	Catholic	Other Religious Affiliation	Private with no Affiliation	Private Non-Catholic[b]
Secondary-level Schools							
Total number with secondary-level grades (9-12)[c]	24,132	17,822	6,310	1,861	1,552	2,296	601
Percentage of total	100.0	73.9	26.1	7.7	6.4	9.5	2.5
Mean number of grades	6.0	4.9	9.2	5.1	10.9	11.2	10.1
Student Enrollment							
Estimated total number enrolled in grades 9-12 (000s)	14,866.4	13,508.4	1,359.0	900.8	168.6	223.8	64.8
Percentage of total enrollment in grades 9-12	100.0	90.9	9.1	6.1	1.1	1.5	0.4
Mean enrollment per school in grades 9-12	616	758	215	484	109	97	108

SOURCE: NORC School Universe Tape.

NOTE: Details may not add to totals because of rounding.

[a] Schools with total enrollments of less than twenty-five students for all grade levels are excluded from these and all subsequent tablulations in this section.

[b] These non-Catholic private schools were on the CIC universe file but not the NCES file. Consequently, no information about affiliation exists beyond the fact that they are not Catholic schools.

[c] The number of schools listed has not been corrected on the basis of information obtained through the High School and Beyond sample. In the original sample of 1,122 schools, 103 were found that were not properly high schools having their own enrollment. (For example, many area vocational schools do not have students enrolled for graduation within them, but instead serve students from other schools, providing the vocational part of their program.) A new estimate was made of the size of the school universe when the schools represented by these schools were eliminated. This estimate gives 21,700 schools rather than 24,132.

vate schools. Of most interest in this table are the numerical division of American high school students between public and private schools (a ratio of about 90/10 public/private, with two-thirds of the students in private schools found in Catholic schools) and the sizes of schools in each sector. As is shown in the sixth row of table 2–1, which contains the average high school enrollments in the different sectors, private secondary schooling tends, on the average, to be carried out in much smaller schools than does public schooling. It should be noted that the estimates of the number of high school students (grades 9 through 12) in each sector are not directly comparable to the enrollment figures that most commonly appear in this sort of tabulation. Those tabulations usually give the number of students enrolled in schools that offer secondary-level programs. As the number of grades in the average school of each sector (row 3 of table 2–1) shows, these two enrollment estimates are likely to differ considerably: The average number of grades in private schools with secondary-level programs is appreciably higher than that in public schools. This, of course, points to yet another sort of diversity, not discussed here, that research might examine—the differences in the age ranges of the average public and private school student's schoolmates.

Turning to geographic distribution, table 2–2 indicates that there is wide variability across regions in the percentage of high school students in private schools, ranging from 4.4 percent in the Mountain states and 5.4 percent in the West South Central region to 13 percent or more in New England and the Middle Atlantic states. The relative shares of the different types of private schools also show some striking differences over this level of aggregation. The Catholic share of American secondary education ranges from a high of 10 percent in the Middle Atlantic region to a low of 2 percent in the Mountain region.

The variability among states is of course more pronounced, as shown in table 2–3. Private education is strongest in Connecticut, where it enrolls nearly 17 percent of all high school students. Wyoming, at the other extreme, has only slightly over 1.5 percent of its students in private schools.

Within the private sector, the Catholic schools are, with few exceptions, strongest in the New England and Middle Atlantic states. Their share falls off dramatically, to under 1 percent, in the Carolinas and in a few of the Western states. Other religious affiliations are generally strongest through the southern Atlantic seaboard, in Tennessee, and in the Midwestern states of Michigan, Wisconsin, and Iowa.

Another distributional breakdown of interest concerns the locations of schools and students in urban, suburban, and rural localities. Table 2–4 gives the percentages of the constituent schools of each of the five school types and the estimated high school enrollments in each of these settings.

TABLE 2-2

Estimated Percentage Distribution of Students in Grades 9–12 in Public and Private Schools for Each of the Nine Census Regions: 1978–79 School Year

Region	Total Enrollment		Public	Private				
	Number in thousands	Percentage		Total	Catholic	Other Religious Affiliation	Private with no Affiliation	Private Non-Catholic
United States total	14,866	100.0	90.9	9.1	6.1	1.1	1.5	.4
New England	876	100.0	86.2	13.8	8.1	.7	4.7	.4
Middle Atlantic	2,650	100.0	87.0	13.0	10.3	1.2	1.2	.3
South Atlantic	2,201	100.0	91.9	8.1	3.3	1.6	2.6	.6
East South Central	959	100.0	91.9	8.1	2.8	1.7	2.9	.8
West South Central	1,427	100.0	94.6	5.4	3.5	.7	.9	.3
East North Central	3,004	100.0	90.7	9.3	7.4	1.1	.6	.3
West North Central	1,180	100.0	91.1	8.9	6.9	1.1	.5	.4
Mountain	682	100.0	95.6	4.4	2.3	.6	.9	.6
Pacific	1,888	100.0	92.4	7.6	4.7	1.1	1.2	.5

Source: NORC School Universe Tape.
Note: Details may not add to totals because of rounding.

TABLE 2–3

Estimated Percentage Distribution of Students in Grades 9–12 in Public and Private Schools by State: 1978–79 School Year[a]

Region	Total Enrollment		Public	Private			
	Number in thousands	Percentage		Catholic	Other Religious Affiliation	Private with no Affiliation	Private Non-Catholic
New England							
Connecticut	230.3	100.0	83.1	9.0	.9	6.2	.8
Massachusetts	409.5	100.0	86.9	9.3	.3	3.4	.2
Maine	81.8	100.0	90.2	1.7	.7	6.9	.5
New Hampshire	60.2	100.0	88.0	4.1	2.3	5.5	.1
Rhode Island	59.2	100.0	85.5	12.0	1.3	1.2	.0
Vermont	35.3	100.0	87.0	4.1	.2	8.8	.0
Middle Atlantic							
New Jersey	550.9	100.0	88.6	9.6	.6	1.1	.1
New York	1,212.8	100.0	86.5	10.1	1.8	1.2	.4
Pennsylvania	886.3	100.0	86.6	11.0	.8	1.2	.4
South Atlantic							
Washington, D.C.	37.1	100.0	79.9	14.1	2.2	3.2	.5
Delaware	46.7	100.0	85.6	10.6	1.3	2.3	.2
Florida	489.1	100.0	89.4	4.2	2.4	3.3	.8
Georgia	343.4	100.0	93.7	1.0	1.4	3.5	.5
Maryland	268.9	100.0	86.5	9.2	1.6	1.7	.9
North Carolina	328.4	100.0	95.3	.5	1.2	2.4	.7
South Carolina	223.0	100.0	94.0	.8	1.5	3.2	.5
Virginia	345.0	100.0	93.5	2.0	1.5	3.2	.8
West Virginia	118.9	100.0	97.0	2.1	.5	.4	.1
East South Central							
Alabama	268.5	100.0	93.7	1.1	1.5	3.1	.5
Kentucky	255.0	100.0	91.6	6.4	.6	1.1	.3
Mississippi	164.7	100.0	90.6	1.5	.8	5.0	2.1
Tennessee	270.6	100.0	91.0	2.0	3.3	3.0	.7
West South Central							
Arkansas	133.2	100.0	96.3	1.6	.6	1.1	.5

Louisiana	270.8	100.0	85.4	10.3	.8	2.5	.9
Oklahoma	190.2	100.0	97.8	1.1	.6	.3	.2
Texas	833.2	100.0	96.6	2.1	.6	.5	.1
East North Central							
Illinois	809.9	100.0	88.2	10.1	.8	.7	.2
Indiana	377.7	100.0	93.7	4.2	.9	.7	.6
Michigan	666.8	100.0	91.5	5.9	2.0	.5	.2
Ohio	815.7	100.0	91.3	7.7	.5	.5	.1
Wisconsin	333.6	100.0	90.4	6.8	1.8	.5	.5
West North Central							
Iowa	194.2	100.0	89.0	8.2	2.6	.0	.3
Kansas	143.5	100.0	93.3	4.9	.3	.6	.9
Minnesota	306.2	100.0	93.4	4.8	1.1	.5	.2
Missouri	337.1	100.0	89.5	8.5	.7	.9	.4
North Dakota	49.2	100.0	94.3	5.3	.3	.1	.0
Nebraska	98.2	100.0	88.2	10.5	.5	.3	.5
South Dakota	51.2	100.0	91.9	4.7	1.0	.9	1.6
Mountain							
Arizona	168.2	100.0	95.2	2.6	.4	1.2	.6
Colorado	174.6	100.0	95.0	2.5	1.0	1.1	.4
Idaho	51.4	100.0	97.7	.9	.4	.4	.6
Montana	54.9	100.0	93.9	4.3	.5	.9	.5
New Mexico	85.2	100.0	94.3	1.9	.9	1.5	1.4
Nevada	40.6	100.0	96.5	3.1	.2	.1	.0
Utah	82.4	100.0	97.5	1.1	.3	.2	1.0
Wyoming	24.8	100.0	98.5	.6	.0	.9	.0
Pacific							
Alaska	27.9	100.0	97.2	.9	2.0	.0	.0
California	1,425.3	100.0	92.0	5.2	1.0	1.3	.5
Hawaii	59.0	100.0	85.0	6.7	4.0	3.4	.9
Oregon	145.2	100.0	95.3	3.0	.6	.5	.6
Washington	230.6	100.0	94.5	3.1	1.2	.6	.6

SOURCE: NORC School Universe Tape.

NOTE: Details may not add to totals because of rounding.

[a] Approximations derived from information on the schools' enrollments, the number of secondary-level grades, and the total number of grades in each school.

TABLE 2-4

Percentage Distribution for Schools and Estimated Enrollments (Grades 9–12) in Urban, Suburban, and Rural Areas[a] by School Sector: 1978–79 School Year

	U.S. Total	Public	Private				
			Total	Catholic	Other Religious Affiliation	Private with no Affiliation	Private Non-Catholic
Total Number							
Schools	24,131	17,822	6,309	1,860	1,552	2,296	601
Students (in thousands)	14,863	13,505.1	1,357.9	900.7	168.6	223.8	64.8
Schools							
Total percentage	100.0	100.0	100.0	100.0	100.0	100.0	100.0
Urban	15.9	11.5	28.2	22.0	26.7	35.6	22.5
Suburban	36.1	33.9	42.1	60.6	34.5	33.4	38.1
Rural	48.1	54.6	29.7	17.4	38.8	31.0	31.4
Students							
Total percentage	100.0	100.0	100.0	100.0	100.0	100.0	100.0
Urban	22.4	22.5	22.2	20.2	30.8	24.5	19.9
Suburban	47.9	46.7	60.0	68.6	45.7	42.3	38.6
Rural	29.7	30.9	17.8	11.3	23.5	33.2	41.5

SOURCE: NORC School Universe Tape, 1979.

NOTE: Details may not add to totals because of rounding.

[a] The urban, suburban, and rural classifications are the standard U.S. Bureau of the Census definitions. "Urban": the school is located in a central city (population of 50,000 or more) of a Standard Metropolitan Statistical Area (SMSA); "suburban": the school is located in an SMSA, but is not a central city; "rural": the school is not located within an SMSA. Bureau of the Census information was not available for a small number of school localities. For these, the school was classified as urban if the population of its locality is 50,000 or more, as suburban if the population is greater than 2,499 and less than 50,000, and as rural if the population is under 2,500.

The Size and Geographical Distributions of Secondary Schools

It is apparent that the public and private sectors are distributed quite differently across these categories, in both schools and enrollments. Comparing public and private schools overall (columns 2 and 3), private schools tend to be substantially more concentrated in urban and suburban areas than do public schools,[3] the majority of which are rural-based. (Of course, as the last row of the table 2–4 shows, a far smaller percentage of students are in rural schools.) Within the private sector, the schools with no religious affiliation are more likely to be urban than the other types. Catholic schools are heavily concentrated in suburban communities and relatively rare in rural areas.

For overall public and private sector enrollments (columns 2 and 3), the differences are found in the suburban and rural areas. Owing largely to the high Catholic enrollments in the suburbs (60.6 percent of the Catholic high school students), the private sector is well above the national suburban average (column 1). When this finding is coupled with the fact that private education enrolls slightly below the national average in urban communities, a pattern somewhat contrary to expectation emerges. Research on Catholic education frequently assumes that Catholic enrollments are concentrated in urban areas (see Erickson, 1978, p. 90). Furthermore, the suburban public schools are commonly believed to be of such quality that private schools are comparatively less distinctive and thus less attractive there. Over against these notions, table 2–4 shows that the private sector enrolls no greater a proportion of its students in the cities than the public sector does of its students, and that private education appears to be at its competitive strongest in the suburbs.

Selected Attributes of Private Secondary Schools

While the analyses presented in this report are carried out on private secondary education as a relatively undifferentiated whole vis-à-vis public

[3] The 1977 National Institute of Education and Council for American Private Education nationally-representative survey of 454 private high schools reports a distribution of private schools across similarly Census-defined urban, suburban, and rural locales that is even more sharply skewed toward the suburbs (16 percent urban, 70 percent suburban, 14 percent rural—Abramowitz and Stackhouse 1980, p. 163). The NIE–CAPE survey also asked school principals to classify the areas where their schools are located, and obtained results more in line with traditional conceptions: 35 percent in large cities (150,000 or more), 19 percent in medium cities (25,000 to 149,999), 28 percent in communities adjacent to large cities, and 16 percent in "nonmetropolitan, non-commuting" locales of less than 25,000 residents (Abramowitz and Stackhouse, 1980, p. 152). Of the Catholic school principals surveyed, 58 percent described their areas as urban, while only a quarter said they served a suburban area. (Abramowitz and Stackhouse, 1980, p. 51). The discrepancies between the two surveys on this point lead us to regard the results presented in table 2–4 as tentative.

TABLE 2–5
Selected Private School Statistics by Affiliation of School: 1978–79 School Year

Affiliation	Number of Schools With Secondary Grade Levels	Percentage of Total Private Schools	Estimated Enrollment in Grades 9–12	Percentage of Total Private Enrollment	Estimated Mean Student Enrollment in Grades 9–12
Total private	6,310	100.0	1,357,725	100.0	215.0
Nonaffiliated	2,296	36.4	223,772	16.5	97.5
Catholic	1,861	29.5	900,776	66.3	484.0
Baptist	510	8.1	42,340	3.1	83.0
Jewish	157	2.5	22,458	1.7	143.0
Lutheran	124	2.0	22,273	1.6	179.6
Episcopal	114	1.8	18,794	1.4	164.9
Other religious affiliation	643	10.2	62,537	4.6	97.3
Non-Catholic unclassified[a]	610	9.6	65,033	4.8	106.6

SOURCE: NORC School Universe Tape.

NOTE: Details may not add to totals because of rounding.

[a] These schools, except four, are schools from the CIC file not found in the NCES file.

TABLE 2–6
Number and Percentage Distributions of Public and Private Schools by Type of School: 1978–79 School Year

Type of School	Total Schools		Secondary Only	Combined Elementary-Secondary	Special Education	Vocational-Technical	Alternative
	Number	Percentage					
All Schools	18,951	100.0	75.0	18.0	4.0	1.5	1.4
Public	13,429	100.0	90.1	7.0	.1	2.2	.5
Private							
No affiliation	2,293	100.0	16.7	50.6	25.2	.2	7.1
Catholic	1,688	100.0	83.1	7.6	7.3	.6	1.2
Baptist	510	100.0	3.9	95.1	.2	.0	.2
Jewish	157	100.0	45.2	48.4	3.8	.6	.6
Lutheran	124	100.0	52.4	39.5	7.3	.0	.8
Episcopal	114	100.0	45.6	49.1	1.8	.0	3.5
Other affiliation	643	100.0	16.0	78.9	2.3	.2	2.3

SOURCE: This table is based only on schools that appeared on the NCES school universe file and excludes schools in the Curriculum Information Center file for which the NCES file had no data.

NOTE: Details may not add to totals because of rounding.

secondary education, further research is clearly needed on the numerous lines of diversity within the private sector. The most important distinctions that can be drawn here appear to be between the religious- ·and nonreligious-affiliated categories and, within the religious-affiliated category, among the schools of the various faiths. This section briefly examines a few of the more striking differences found in the structural arrangements of some of these principal divisions within private education.

Table 2–5 gives the numbers of schools and secondary enrollments for the nonreligious-affiliated and the five largest religious-affiliated categories. Although the numbers of schools in the two categories are not greatly different, over 80 percent of the students are in religiously affiliated schools. (For discussions of the historical and doctrinal backgrounds of the various types of schools given in table 2–5, as well as others not included here, see Kraushaar, 1972 and Erickson, 1978).

Table 2–6 shows the distribution of various types of schools, classified by grade levels covered and curriculum. In general, the table shows, for types of curriculum, that there are few vocational-technical schools outside the public school system, but there are comparable percentages of special education schools and alternative schools, with some of each to be found in all types of schools.

Finally, table 2–7 shows the percentage of male, female, and coeducational schools among private schools of all affiliations, and table 2–8 shows the percentage of boarding schools among them. As indicated earlier, the

TABLE 2–7

Number and Percentage Distribution of Private Schools with Different Affiliations, by Sex of Students Served: 1978–79 School Year[a]

Affiliation	Total Schools		Males Only	Females Only	Both Males and Females
	Number	Percentage			
Total private	5,529	100.0	9.2	9.7	81.1
No affiliation	2,292	100.0	5.9	2.6	91.5
Catholic	1,691	100.0	16.6	25.6	57.9
Baptist	508	100.0	.8	0	99.2
Jewish	157	100.0	40.1	14.7	43.2
Lutheran	124	100.0	1.6	0	98.4
Episcopal	114	100.0	14.0	11.4	74.6
Other	643	100.0	1.2	1.1	97.7

SOURCE: NORC School Universe Tape.
NOTE: Details may not add to totals because of rounding.
[a] This table is based only on schools that appeared on the NCES school universe file; it excludes schools in the Curriculum Information Center file for which the NCES file had no data.

TABLE 2–8

Number and Percentage Distribution of Schools with Different
Affiliations by Day-Boarding Mix: 1978–79 School Year[a]

Affiliation	Total Schools		Day Only	Boarding Only	Mixed: Day and Boarding
	Number	Percentage			
Total private	5,528	100.0	82.9	3.9	13.2
No affiliation	2,293	100.0	77.5	6.0	16.6
Catholic	1,691	100.0	89.8	2.7	7.6
Baptist	507	100.0	97.6	.6	1.8
Jewish	157	100.0	65.0	3.2	31.9
Lutheran	124	100.0	84.7	1.6	13.7
Episcopal	114	100.0	50.0	7.0	43.0
Other affiliation	642	100.0	82.1	2.7	15.3

SOURCE: NORC School Universe Tape.

NOTE: Details may not add to totals because of rounding.

[a] This table is based only on schools that appeared on the NCES school universe file; it excludes schools in the Curriculum Information Center file for which the NCES file had no data.

affiliation breakdowns used here are not used in later chapters, which are based on the High School and Beyond sample of schools and students. These tables thus serve to give some sense of the kind of schools contained within the private sector, especially the non-Catholic private sector (or, as it is called later, the "other private" sector).[4]

---

[4] Data from NCES on private school enrollments for the 1978–79 school year show that about 80 percent of all students who attend private "secondary only" schools are in Catholic schools. The figure of 66 percent given in table 2–5 reflects the fact that a great number of private, non-Catholic high school students attend schools that are classified as "combined elementary and secondary."

We are indebted to Roy Nehrts of NCES for the tabulations on private schools, and to the technical report of the SAGE group (McLaughlin and Wise, 1980).

27

3

The Student Composition of
Public and Private Schools

IN this chapter, a series of questions about the student composition of public and private schools will be examined. There are two wholly different issues of economic, religious, and racial segregation raised by the existence of private schools. The first, and the one to which most attention has been given, is the segregation between the public sector and the private sector. The second is the segregation that exists among schools within each sector.

Although these issues are different, they are related, for the criticism that private schools are divisive along economic, religious, or racial lines is a criticism that points to both forms of segregation. First, the existence of a private school alternative allows those with financial resources to segregate themselves from the remainder in public school; second, the existence of choice among private schools facilitates segregation along these lines within the private sector itself. If, for example, minorities who do attend private schools are concentrated in schools enrolling a small proportion of whites, then even a large proportion of minority students in the private schools is hardly a rebuttal to the charge that private education functions to increase social divisiveness along racial lines.

Yet matters are not so clear as this criticism would suggest, because choice exists within the public sector as well. Residential mobility, the principal way in which such choice is exercised, has increased over the years, and, along with it, the potential for families with sufficient resources to segregate children from others, wholly within the public sector. An examination, therefore, of these issues is not merely to document the obvious. It is rather to examine segregating tendencies as they are manifested both within and between the sectors of education. For each issue area, then, the analysis begins with a comparison of segregation between sectors and moves on to a comparison of within-sector segregation. The basic method used for assessing the extent of within-sector segregation is described in appendix A.

In addition to the issues related to the racial and ethnic, economic, and religious compositions of private and public schools, a fourth substantive area, one that has been growing in importance in recent years, is the education of handicapped children. Summary tables and a brief discussion of the role of the private sector in the education of the handicapped follows discussion of the other three issues.

Finally, in the areas of racial and economic segregation of the three sectors, it is useful to gain some sense of the impact of changes in family resources on the movement of different groups into or out of the private sector. Of most interest from a policy perspective would be the impact of reduced tuition, through something like an educational voucher or a tuition tax credit. Data from this study are not appropriate for examining this question. It is possible, however, to show the social mix of students who would change sectors with change in family income. This is shown for a very small increment of income, a $1,000 change for all income groups.

The Racial and Ethnic Backgrounds of Public and Private School Students

Issues related to the racial and ethnic compositions of the private schools constitute a major component of the controversy surrounding private education. Policies designed to facilitate private education are frequently opposed because private schools have sometimes functioned as a means for whites to escape the racial integration that has been imposed in the public sector. And it is generally recognized that private schools enroll proportionately smaller numbers of minority students, particularly blacks and Hispanics.

Past research supports this claim. Kraushaar's (1972) survey of 251 private secondary schools found that, overall, less than 5 percent of the total enrollment was of racial or ethnic minority status. Higher proportions are estimated by more recent studies, however. Abramowitz and Stackhouse (1980, p. 149), in a 1977 survey of 454 representively sampled private schools, estimate 5.7 percent Hispanic students and 8.3 percent black students in the private sector. The National Assessment of Educational Progress (1981) estimates 4 percent Hispanic students and 12 percent black students of the thirteen-year-old age group in private schools in 1980. Estimates for 10th and 12th grades from the High School and Beyond survey were somewhat lower.

The High School and Beyond survey was designed to provide accurate representation of the black and Hispanic student population in American secondary education. The two-stage probability sample that was employed drew schools as the first-stage unit and a random sample of students within the selected schools as the second stage. Oversampling was carried out on seven types of schools, four of which were included to facilitate analyses concerned with black or Hispanic students. The normally sampled public schools included school racial composition as one of the stratification criteria.

Table 3–1 shows the distribution of white, black, and Hispanic students among the three school types, as well as the distributions for the sophomores and senior classes.[1] As prior research and public opinion suggest, blacks are proportionately overrepresented in the public sector and underrepresented in the private sector. Averaging over grades 10 and 12 shows that the percentage of blacks in Catholic schools is a little under half that in the public schools, while the percentage of blacks in the other private schools is only about a fourth that in the public schools. The percentage of Hispanics in the private schools is much closer to that in the public schools than is the case for blacks. The percentage in the Catholic schools is as

[1] The race/ethnicity variable is constructed from items BB089 and BB090 in the codebook. Students are classified here as Hispanic if they gave as their origin or descent any one of the four classes under the heading of "Hispanic or Spanish" on BB090, regardless of how they responded to BB089. Students are classified as white if they listed themselves as "white" on BB090. Similarly, students are identified as black if they listed themselves as "black" on BB089 and did not mark Hispanic or Spanish origin on BB090. Thus constructed, this variable includes over 95 percent of the students surveyed. (Nearly all the remainder consists of persons who classified themselves in a racial category other than black or white.)

In the discussion of segregation between Hispanics and non-Hispanic whites, the latter are sometimes referred to as "whites" (as in table 3–2), and sometimes as "Anglos" (as in portions of the text).

TABLE 3–1

Percentage Distributions of Whites, Blacks, and Hispanics in Public and Private Schools by Grade: Spring 1980

	U.S. Total Grade		Public Grade		Private Total Grade		Private Catholic Grade		Private Other Private Grade	
Race-Ethnicity[a]	10	12	10	12	10	12	10	12	10	12
Total Enrollment										
Number (in thousands)	3,727.2	3,020.7	3,378.5	2,717.0	348.7	303.7	227.2	200.1	121.5	103.6
Sample number	29,504	27,412	25,754	23,902	3,750	3,510	2,783	2,656	967	854
Percentage[b]	100.0	100.0	100.0	100.0	100.0	100.0	100.0	100.0	100.0	100.0
White	74.9	78.8	73.7	78.0	86.2	86.2	83.9	85.4	90.4	87.9
Black	13.9	11.5	14.8	12.2	4.5	5.0	5.8	5.5	2.2	4.1
Hispanic	7.6	6.2	7.7	6.3	6.5	5.8	7.5	6.7	4.6	4.2
Other	3.6	3.5	3.7	3.6	2.9	2.9	2.9	2.5	2.9	3.9

NOTE: Details may not add to totals due to rounding.
[a] See footnote 1, p. 30, for construction of the race/ethnicity variable.
[b] Percentages are based on the population numbers.

great as that in the public schools, and the percentage in the other private schools is about two-thirds that in the public schools.[2]

Table 3–1 shows that the proportional representation of blacks differs considerably in the public and private sectors, but that percentages of Hispanics are similar in the public and private sectors. An equally important question however, is just how the sectors compare in the segregation among different schools within each sector. On the one hand, even if there were a high proportion of minorities in private schools, a high degree of internal segregation among these schools would have the same segregating consequences as if the proportion of minorities were low. On the other hand, even if the public schools contain a high proportion of minorities, a high degree of internal segregation within the public schools would have the same segregating consequences as if the whites were segregated in private schools. It is important to recognize, in examining the measures of segregation to be presented next, that these address only one of the two components of the overall impact of the private sector on segregation. For this component, that is, internal segregation within the sector, the proportion of each racial or ethnic group in the sector is irrelevant. For segregation between sectors, it is only these proportions that are relevant. The overall impact resulting from the combination of these two components will be discussed after examining internal segregation of each sector.

Measures of intergroup contact and of intergroup segregation have been constructed to examine internal segregation. (See the appendix for methods of calculation.) The measure of contact is a measure of the average proportion of a student's schoolmates who are from another group. It is affected both by the proportion of students of the other group in that sector and by their distribution among the schools of that sector. The measure of segregation was constructed by standardizing the measure of contact by the proportion of students of the other group in the sector. Thus it reflects only the distribution of students among the schools in the sector, given their overall numbers.[3]

---

[2] The sampling error on the proportion of Hispanics in other private schools is especially high because over half of the Hispanic students sampled in this sector were in a single school.

[3] These measures are taken from Coleman, Kelly, and Moore (1975, p. 22), where they were developed and used to measure interracial contact and interracial segregation. Since their development they have been used by a number of investigators, and they now constitute one of the standard ways of measuring segregation in schools. See Zoloth (1976), Cortese et al. (1976), Becker et al. (1978), Thomas et al. (1979). In reactions to the draft report, these measures of segregation have been subject to extensive discussion and debate. The final report contains differently calculated measures (dissimilarity indices, entropy measures, and Gini coefficients), but they lead to the same qualitative conclusion stated in the text.

TABLE 3–2

Indices of Interracial and Interethnic Contact and Segregation in
Public and Private Schools: Spring 1980

| | | | | Private | |
Measure	U.S. Total	Public	Total	Catholic	Other Private
Overall Proportions					
Non-Hispanic whites	.767	.756	.862	.846	.893
Non-Hispanic blacks	.128	.137	.047	.056	.030
Hispanics	.070	.071	.062	.071	.044
Index of Contact, s_{ij}					
For Whites and Blacks:					
Proportion of the average black's schoolmates who are white, s_{bw}	.39	.38	.61	.58	.71
Proportion of the average white's schoolmates who are black, s_{wb}	.07	.07	.03	.04	.02
For Whites and Hispanics:					
Proportion of the average Hispanic's schoolmates who are white, s_{hw}	.53	.53	.57	.63	.40
Proportion of the average white's schoolmates who are Hispanic, s_{wh}	.05	.05	.04	.05	.02
Index of Segregation, r_{ij} *(ranges from 0 = no segregation to 1 = complete segregation)*[a]					
Segregation of blacks and whites	.49	.49	.29	.31	.21
Segregation of Hispanics and whites	.30	.30	.34	.25	.55

[a] For the method of calculating the values of s_{ij} and r_{ij} see appendix A. Although the value of r_{ij} is theoretically identical to the value of r_{ji}, slight discrepancies will occur because of rounding.

Table 3–2 presents the indices of intergroup contact and segregation as applied to racial and ethnic groups. The measure of interracial contact of blacks with whites is a measure of the proportion of the average black student's schoolmates who are white; the measure works in reverse for the contact of whites with blacks. The values of .38 and .07 in column 2 of table 3–2, for example, mean that about 38 percent of the average black child's classmates in public schools are white, and that about 7 percent of the average white student's classmates are black.

The results tell something about the racial distribution within the school sectors. Looking first at the measures of contact, we see that the proportions are generally consistent with what we would expect, given the overall proportions at the top of the table. That is, since the public sector has about 11 percent fewer whites than the private sector, we would expect that the proportion of the average black's and the average Hispanic's schoolmates who are white would be lower in the public than in the private sector. Comparison of the second and third column of table 3–2 makes it clear that this is in fact the case; but, for the average black student, the difference is much greater than 11 percent. About 60 percent of the classmates of the average black student in the private sector are white, as compared with about 38 percent for the average black student in the public schools, a difference of 22 percent. For Hispanics, the figures are much closer: the average Hispanic student has 53 percent white classmates in the public sector and 57 percent in the private sector. The pattern generally holds when the Catholic and other private schools are considered separately, the only exception being the low proportion of white schoolmates for the average Hispanic in the other private schools (.40).

Following the same logic, we would expect that the proportions of the average white student's classmates who are black and Hispanic would be higher in the public schools (except in the public-Catholic comparison for Hispanics, where the proportions should be about equal). The measures of contact are consistent with expectation on this point as well.

The measures of intergroup segregation within each sector are given in the bottom two rows of table 3–2. Comparing columns 2 and 3, we see that blacks and whites are substantially less segregated in the private sector than in the public sector: the black-white segregation index takes on a value of .49 in the public sector versus only .29 in the private. For Hispanics, the sectors are much closer, with the private sector index (.34) indicating slightly greater segregation than is found in the public sector (.30).

Examining black-white segregation and Hispanic-Anglo segregation within the Catholic sector alone (where most of the private-sector minorities are to be found) shows that in both cases, the internal segregation of the Catholic sector is less than that in the public sector—substantially so for blacks and whites, slightly so for Hispanics and Anglos.

The information given by the measures of within-sector intergroup contact and segregation is displayed in another form in tables 3–3 and 3–4, which show, respectively, the percentages of blacks and Hispanics attending schools of four different racial compositions. Table 3–3 indicates that

The Student Composition of Public and Private Schools

TABLE 3-3

Percentage Distribution for Black Students in Public and Private Schools by Level of Black Enrollment: Spring 1980

Percentage of Black Enrolled	U.S. Total	Public	Private		
			Total	Catholic	Other Private
Totals					
Number	863,629	832,767	30,862	24,045	6,817
Sample number	7,850	6,991	859	783	76
Percentage[a]	100.0	100.0	100.0	100.0	100.0
0 to 19 percent	20.6	19.4	53.3	54.6	48.8
20 to 49 percent	35.2	35.4	30.0	24.0	51.2
50 to 79 percent	21.3	21.8	6.6	8.5	0
80 to 100 percent	22.9	23.4	10.0	12.9	0

NOTE: Details may not add to totals because of rounding.
[a] Percentages are based on the population numbers.

TABLE 3-4

Percentage Distribution for Hispanic Students in Public and Private Schools by Level of Hispanic Enrollment: Spring 1980

Percentage of Hispanic Enrolled	U.S. Total	Public	Private		
			Total	Catholic	Other Private
Totals					
Number	470,856	430,660	40,196	30,344	9,852
Sample number	6,680	5,613	1,067	997	70
Percentage[a]	100.0	100.0	100.0	100.0	100.0
0 to 19 percent	59.1	59.7	52.7	58.8	34.1
20 to 49 percent	18.2	18.4	16.2	21.0	1.6
50 to 79 percent	17.5	16.7	26.6	14.4	64.3
80 to 100 percent	5.2	5.3	4.4	5.8	0

NOTE: Details may not add to totals because of rounding.
[a] Percentages are based on the population numbers.

over half of the black students in the private sector attend schools that are less than 20 percent black, but only about a fifth of the public school blacks attend such schools. About 45 percent of the black students in the public sector attend predominantly black schools, compared to 17 percent in the private sector. Table 3-4 shows that, although over half of all Hispanics in both sectors are in schools that are less than 20 percent Hispanic, a somewhat higher percentage of Hispanics in the private sector are in predominantly Hispanic schools. However, the pattern in the Catholic sector is similar to that in the public sector.

Summarizing our examination of private schools and racial and ethnic segregation, we can say the following. For Hispanics, there is very little difference between the public and private sectors, either with respect to the proportions of Hispanics in each sector, or with respect to the internal distribution of Hispanics within the schools of each sector. The distribution of Hispanics between public and private schools is about the same as that of non-Hispanic whites. Within each sector the degree of segregation between the two groups is not especially high, and it is about the same in the public and private sectors.

The results for black-white segregation are more complex. There is a substantially smaller proportion of blacks in the private sector than in the public sector—less than half as high a proportion in the Catholic schools, and less than a quarter as high in the other private schools. But information on the internal segregation between blacks and whites tells a different story: The public sector has a substantially higher degree of segregation than the private sector (or either of its two components separately). Thus, the integrating impact of the lesser degree of segregation within the private sector counteracts the segregating impact of the lower proportion of blacks in that sector.

What is the end result of these conflicting tendencies, the overall impact of private schooling on black-white segregation? An answer can be obtained by comparing the overall black-white segregation among all high schools, public and private considered together, as it currently stands, to the segregation we would expect if the students currently in private schools were absorbed into the public system. We assume that they would be distributed among schools within the public sector in exactly the way whites and blacks are currently distributed in the public sector.[4] Any differences found in such a comparison would of course be quite

[4]This assumption may be questioned on two grounds: These students may live in areas that are closer to or further from blacks than is true for whites currently in public schools; and their family incomes may allow them more resources to move to higher income areas with smaller proportions of blacks. Table 3–11 shows that private schools are located in areas with slightly smaller proportions of blacks than is true for the average public school. And, in the next section, table 3–5 shows that the incomes of parents of private school students are somewhat higher than those of parents of public school students. Thus, on both these grounds, both black and white students currently in private schools would tend to enter public schools that were more white than the public schools attended by black and white students in the public sector. Since the proportion of white students in private schools is higher than in the public sector, we would expect that absorption of private school students into public schools would result in a slightly more segregated public sector than found at present. Thus the comparison in the text may slightly understate the degree of segregation to be expected if private schools were absent.

For a much more extensive discussion of the rationale behind this way of assessing the overall impact of private schooling on racial segregation, see Coleman, Hoffer, Kilgore, 1982.

small, since only 10 percent of the student population would change schools; but the direction is important.

If we assumed that no private schools existed, and that blacks and whites currently in private schools were absorbed into the public schools with exactly the same distribution among schools as is currently found in the public schools, the degree of segregation for the total U.S. student population would be that given by the segregation index for the public sector, .49. Comparing this to the current segregation index for all U.S. students, also .49, suggests that the two tendencies cancel each other out.

The Economic Backgrounds of Public and Private School Students

Although much attention has been directed to the possible divisiveness of private schools along racial lines in recent years, the first such concern was with economic divisiveness. This is the most natural form that public-private stratification would take, since private schools are costly to the user, and public schools are free to the user. And it is this stratification that usually comes to mind when the elite private schools are discussed.

We know, however, that a large number of private schools do not fit this image. The Catholic schools were not designed for an upper-class elite, and many of the other private schools are also based on religious rather than social class homogeneity. Consequently, despite the fact that sending a child to a private school costs parents money while sending a child to a public school does not, the diverse origins and affiliations of private schools suggest that private schools as a whole may serve students with economic backgrounds not greatly different from those of students served by public schools.

But even if this is true, it addresses only the question of economic segregation between the public and private sectors, not economic segregation within the private sector. And, if there are elite schools and nonelite schools in the private sector, there must be a considerable degree of economic segregation among schools within that sector.

Yet the questions of economic segregation between the private and public school sectors and within the private sector do not exist in a vacuum. They exist, rather, within the framework of some degree of economic stratification among schools in the public sector itself. The geographic mobility by residence that facilitates a degree of racial homogeneity in public schools, as shown in the preceding section, also facilitates a degree of economic homogeneity. Thus the tendencies of private schools to lead to economic stratification between the private and public sectors or within the private sector must be seen in a context of economic stratification within the public school sector.

The task, then, is first to examine the degree of economic stratification between the private and public sectors of education, then to examine the degree of stratification within the private sector as compared to that within the public sector, and, finally, as in the case of race and ethnicity, to ask what the overall contribution of the private sector is to economic segregation.

Looking first at the distributions of students between sectors, table 3–5 and figure 3–1 reveal that the directions of the economic differences among students in the public and private sectors are consistent with what past research and popular conception lead us to expect. The private sector as a whole has an income distribution somewhat higher than that of the public sector, with a median income of $23,200, compared to $18,700 for the public sector. Within the private sector, the differences are also in the expected direction: $22,700 for the students in Catholic schools, compared

TABLE 3–5

Percentage Distribution of Students From Various Economic Backgrounds and Median Family Incomes in Public and Private Schools: Spring 1980

Amount of Money Family Makes in a Year[a]	U.S. Total	Public	Private		
			Total	Catholic	Other Private
Totals					
Number	5,798,420	5,246,991	551,429	361,250	190,179
Sample number	49,567	43,391	6,176	4,614	1,562
Percentage	100.0	100.0	100.0	100.0	100.0
$6,999 or less	7.2	7.7	2.6	2.4	2.9
$7,000 to $11,999	11.9	12.5	6.3	6.3	6.3
$12,000 to $15,999	16.7	17.2	12.4	12.8	11.5
$16,000 to $19,999	18.7	19.0	16.6	17.3	15.2
$20,000 to $24,999	18.1	18.0	19.2	20.7	18.1
$25,000 to $37,999	15.0	14.6	18.5	20.4	15.0
$38,000 or more	12.4	11.1	24.5	20.1	32.8
Median Income[b]	$19,000	$18,700	$23,200	$22,700	$24,300

NOTE: Details may not add to totals because of rounding.

[a] Taken from responses to BB101, "Which (of seven groups) comes closest to the amount of money your family makes in a year?".

[b] Median income is obtained by linear interpolation within the income category in which the 50th percentile falls.

The Student Composition of Public and Private Schools

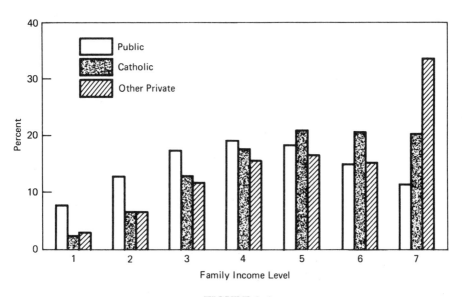

FIGURE 3–1

Percentage of Students in Public, Catholic, and Other Private Schools, by Family Income Level: Spring 1980.

to $24,300 for the students in other private schools. At the same time, the income distribution in each sector is quite broad. Of particular interest is the fact that the private sector does not contain students from homogeneous economic backgrounds; nor does either of its two major subsectors. The greatest differences between the public and private sectors occur, as one might expect, at the extremes: At the lower extreme, both of the private subsectors have proportions of students from families with incomes of less than $12,000 that are less than half as high as those in the public sector; at the upper extreme, the Catholic schools have almost twice as high a proportion and the other private schools have almost three times as high a proportion of students from families with incomes of $38,000 or more.

These differences suggest that there are a number of possible factors at work functioning to reduce the accessibility of lower income students to private education. Foremost among these, of course, is simply the cost of private education. But it may also be that private schools tend to be located at some distance from residential concentrations of lower income families, thus further reducing their accessibility. While an analysis comparable to that carried out on the local distributions of racial and ethnic groups (see pp. 49–51) cannot be included in this report, further research in this direction would be useful.

The second question relevant to an examination of the contribution of private schools to economic stratification concerns the distributions of students from different income levels within the sectors and school types. While we have seen that poorer students are underrepresented and wealthier students overrepresented in the private sector taken as a whole, it is quite another question to ask whether students from different economic backgrounds who are enrolled in each sector attend the same schools or different ones. To address this question, we can use the measures of contact and segregation that were used for race and ethnicity. The variable identifying student economic backgrounds, BB101, is collapsed into three categories for this analysis: below $12,000, between $12,000 and $20,000, and above $20,000. The segregation examined is that between those below $12,000, about 19 percent of the total, and those above $20,000, about 46 percent of the total.

Table 3–6 gives the results of the computations. As the overall propor-

TABLE 3–6

Indices of Contact and Segregation of Pupils From Higher and Lower Income Families in Public and Private Schools: Spring 1980

Measure	U.S. Total	Public	Private		
			Total	Catholic	Other Private
Overall Proportions					
High income ("over $20,000" on BB101)[a]	.429	.411	.595	.577	.629
Low income ("under $12,000" on BB101)[a]	.178	.188	.084	.082	.086
Index of Contact, s_{ij}[b]					
Proportion of the average low-income student's schoolmates who are from high-income families	.331	.323	.499	.476	.542
Proportion of the average high-income student's schoolmates who are from low-income families	.137	.148	.070	.068	.075
Index of Segregation, r_{ij}[b]					
Segregation of high-income students from low-income students	.23	.21	.16	.18	.14

[a] Taken from responses to BB101, "Which (of seven groups) comes closest to the amount of money your family makes in a year?".

[b] For the method of calculating the values of s_{ij} and r_{ij} see appendix A. Although the value of r_{ij} is theoretically identical to the value of r_{ji}, slight discrepancies will occur due to rounding.

tions (given at the top of the table) would lead one to expect, the measures of contact, s_{ij}, show that the average low-income student in the public sector has a lower proportion of schoolmates from high-income families than such a student in the private sector (.323 versus .499, columns 2 and 3). The disparity between the proportions of low-income schoolmates for the average high-income student in the two sectors is even more pronounced—the high-income student in the private sector has less than half as high a proportion of lower income schoolmates as the high-income student in the public sector (.070 versus .148).

These values of the measure of contact reflect both the proportions of high- and low-income students in the sector as a whole and the distribution of these students within each sector. The values on the index of segregation given at the bottom of the table, which standardize on the proportion of each group in the sector, shown the economic segregation within each sector of students from the two different income backgrounds. As in the case of race and ethinicity, the degree of economic segregation is lower in the private sector as a whole, and in the Catholic and other private sectors separately, than in the public sector. But the differences between the public and private sectors in internal segregation are much less here than in the case of black-white segregation.

With economic segregation, then, there is the same counterbalancing tendency as found in the case of racial segregation: Higher economic backgrounds are overrepresented in the private sector, but the private sector is less internally segregated than is the public. The overall levels of economic segregation are considerably lower than those of black-white segregation (for example, in the public sector, .21 versus .49), but a similar counterbalancing pattern holds.

We can ask, then, as in the case of black-white segregation, what the overall impact is of these two counterbalancing tendencies. Again, this is done by comparing the economic segregation among schools for all sectors together (the U.S. total in the table) to that for the public sector. This comparison shows the economic segregation among U.S. schools as a whole that would result from private school students being absorbed into the public schools and distributed among public schools as current public school students are. Here the comparison of .23 to .21 shows that the overall impact of the private sector is to increase slightly the degree of economic segregation, not, as in the case of black-white segregation, to effect an exact counterbalancing.

The similarity of pattern in the cases of racial and economic segregation raises a question about whether there might be a common cause. That is, in both areas, the segregation within the private sector is less than that within the public sector, while in both areas the private sector has higher proportions of the population group with greater resources (in the black-white comparison, whites; in the economic comparison, higher income groups).

Two related explanations seem plausible, both based on the assumption that parents will attempt to have their children in schools with others who are likely to do well in school, and that those parents with greater resources (higher incomes, or whites) will be better able to do this. The explanations are:

1. The proportion of lowest income students and the proportion of black students are lower in the private schools than in the public schools. Thus the parent who has chosen the private sector will be less concerned that the norms of the school and the standards of instruction will be brought down by students that the parent a priori assumes are more likely to have such an impact, that is, students from low-income families and black students (who, of course, are often from low-income backgrounds). Public school parents will have the same general concerns, but, with a higher proportion of low-income or black (or both) students in the sector as a whole, will manifest those concerns by moving their children to schools where the proportions are lower, if they have the resources to do so. It is white, higher income families who more often have such resources, and the end result is a higher degree of internal segregation.

2. Private schools, as will be evident in the subsequent chapters, have greater control of their students and exercise stronger discipline than do public schools. This is, of course, based to a considerable degree on the fact that private schools can expel students or use other disciplinary measures with much less legal constraint and much more parental acquiescence than the public schools. This stronger discipline means that a parent concerned about the norms and standards in the school will be more assured in the private sector that those norms and standards are maintained by the staff, rather than being shaped by the type of student body. Consequently, the private school parent will be less concerned about the student body composition, since that student body is "kept in hand" by the staff. Public school parents with the same general concerns, but seeing the norms and standards more shaped by the composition of the student body, will exert greater effort to have their children in schools where they see that composition favorable to school achievement. Parents with greater resources will be more successful in this, thus leading to

greater racial and economic segregation in the public than in the private sector.

The Religious Backgrounds of Public and Private School Students

Historically, issues of religious divisiveness have been central to debates concerning private education. Although economic differences are an important factor in private school enrollment, religious concerns have been, and continue to be, probably the strongest motivating force in parents' decisions to send their children to private schools. This motivation can be seen better, perhaps, in other countries. For a number of countries have, as well as secular schools, state-supported schools operated by religious groups; and, in some countries, the major sectors of publicly-supported education are those operated by different religious denominations.

As pointed out earlier (chapter 2), about 80 percent of private sector students are enrolled in schools affiliated with some specific religious denomination, and it is probably safe to assume that an interest in affirming basic religious values within the context of formal education is a major motivation for private school enrollment. This choice usually presents no problem. But when the question of public aid to private education is raised, many see a conflict with the separation of church and state mandated by the United States Constitution. In addition to the constitutional question, there is a social issue in the potential divisiveness of the orientations of religiously affiliated schools. Specifically, it is sometimes argued that the existence of religiously affiliated schools isolates youth of different faiths and generates intolerance of other religious faiths. Traditionally, this argument has been applied primarily to Catholic schools, and, because only the numbers of Catholic schools in the sample are sufficient to allow analysis in this area, the analyses conducted here will focus on Catholic schools. In particular, we will examine the extent to which Catholic and non-Catholic students are segregated from each other as a result of private education.

Table 3–7 gives a picture of the proportions of students from each of the major religious groups in each school sector. With the exception of Episcopalians, Catholics, and Jews, the public and the non-Catholic private sectors tend to be quite similar. While Catholics make up the overwhelming majority of the student enrollment in the Catholic school sec-

TABLE 3–7

Percentage Distribution of Students From Various Religious
Backgrounds in Public and Private Schools: Spring 1980

Religious Background	U.S. Total	Public	Private		
			Total	Catholic	Other Private
Totals[a]					
Number	6,280,304	5,652,648	627,656	413,264	214,392
Sample number	53,490	46,481	7,009	5,240	1,769
Percentage	100.0	100.0	100.0	100.0	100.0
Baptist	21.0	22.5	7.4	1.9	18.0
Methodist	8.6	9.3	3.0	1.0	6.8
Lutheran	6.2	6.7	2.0	1.0	4.0
Presbyterian	4.5	4.7	2.8	1.1	6.1
Episcopalian	2.1	2.0	3.1	0.7	7.8
Other Protestant	4.1	4.2	3.1	0.7	7.7
Catholic	34.2	30.7	65.8	90.9	17.4
Other Christian	6.5	6.8	3.6	0.9	8.9
Jewish	2.1	1.9	4.2	0.3	11.9
Other religion	4.3	4.5	1.8	0.4	4.5
None	6.4	6.8	3.1	1.2	6.9

NOTE: Details may not add to totals because of rounding.

[a] The total number reflects the usable responses to BB091 ("What is your religious background?"). Percentages are based on the population numbers.

tor, the Catholic contingent in the public schools (30.7 percent) means that, given the numerical bases, most Catholics are in the public schools. Also, perhaps contrary to general assumptions, the relative percentages of Baptists and Lutherans are smaller in the non-Catholic private sector than they are in the public sector, despite the traditionally strong Lutheran schools and the increasing numbers of Baptist schools.

Table 3–7 shows that there are sharply different proportions of Catholic students in the public, Catholic, and other private sectors. The next question concerns the distribution of Catholic students within each of the sectors (and, if the sample of other private schools were much larger, would also include the distribution of students of other religious backgrounds among the schools in that sector). Information on this distribution is given in table 3–8. This table shows that the average Catholic student in the Catholic school sector indeed has a very low proportion of schoolmates who are non-Catholic (.081), and that the average non-Catholic student in the public and other private sectors has a much smaller proportion of Catholic schoolmates (.240 and .125 compared to .805). Turning to the index of segregation, which standardizes on the differing proportions in each sector, the results are given in the last row of the table. It is not the

TABLE 3–8

*Indices of Catholic/Other Religious Background Contact and
Segregation in Public and Private Schools: Spring 1980*

Measure	U.S. Total	Public	Private		
			Total	Catholic	Other Private
Overall Proportions					
Catholics	.342	.307	.658	.909	.174
Other religious background	.658	.693	.342	.091	.826
Index of Contact, s_{ij}, for Catholics and "Others": Proportion of the average Catholic's schoolmates who are "Other"	.462	.541	.127	.081	.590
Proportion of the average "Other's" schoolmates who are Catholic	.241	.240	.244	.805	.125
Index of Segregation, r_{ij} (ranges from 0 = no segregation to 1 = complete segregation)[a]	.30	.22	.63	.11	.28

[a] For the method of calculating the values of s_{ij} and r_{ij} see appendix A. Although the value of r_{ij} is theoretically identical to the value of r_{ji} slight discrepancies will occur because of rounding.

case that non-Catholics and Catholics are more segregated within the Catholic sector than are non-Catholics and Catholics in public and other private schools. The opposite is true: Non-Catholic and Catholic students are the least segregated from one another in the Catholic schools (.115). Somewhat surprisingly, Catholic students are the most segregated in the non-Catholic private schools, though in no case is the extent of segregation very high.

The overall religious segregation in U.S. schools as a whole is higher than that in any single sector because of the concentration of Catholics in Catholic schools. However, it is lower than black-white segregation and about the same as Hispanic-Anglo segregation (.30 compared to .49 or .30).

We would expect the Catholic/non-Catholic segregation within the private sector as a whole to be higher than that in the public sector or either of the private sectors separately, and it is (.63). This means that, in contrast to the case of black-white segregation, policies that would draw children from the public sector to the private sector would move them from a sector of lower religious segregation to a sector of higher religious segregation.

We can also ask, as we did for racial, ethnic, and economic segregation, just what the overall contribution of the private schools is to religious segregation among schools in the United States. The current degree of segregation is, as shown in the table, .30. If students from the private sector were absorbed into the public sector and were distributed exactly as those currently in the public sector are distributed, the degree of segregation would be .22. Thus the private schools do contribute to the segregation of Catholic and non-Catholic students, raising the segregation index from .22 to .30. At the same time, this degree of segregation is, as noted earlier, not high, primarily because most Catholic students attend public schools.

Handicapped Students in Public and Private Schools

The final category of students that this chapter examines is the handicapped. Information about handicapped students in the schools is obtained from students' self-reports and from the school questionnaire. Neither of these is a wholly satisfactory information source, but use of both will give some information about handicapped students. Although table 2–6 in the preceding chapter shows that there is a considerably higher proportion of special education schools in the private sector than in the public, table 3–9, based on student reports, indicates that the public schools enroll a somewhat higher proportion of handicapped students than the private schools in our sample. However, the differences between sectors in table 3–9 are rather small for those reporting "some" kind (that is, including less severe kinds) of handicap.[5] The third row in the table, which reflects more serious handicaps, shows a somewhat greater difference, with about three-fifths as high a proportion of the Catholic and other private school students as of the public school students reporting a limiting handicap.

If principals' responses are used to estimate the percentages of handicapped children in these schools the differences are more pronounced (table 3–10). These reports indicate that in the public sector the average percentage of the student body that is handicapped is more than double that in the non-Catholic private schools, and over four times that in the

[5] Some of the students in private special education schools are paid for by public funds. Where the students' handicaps were severe enough so that they could not fill out a questionnaire, or where schooling did not terminate with a high school diploma, the school was ineligible by definition from the population of schools and students to be studied.

TABLE 3–9
*Percentage of Students Reporting Handicaps in Public
and Private Schools: Spring 1980*

			Private		
	U.S. Total	Public	Total	Catholic	Other Private
Percentage with some handicap other than visual (BB087A, C, D, E, F, or G)	12.0	12.2	9.4	8.5	11.2
Percentage with visual handicap (BB087B)	13.0	12.7	16.1	17.2	13.8
Percentage with a physical condition limiting work or education (BB088)	7.1	7.4	4.7	4.7	4.6

TABLE 3–10
*Mean Percentage of School's Student Body That Is Handicapped,
as Reported by Principals, and Criteria Used to Classify
for Public and Private Schools: Spring 1980*

			Private		
	U.S. Total	Public	Total	Catholic	Other Private
Mean Percentage of Students Classified as Handicapped (SB034 ÷ SB002A)	4.2	4.9	1.5	1.1	2.3
Percentage of Schools Using Various Criteria to Classify Students					
Standard test	74.9	90.1	28.1	33.0	18.2
Federal guidelines	74.6	91.7	18.0	23.4	7.1
State guidelines	79.6	96.6	23.0	28.0	12.9
Counselor's judgment	90.8	94.5	85.4	94.2	85.4

Catholic schools. The reason for this discrepancy between school reports and student reports is not clear. The comparison with table 3–9, which shows much less difference between sectors, suggests the possibility that in public schools students classified as handicapped would not be classified as handicapped in private schools. Three reasons for such a difference in classification seem possible: (1) in the larger schools found in the public sector, children who would be able to function normally in a smaller school must be classified as special and treated in a different fashion; (2) there is in the public sector an administrative incentive in the form of government aid for classifying children as handicapped—an incentive that does not exist or less often exists in the private sector; and (3) the more severely handicapped students, who would not respond to the survey, may be more numerous in the public sector. In any case, the data are clearly not sufficient for drawing inferences about the relative proportions of handicapped children in public and private schools.

Factors Affecting Access to Private Education

The examination of private school student composition has thus far focused on the distributions of students from various backgrounds between and within the educational sectors. An important general conclusion is that the extent of within-private sector segregation along racial and economic lines is lower than that found in the public schools, but that there is between-sector segregation because blacks and lower-income students are substantially underrepresented in private education. The higher degree of within-sector segregation in the public sector over the private sector is striking, because it is ordinarily overlooked when asking about the impact of private schools on segregation. The data serve as a reminder that the public schools of the United States constitute a rather highly stratified and differentiated set of schools, not the common school envisioned by Horace Mann.

In this section we will make an effort to address the analytical question of what factors affect different students' chances of enrolling in a private school, focusing primarily on the issue of the underenrollment of blacks in private education. Three factors in particular are worth examining as hypotheses amenable to empirical test. First, the geographic location of private schools may account for some part of the difference between public and private schools in their proportion of black students. Private schools may tend to be located in areas that have lower proportions of blacks than the areas in which public schools are located. Second, income differences between black and white families are likely to account for another part of the difference. Third, religious differences among racial or ethnic groups may play a part. The fact that blacks are less likely to be Catholic than are Hispanics and non-Hispanic whites may account for some part of the underrepresentation of blacks in the Catholic schools compared to the public schools—though not, of course, for the underrepresentation of blacks in the other private schools. Part of this difference between Catholic and other private schools in the proportion of blacks enrolled may be due to the first two of these three factors, rather than religion, that is, a greater proportion of Catholic schools may be located in or near concentrations of black students in large cities, and tuition may be lower in Catholic schools.

The first of these hypotheses can be tested by data on the racial and ethnic composition of the local areas in which the sampled schools are found. The data that come closest to fitting this description are the 1970 U.S. Census counts aggregated according to U.S. Postal Service zipcodes.[6] Because the available information on the schools includes their zipcodes, it is possible to compare the racial and ethnic composition of a school to the racial and ethnic composition of the same age group in the area covered by that zipcode. The Census classification closest to the ages of high school sophomores and seniors is the sixteen- to twenty-one-year age category.

To make such a comparison, the numbers of blacks, Hispanics,[7] and all sixteen- to twenty-one-year-olds in zipcode areas containing sampled schools of a given sector are aggregated, weighted by the numbers of sophomores and seniors in schools of that sector in the zipcode. (Methods of carrying out these calculations are described in appendix A).

Table 3–11 presents the results of these comparisons.[8] The first and fourth rows show the proportion of blacks and Hispanics aged sixteen to

[6] The data employed are from the U.S. Bureau of the Census Population and Housing Fifth Count Summary Tapes, 15 and 20 percent samples, Files A and B. File A consists of summaries for three-digit zipcode areas, and represents the entire United States population. File B consists of summaries for the five-digit zipcode areas within Standard Metropolitan Statistical Areas (SMSAs) only. Because the areas represented by the five-digit codes are likely to coincide more closely with the drawing areas of schools located in SMSAs, these codes are used for all schools that could be matched with them. Of the 1,015 schools in the High School and Beyond sample, 548 have five-digit zipcode information, 456 have only three-digit, and 11 could not be matched with either of the Census files because of missing information on the latter.

[7] There is of course no Hispanic category in the Census race question, and Hispanics do not enter into the "other" category of that question. For present purposes, we have equated "Hispanic" with the Census category "Spanish American." The latter refers to people of "Spanish language," of Spanish surname, or of Puerto Rican birth or parentage, depending on the area of the country. In order to obtain mutually exclusive white, black, and Hispanic categories, we assume that most of those that the Census Bureau classified as "Spanish American" classified themselves as "white" on the race question. Thus, for each zipcode area, the number of non-Hispanic whites is obtained by simply subtracting the number of Spanish Americans from the number of whites. Proportions are calculated by dividing the numbers of non-Hispanic whites, Spanish Americans, and blacks by the count of all sixteen- to twenty-one-year-olds in the area.

[8] The U.S. total 1970 proportions of sixteen- to twenty-one-year-old blacks and Hispanics differ somewhat from the totals for the 1980 High School and Beyond survey. The 1970 zipcode data show 10.2 percent black and 5.0 percent Hispanic. Table 3–1 shows that the 1980 sample is 12.8 percent black and 7.0 percent Hispanic. Assuming no measurement error, the differences between these figures point to demographic changes over the last decade. In the absence of detailed information about where the local changes have oc-

TABLE 3-11

Proportional Racial and Ethnic Composition of the Surveyed High Schools' Local Geographic Areas, Weighted by School Enrollments, and Differences Between Local Areas and Schools, by Educational Sector: Spring 1980

			Private		
Measure	U.S. Total	Public	Total	Catholic	Other Private
1. Proportion of local population that is black[a]	.128	.128	.124	.132	.110
2. Proportion of sector enrollment that is black[b]	.128	.137	.047	.056	.030
3. Over- or underrepresentation in proportion black		.009	−.077	−.076	−.080
4. Proportion of local population that is Hispanic[a]	.070	.069	.075	.080	.067
5. Proportion of sector enrollment that is Hispanic	.070	.071	.062	.071	.044
6. Over- or underrepresentation in proportion Hispanic		.002	−.013	−.009	−.023
7. Sum total of school enrollments used for weighting local population proportion[c]	6,852,696	6,195,338	658,158	429,224	227,934

SOURCE: (1) High School and Beyond, 1980; (2) U.S. Bureau of the Census, 1970 Census of Population and Housing Fifth Count Summary Tapes (15 and 20 percent samples): Files A and B: Population and Housing Summaries for three- and five-digit Zipcode Areas.

NOTE: Details may not add to totals because of rounding.

[a] Local proportions are adjusted for overall changes in proportion black, white, and Hispanic from 1970 to 1980, see footnote 8, p. 49 for further discussion.

[b] Sector proportions are obtained by combining the figures for sophomores and seniors given in table 3-1.

[c] These figures represent the sum of student weights without reference to any other variable; because of the absence of missing values the sums are higher than any of the total numbers given in other tables.

twenty-one that live in the local areas of the school of the average student in each of the different school types; the second and fifth rows show the proportions of blacks and Hispanics, respectively, in the schools of each

---

curred which, when aggregated, account for these overall shifts, we assume as a first approximation that the changes are distributed uniformly. The figures given in table 3-11 are derived on this assumption. They are computed by simply adding the differences between the overall proportions of blacks and Hispanics in 1980 and their respective 1970 overall proportions to the proportional local compositions for the average students in each school type. The Census data show that the average public school student attends a school located in an area that is .102 black and .049 Hispanic, and that the average private school student attends a school located in an area that is .098 black and .055 Hispanic. Thus, since the difference between the 1980 and 1970 overall proportions of blacks is .128 − .102 = .026, the corrected proportion of blacks in the community for the average public school student is .102 + .026 = .128, while for the average private school student it is .098 + .026 = .124. For Hispanics the overall difference is .070 − .050 = .020, and the corrected proportions are .049 + .020 = .069 for the average public school student and .055 + .020 = .075 for the average private school student.

sector. Comparing the public and private sectors as wholes, we see that private schools are located in areas where the black population is very slightly lower than the average for the public schools (12.4 percent versus 12.8 percent) and where the Hispanic population is very slightly higher (7.5 percent versus 6.9 percent). The differences in both cases are so small that they can be regarded as approximately the same.

From these data, then, we cannot conclude that private schools under-enroll blacks because the schools are not located close to where blacks live. If the geographic distribution of schools were the only constraint on black enrollment, we would expect to find a black enrollment in the private sector about the same as that in the public sector. As the third row of table 3–11 shows, the average private school student attends a school that has about 7.7 percent fewer blacks enrolled in it than there are blacks in the area in which the school is located, while the average public school student attends a school with 0.9 percent more blacks in it than in the surrounding area.

For Hispanics, we would again expect to find about the same proportions in the public and private sectors. Line 6 in the table 3–11 shows that there is only a small underrepresentation of Hispanic students, 1.3 percent, in the private sector.

Taking Catholic and other private schools separately, there are more blacks in the areas surrounding Catholic schools (13.2 percent on average) than in the areas surrounding other private schools (11.0 percent). This partially accounts for the greater numbers of blacks in Catholic schools (5.6 percent compared to 3.0 percent). Similarly, Catholic schools are located in areas with greater concentrations of Hispanics; but line 6 shows that the Catholic schools contain approximately the same proportion of Hispanics as reside in those areas (7.1 percent compared to 8.0 percent), while the other private schools have 2.3 percent fewer Hispanics than are found in the local areas.

Altogether, although other private schools are located in areas with somewhat fewer black residents, which partly accounts for their lower black enrollments, the low enrollment of blacks in private schools as a whole cannot be accounted for by the geographic distribution of black residence. For Hispanics, the enrollment in Catholic schools is slightly below the local proportion of Hispanics, but slightly above the national average. The lower enrollment in other private schools again cannot be accounted for by geographic distribution, though, as before, these schools are located in areas with somewhat fewer Hispanic residents.

The second hypothesis, that income differences are responsible for the lower enrollments of blacks and Hispanics in Catholic and other private schools, can be examined by looking at the proportion of Hispanics, blacks, and non-Hispanic whites in each of these sectors at each income level.[9] These subgroups in the private sector are small, so the data show some erratic variability; the general results should be regarded as suggestive but not conclusive. Figures 3–2 and 3–3 show the proportions of each group at each income level in the Catholic and other private schools, respectively. Table 3–12 gives the sample numbers and percentages upon which the graphs are based.

Figure 3–2 shows that income differences do account for a large part of the lower enrollments of blacks in Catholic schools. At the lower- and middle-income levels, the difference in enrollments of blacks and whites in Catholic schools is 2 to 3 percent; it is 1 percent at the highest level. This compares with a difference of 4.2 percent when income is not taken into account. (The column headed "Total" in table 3–12 shows that 7.1 percent of all non-Hispanic whites and 2.9 percent of all blacks are enrolled in Catholic schools.) Assuming that the differences represent a true income effect, these data indicate that the public-Catholic difference in proportions of blacks would be reduced to less than half its size if blacks had the same income distribution as whites.

There is a higher percentage of Hispanics than of non-Hispanic whites in Catholic schools at nearly every income level, increasingly so at higher income levels. Thus, if the incomes of Hispanics and non-Hispanic whites were the same, Hispanics would be somewhat overrepresented in Catholic schools.

Figure 3–3 shows that the increase in percent enrolled with increase in income is much less for all three groups in other private schools than in Catholic schools. The gradient is small and about the same for Hispanics and non-Hispanic whites, except for those at the highest income level, and it is nearly zero for blacks, again excepting the highest income level. Over most of the income range, the difference between the percentage of all non-Hispanic whites enrolled in these schools and the percentage of all Hispanics enrolled is about 1 percent. The difference between whites and blacks is about 2 percent at lower income levels, 3 percent or more at higher levels.

These differences can be compared to the overall differences when income is not controlled. The column headed "Total" in Table 3–12 shows

[9] Information on the family income level of students was obtained from variable BB101, which asked which one of seven different annual income ranges the respondent's family income was in: (1) less than $7,000, (2) $7,000 to $11,999, (3) $12,000 to $15,999, (4) $16,000 to $19,999, (5) $20,000 to $24,999, (6) $25,000 to $37,999, and (7) $38,000 or more. The seven levels on figures 3–1, 3–2, 3–3, 3–4, and 3–5 correspond to these ranges. The numbers and percentages on which figures 3–2 and 3–3 are based are given in table 3–12.

TABLE 3–12

Percentages of Whites, Blacks, and Hispanics From Each Family Income Level in Catholic and Other Private Schools,[a] and Total Numbers Sampled: Spring 1980
(Standard errors of percents in parentheses[b])

	Income groups							Total
	1	2	3	4	5	6	7	
A. Total Numbers in Sample								
Non-Hispanic white	1,566	3,372	5,760	6,858	6,879	5,979	5,079	35,493
Non-Hispanic black	1,255	1,393	1,148	954	852	512	357	6,471
Hispanic	900	1,139	1,108	963	787	458	348	5,703
B. Percentages in Catholic Sector								
Non-Hispanic white	3.0	3.7	5.2	6.0	7.3	8.7	10.2	7.1
	(.65)	(.49)	(.44)	(.43)	(.47)	(.55)	(.64)	(.20)
Non-Hispanic black	.8	1.9	2.1	2.8	4.3	5.9	8.9	2.9
	(.38)	(.55)	(.63)	(.80)	(1.04)	(1.57)	(2.27)	(.31)
Hispanic	2.0	4.2	5.6	7.1	9.0	9.0	13.9	6.5
	(.71)	(.90)	(1.04)	(1.24)	(1.53)	(2.01)	(2.78)	(.49)
C. Percentages in Other Private Sector								
Non-Hispanic white	2.3	2.0	2.7	2.9	3.4	3.5	9.2	3.9
	(.57)	(.36)	(.33)	(.30)	(.33)	(.35)	(.61)	(.15)
Non-Hispanic black	.4	1.0	.5	.9	.6	.7	1.9	.8
	(.26)	(.40)	(.30)	(.46)	(.39)	(.56)	(1.08)	(.16)
Hispanic	.3	1.5	1.7	2.2	2.0	3.7	4.3	2.1
	(.26)	(.54)	(.58)	(.71)	(.75)	(1.17)	(1.8)	(.28)

[a] The percentages signify the percentage of each of the twenty-one subpopulations defined by cross-classifying students in terms of family income and race-ethnicity that are enrolled in Catholic and other private schools. The percentages are based on the weighted numbers of students.

[b] Standard errors are calculated according to the formula

$$\text{s.e. } (p) = 1.5[p(100-p)/(\text{unweighted } N)]^{\frac{1}{2}}$$

where the number 1.5 is a correction factor that adjusts for the effect of clustering in the sample design of the High School and Beyond survey. The p's are the percentages given in the table, and the unweighted N's are the total numbers in the sample shown above. Correction factors for standard errors of these and other subpopulations are found on p. 12, Table 2 of the High School and Beyond codebook, *Information for Users: Base Year (1980) Data*, available from the National Center for Educational Statistics.

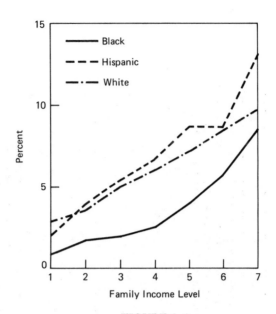

FIGURE 3–2

Percentage of Students From Differing Income Levels in Catholic Schools,
by Race and Ethnicity: Spring 1980.

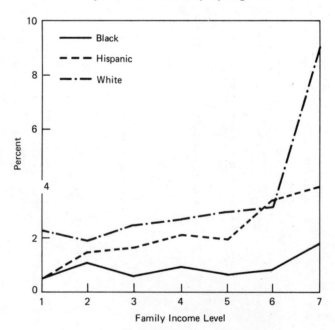

FIGURE 3–3

Percentage of Students From Differing Income Levels in Other Private Schools,
by Race and Ethnicity: Spring 1980.

that 3.9 percent of the non-Hispanic whites, 2.1 percent of the Hispanics, and .8 percent of the non-Hispanic blacks are in the other private schools. The differences with income uncontrolled are 1.8 percent for Hispanics and 3.1 percent for blacks; controlling for income reduces the difference between non-Hispanic whites and Hispanics from 1.8 percent to about 1 percent, but reduces the white-black difference by a lesser amount. Thus, income accounts for some part of the difference in enrollment of non-Hispanic whites and Hispanics in other private schools, for a smaller part of the difference in enrollment of whites and blacks.

These comparisons, of course, do not take religion into account. The fact that about 9 percent of blacks, about 35 percent of whites, and over 65 percent of Hispanics are Catholic[10] means that the enrollment rates of Catholics in each of these three groups in Catholic schools must be different from that shown in the graphs. In fact, as table 3–13 shows, there is a reversal among the groups in the enrollment rates of Catholics and non-Catholics in Catholic schools. Among Catholics, Hispanics are least likely to be enrolled in Catholic schools, and blacks and whites are equally likely to be enrolled. Among non-Catholics, the rates are of course low for all groups, but here blacks are most likely to be enrolled in Catholic schools, and Hispanics and whites are about equally likely to be enrolled.

Again, because there are differences in income distribution among blacks, whites, and Hispanics, Catholics from these three groups who have the same income levels should be enrolled at rates somewhat different from those shown in figure 3–2. Figures 3–4 and 3–5 show, for blacks, whites, and Hispanics at each income level, the enrollment rates for Catholics and non-Catholics separately.

The results are striking, although the small numbers of cases among

TABLE 3–13

Number and Percentage of Catholic and Non-Catholic Whites, Blacks, and Hispanics Who Are in Catholic Schools[a]*: Spring 1980*

Religious Background	Whites		Blacks		Hispanics	
	Number in thousands	Percentage	Number in thousands	Percentage	Number in thousands	Percentage
Catholic	326.0	18.8	12.0	18.7	28.1	10.3
Non-Catholic	35.4	1.0	12.1	1.5	2.2	1.1

[a] The numbers reported here are weighted to the population.

[10] These figures are obtained from the crosstabulation of the constructed race-ethnicity variable with BB091, which asked students to identify their religious background. About 13 percent of students left this question unanswered or answered "none" so that the percentages in the text are lower bounds as measures of religious background.

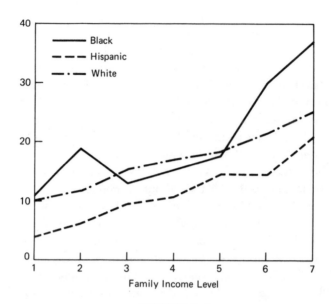

FIGURE 3–4

Percentage of Catholic Students From Differing Income Levels in Catholic Schools, by Race and Ethnicity: Spring 1980.

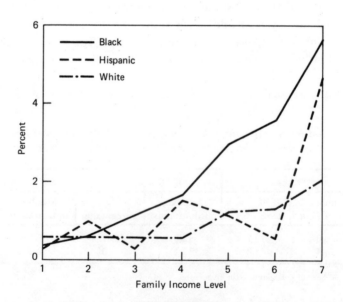

FIGURE 3–5

Percentage of Non-Catholic Students From Differing Income Levels in Catholic Schools, by Race and Ethnicity: Spring 1980.

black Catholics at each income level make the location of particular points erratic. Generally, with income controlled, black Catholics have higher enrollment rates in Catholic schools than white Catholics, and both groups have higher rates than Hispanics. Similarly, among non-Catholics, the black enrollment rate in Catholic schools is higher than the white rate, and again both are higher than the Hispanic rate.

Among both Catholics and non-Catholics, the Catholic school enrollment rate rises much more sharply at high-income levels for blacks than for whites, a result that is strengthened by consistency across the two religious groups. The evidence indicates that enrollment rates of high-income blacks are especially high compared to those of whites of the same religious group.

Thus, when the effects of both income and religious background are controlled for, blacks are enrolled in Catholic schools in higher proportions than are whites and Hispanics. Two caveats should be entered with respect to these findings. First, the numbers of blacks and Hispanics at the higher income levels are not large, as is seen in the panels A and B of table 3–12. This results in relatively high standard errors for the percentages of blacks and Hispanics in Catholic schools from these income levels. The confidence bands around the curves are quite wide, especially in figures 3–4 and 3–5, and it is possible that the true population figures could be substantially larger or smaller than our estimates. While the findings must be thus qualified, the striking consistency of the results across income levels represents an important finding.

A second caveat concerns the limitations of the method of analysis. The question addressed asks about the factors that influence enrollment in private versus public schools. Thus far the analysis has examined three factors (race-ethnicity, family income, and religious background) in some detail. But it is likely that other factors which are correlated with these three also influence the probability of attending private school. In so far as this is true, the effects that have been estimated thus far are inaccurate, either in the direction of being too low or of being too high.

In order to address these issues, a more rigorous method of analysis is required. Since our sample of private schools is more adequate for the Catholic sector, the examination that follows is restricted to an analysis of factors affecting the probability of Catholic as opposed to public school enrollment. The general questions of concern are, first, what are the effects of race and ethnicity on enrollment, controlling on other factors presumed to affect a student's chances of enrolling in Catholic school; and second, how do differences in family income affect the enrollment rates of the different racial and ethnic groups? Because the dependent variable of interest is categorical (Catholic versus public school enrollment) and because the numbers of students in Catholic schools are relatively small compared with those in public schools, the ordinary least squares estimation procedure that is typically employed in multivariate analysis is inappropriate here. The method chosen for use here is logit analysis, a method particularly well suited to the problem at hand (see Hanushek and Jackson, 1977: ch. 7 or Fienberg, 1977).

The model that is to be estimated specifies a number of social and economic background variables that are likely to affect the probability of enrollment in Catholic school. For this analysis, the sample is stratified by race and ethnicity, and the same model is estimated separately for whites, blacks, and Hispanics.[11] In addition to the factors of income and religious background, it is reasonable to include controls for other aspects of parental social status and for parental aspirations for their children's education. Of the measures available in the High School and Beyond base year survey, the following are included in the model of selection into the Catholic sector:

1. Parental income (thousands of dollars) (each of the seven income ranges shown in table 3–5 is identified with its midpoint. The midpoint of the "below $7,000" category is set at $3,500, and that for the "above $38,000" at $45,000);
2. Mother's education (coded to range from 1 to 9, with 1 = less than high school and 9 = advanced professional degree);
3. Mother's expectations for student's future education (coded 1 = college, 0 = other);
4. Respondent's number of siblings ("Sibs");
5. Religious background (coded 1 = Catholic, 0 = other);
6. Region of the country (coded 1 = Northeast, 0 = other);
7. Whether or not the student lives with a male and a female parent or guardian (coded 1 = both, 0 = other);
8. Whether or not the student planned to go to college when in the 8th grade (coded 1 = planned to go, 0 = did not plan to);
9. Family possessions: typewriter, more than 50 books (both coded 1 = family owns, 0 = family does not own).

---

[11] Because the effects of the independent variables on a students' probability of enrolling in Catholic school differ for blacks, Hispanics, and whites, it is methodologically appropriate to either estimate a single equation for all students that includes race and ethnicity interaction terms, or to stratify the sample by race and ethnicity. The latter approach has the drawback of complicating the presentation of results, but for the problem at hand no computer programs were available which simultaneously allowed the use of the student weights and the full number of cases in the sample. While omitting the weights does not seriously bias the estimates for whites, the oversampling of blacks and Hispanics in the Catholic sector necessitates the use of the weights. Since a program allowing the use weights for samples of sizes equal to the High School and Beyond samples of blacks and Hispanics is available (Coleman 1981: 53–62), we stratified by race and ethnicity. The models for blacks and Hispanics are thus estimated for the weighted sample, and the model for whites for the unweighted sample.

The region variable is included since Catholic schools tend to be dispor-
tionately located in the Northeast. The family possessions variables are
included as additional proxies for parental social status and aspirations for
their child. A more complete specification of the model would include
father's occupation and education, but since these variables have relatively high nonresponse rates in this survey, they were omitted from the
analysis.

Sophomores and seniors are combined to form the three samples for
which the model is estimated. Since the maximum likelihood method used
in estimating parameters in logistic analysis requires that only students
with usable responses to all variables in the model can be used, the number of deleted cases is large here despite the restrictions imposed on the
model. Of the total sample of public and Catholic sophomores and seniors
88 percent of the whites, 64 percent of the blacks, and 71 percent of the
Hispanics entered the analysis.

Table 3–14 shows the results of the multivariate logistic estimation.
Although logit model coefficients do not directly admit of a precise substantive interpretation,[12] the signs and strengths of the parameter estimates tell an interesting story. Consistent with crosstabular analyses, the
statistically significant coefficient for the income variable in each sub-
population indicates that family economic resources effect the probability
of Catholic school enrollment independently of social status influences.
Moreover, comparing the sizes of the income coefficients for the three
groups indicates that the effect of income is stronger for blacks and Hispanics than for whites. The additional effects of income that are specific
to blacks and Hispanics suggest that changes in the cost of Catholic education may lead to relatively greater changes in the enrollment of these
groups.

To describe the results of the logit analysis more concretely, estimates
of the Catholic school enrollment probabilities for students of different
backgrounds can be made. The primary interest here is in the different
effects of income on the probability of Catholic school enrollment for
whites, blacks, and Hispanics. To illustrate these effects, predicted enrollment rates for each of the three groups at seven different income levels
are shown in table 3–16. (The income levels used here are the midpoints
of seven categories of BB101. These levels are chosen to enable compari-

---

[12]A logit coefficient signifies the change in the log of the odds resulting from a unit
change in the independent variable. The log odds are transformed into ordinary probabilities by the equation:

$$P = 1/(1 + e^{-XB})$$

where e is the natural logarithm base, X is a vector of determined values for the independent variables, and B is the vector of logit coefficients.

TABLE 3–14
Logistic Model of Factors Affecting Probability of Enrollment in Catholic Schools[a]: Spring 1980

Dependent Variable: Catholic school enrollment (=1) versus public school enrollment (=0)

Independent Variables	White (N=29,911) b	Black (N=4,093) b	Hispanic (N=3,987) b
Intercept	−6.153	−6.176	−7.206
Income	.014	.028	.023
Mother's education	.041	.098	.104
Mother's expectation	.492	.690	.450
Sibs	.004*	−.200	−.114
Catholic religion	3.145	2.396	3.252
Northeast region	.292	.379	.455
Both parents present	.023*	.115*	.091*
8th grade college expectations	.487	.487	.553
Typewriter	.329	.662	.057*
Books	.215	.390*	.725
R²	.135	.141	.101

[a] Sophomores and seniors are pooled in the analysis. Due to computer program availability, the white students in the analysis are unweighted (see footnote 11, p. 58).

*Coefficient not significant at .05 level.

son with the tables and figures presented earlier in this section.) The rates are calculated by standardizing the logit equations to the average backgrounds given in table 3–15 on all variables except income. Two sets of estimates are obtained for each of the three racial and ethnic subpopulations. The first set is the predicted proportions of each group with backgrounds equal to that of the average U.S. high school student who would enroll in Catholic schools. (This background is represented by the means in the "total" column of table 3–15.) These predicted proportions thus indicate the rates that students from each of the family income levels who are white, black, or Hispanic would enroll in Catholic schools were they otherwise the same.

Comparison of the first and third columns of table 3–16 shows that blacks with an average background are, at all but the lowest income levels, more likely than whites to be enrolled in Catholic school. Blacks with a family income of $3,500 and a background that is average in the other measured respects are about equally likely as whites to be in Catholic school. The percentage differences between blacks and whites steadily increase across the income levels so that at the highest level ($45,000) blacks are 2.6 percent more likely than whites to enroll in Catholic school, other things equal. Hispanics exhibit the lowest enrollment rates of the three groups. But because the coefficient for income is larger for Hispanics than for whites, Hispanic enrollment rates increase with rising income more than the rates for whites.

The second set of estimates addresses a somewhat different question than the first. Here we ask about the effects of income on Catholic school enrollment for the average members of each of the social and ethnic subpopulations. Thus instead of standardizing the logit equation to the background of the average U.S. high school student, we now standardize the equation separately for the backgrounds of the average white, black, and Hispanic student. The average values of the background variables for each of the three subpopulations are given in table 3–15.

The results of carrying out these standardizations are found in the second, fourth, and sixth columns of table 3–16. Compared to the first set of standardizations, the proportions of whites and Hispanics at each income level are larger. The difference is more pronounced for Hispanics, reflecting the fact that Hispanics are about twice as likely as the average U.S. student to have a Catholic religious background. The predicted enrollments of blacks at each income level, in contrast, decline sharply from what was predicted for blacks with an average U.S. student background. This is in large part a reflection of the fact that blacks are far less likely to have a Catholic religious background than the average student.

TABLE 3–15
Means and Standard Deviations of Variables Used in Logistic Model of Factors Affecting Probability of Enrollment in Catholic Schools[a]: Spring 1980

Variable	Total		Whites		Blacks		Hispanics	
	Mean	Standard Deviation	Mean	Standard Deviation	Mean	Standard Deviation	Mean	Standard Deviation
Enrollment in Catholic school	.065		.071		.029		.065	
Income (000)	21.221	11.508	22.468	11.379	15.420	10.427	17.244	10.720
Mother's education	4.180	2.201	4.263	2.209	4.008	2.195	3.399	1.929
Mother's expectation	.616	.486	.617	.486	.618	.486	.593	.491
Sibs	3.034	2.045	2.881	1.915	3.807	2.475	3.518	2.311
Catholic religious background	.325	.466	.347	.472	.089	.262	.654	.494
Northeast region	.225	.418	.234	.423	.203	.402	.167	.373
Both parents present	.819	.385	.851	.356	.571	.495	.786	.410
8th grade college expectations	.532	.499	.532	.499	.554	.497	.491	.500
Typewriter	.678	.467	.719	.450	.481	.500	.575	.494
Books	.763	.425	.810	.399	.611	.487	.612	.487

[a] Sophomores and seniors are pooled for these estimates, which are based on the weighted sample. The means and standard deviations for each variable are calculated using all valid student responses.

TABLE 3-16

Predicted Catholic School Enrollment Rates for Whites, Blacks, and Hispanics at Different Family Income Levels, Otherwise Standardized to Average Backgrounds[a]: Spring 1980

Family Income Level	White		Black		Hispanic	
	Standardized to Average U.S. Student	Standardized to Average White Student	Standardized to Average U.S. Student	Standardized to Average Black Student	Standardized to Average U.S. Student	Standardized to Average Hispanic Student
$3,500	.021	.023	.020	.008	.010	.020
$9,500	.023	.025	.024	.009	.011	.023
$14,000	.024	.026	.027	.011	.012	.026
$18,000	.025	.028	.030	.012	.013	.028
$22,500	.027	.029	.034	.013	.015	.031
$31,500	.030	.033	.043	.017	.018	.038
$45,000	.036	.040	.062	.025	.025	.051

[a] Predicted rates are calculated from the b coefficients and background variable means presented in tables 3–14 and 3–15. The family income values listed in the first column above are substituted into the equation in place of the four income means shown in table 3–15. The totals derived by this procedure are converted to probabilities by the formula given in footnote 12, p 59.

Compared to the actual rates presented in tables 3–12 and 3–13 and figures 3–2 through 3–5, the predicted rates shown here are substantially lower. The differences are accounted for by the fact that the average backgrounds of the different types of students are higher in the Catholic sector than in the population as a whole. Thus a student at a given level of family income with a background otherwise equal to one of the average profiles shown in table 3–15 is less likely than average to enroll in a Catholic school, and the predicted rates given by the logistic model reflect this lower probability. The absolute magnitudes of the predicted rates, of course, are not the focus of the analysis presented in tables 3–14 through 3–16, but rather the relative enrollment rates of different groups.

To summarize the results of this section, the analysis has pointed to a number of factors related to private school enrollment. The examination has focused on the Catholic sector, since the High School and Beyond data are more complete for this part of private secondary schooling.

Not surprisingly, the analysis has shown that family income bears a consistent relationship to private school enrollment. This relationship does not appear to be reducible to differences in social background correlated with economic differences. The multivariate analysis provides strong evidence that the availability of economic resources exerts a significant independent effect on Catholic school enrollment.

By one commonly voiced view, interest in the private alternative is explained by a desire on the parts of some groups to avoid having their children attend schools with students of other backgrounds. This segregative intention is most frequently identified with whites vis-à-vis minorities. But this chapter has shown that, at least in the Catholic schools, minorities are enrolled at nontrivial rates. Moreover, these minorities tend to be more evenly distributed, or less segregated, in private than in public schools. Finally, the present section has shown that, other things equal, blacks are more likely to enroll in Catholic school than whites. The significance of this fact is heightened when one considers the relative absence of tradition for this pattern, except in the South. The data presented here strongly suggest that such a tradition is developing rapidly; blacks with the means to do so enroll in Catholic schools at rates that are generally higher than rates for other groups, when the effects of religious and other measured aspects of family background are controlled for. In light of these findings, any global characterization of private schools as racially segregative is ill founded.

These comparisons in the Catholic and other private schools indicate not only the degree to which income and religious differences can account for enrollment differences among whites, blacks, and Hispanics, but also what might be the consequences of lowering the economic barriers to private schools for lower income families, or of raising those barriers. An examination of this question is offered later in this chapter.

The Predicted Impact of Income Changes on Enrollment in Private Schools[13]

Some have argued that any changes which facilitate enrollment in private schools, even a general increase in affluence, would differentially benefit the white, upper-middle class, who use private schools more. Such changes would, in this view, extend still further the skimming process which leaves the poor and minorities in the public schools. Others argue that such changes place private schooling in the reach of those who cannot now afford it, and thus differentially benefit minorities and those less well off financially.

It is possible with these data to predict what students would be recruited into private schools by a marginal increase in family income, assuming no changes in tuition or other costs. We know for each income level the proportions of students from a given group (say, Hispanics or blacks) in private schools (table 3–12). This tells us the income elasticity of private schooling for each of these groups. We can, then, predict the recruitment into private schools from each group that would take place if there were a change that increased income by a fixed amount for all, as well as the defection from private schools that would take place if income were reduced by a fixed amount for all. We ask the former question, first with respect to whites, blacks, and Hispanics, and second with respect to students from families with different income levels.

It is possible to go a step further than we have gone thus far and ask about the social mix of those shifting between sectors with changes in income, assuming constant tuition levels. In particular, what we will ask in this section is what is the racial, ethnic, and economic mix of students who would come into the private sector if family income were to be greater by $1,000. Suppose incomes were increased by $1,000 for all, for example by a tax rebate or by a general increase in the standard of living. Would this mean that racial and economic segregation between public and private schools would be increased, by increasing the flow of white and middle- and upper-middle-class children into the private schools? Or would it mean that racial and economic segregation between these sectors

---

[13] The title of this section in the draft report was, "The Predicted Impact of a Policy Change Facilitating Enrollment in Private Schools." But there was extensive confusion among some who read the draft report, with some understanding the $1,000 income change to mean a $1,000 tuition tax credit. The title and some of the text of this section have been changed to prevent such misunderstanding. In effect, the hypothetical experiment here could be thought of as a $1,000 rebate to all families, to be used for any purpose, or a $1,000 increase in income, without change in private school tuition.

would be decreased, as relatively more blacks and Hispanics and lower income students would shift?

This is, in effect, asking the consequence of a hypothetical experiment. But it is important to distinguish this from a policy change such as tuition tax credits or vouchers, in which any benefit would be contingent on enrollment in private school. Such policy changes could be expected to have much greater effects than the incremental increase in overall affluence examined here. Here, we are asking only the social composition of the marginal students who would change sectors with the marginal increase in affluence.

This question can be answered by use of two items of information: the number of Hispanics, blacks, and non-Hispanic whites and the number of all children in the total 10th and 12th grade student population at each income level; and the increment in the proportion of students in private schools per $1,000 income increase at each income level for each group. Following the order of presentation of the earlier parts of this section, we will first examine the effects of this hypothetical income change on the distribution of blacks, Hispanics, and whites among the school sectors.

Figure 3–2 shows that the increase in the proportion of students attending Catholic schools with increase in income (the slope of the curve) is greatest for Hispanics. It is greater for whites than for blacks at low income levels, but greater for blacks than for whites at high income levels. Figure 3–3 shows that for all three racial and ethnic groups the increase in the proportion attending other private schools is lower than that for Catholic schools, except at the highest income levels for non-Hispanic whites. The curve is especially flat for blacks, except at the upper extreme of income.

Table 3–17 gives the numbers on which figures 3–2 and 3–3 are based. For example, the figure of 3 percent in the upper left corner means that 3 percent of all the non-Hispanic whites from families earning below $7,000 in the United States are enrolled in Catholic schools. Coupled with the total numbers of students at each income level, shown in the lower panel of table 3–17 these percentages make it possible to calculate the frequencies at which whites, blacks, and Hispanics currently within the public sector could be expected to shift into the private sector, given an increase in income of $1,000.

To illustrate how such a calculation is made, let us suppose that 3 percent of the students from families earning between $7,000 and $8,000 and 5 percent of the students from families earning between $8,000 and $9,000 are enrolled in private schools. Then, if income is increased by $1,000, the rates of private school enrollment for students from the fam-

TABLE 3-17

Percentages of White, Black, Hispanic, and All Students from Each Family Income
Level in Catholic and Other Private Schools, and Total Numbers: Spring 1980

School	Income Groups							(No Income Data)
	Below $7,000	$7,000–12,000	$12,000–16,000	$16,000–20,000	$20,000–25,000	$25,000–38,000	Above $38,000	
Catholic Schools								
Total Percentage[a]	2.0	3.3	4.8	5.7	7.1	8.5	10.1	
Non-Hispanic white	3.0	3.7	5.2	6.0	7.3	8.7	10.2	
Non-Hispanic black	.8	1.9	2.1	2.8	4.3	6.0	9.0	
Hispanic	2.0	4.2	5.6	7.1	9.0	9.0	13.9	
Other Private Schools								
Total Percentage[a]	1.3	1.7	2.3	2.7	3.0	3.3	8.7	
Non-Hispanic white	2.3	2.0	2.7	2.9	3.3	3.5	9.2	
Non-Hispanic black	.4	1.0	.5	.9	.6	.7	1.9	
Hispanic	.3	1.5	1.7	2.2	2.0	3.7	4.3	
Total Numbers in 10th and 12th Grades								
Total[a]	417,649	689,126	968,817	1,086,308	1,051,440	868,692	715,815	966,952
Non-Hispanic white	196,133	427,056	733,380	876,857	869,386	755,005	622,285	696,363
Non-Hispanic black	143,069	157,914	123,900	102,581	88,986	52,990	36,714	157,539
Hispanic	57,761	75,257	73,302	70,126	61,046	36,467	27,570	69,383
Other	19,281	28,024	36,985	35,399	29,465	22,051	26,193	43,667

[a] Total numbers and percentages are for students who gave a usable response to the question about family income (BB101). As these totals include students who did not give a usable response to the race-ethnicity variable, the sum of the numbers of whites, blacks, Hispanics, and others in the public schools at each income level is slightly smaller than the totals listed.

ilies who had had income levels of $7,000 to $8,000 would increase from 3 percent to 5 percent. If there are 100,000 students from families at that income level, the increase in the number of students in private schools would be 100,000 × .02, or 2,000. As the seven income categories that our data provide have intervals larger than $1,000, adjustments must be made to carry out the calculations. This procedure is described in the note to table 3–18.

Table 3–18 gives the results of the calculations: the expected numbers of whites, blacks, and Hispanics who would shift from the public schools to private schools with an increase of $1,000 in family income, and the racial and ethnic compositions of the group shifting. The results of this hypothetical experiment are interesting. Since this is a marginal income change, we are not interested in the size of the predicted shift, but its social composition, to indicate the compositional direction to which increased affluence would lead. First, the greatest shift would come among the Hispanics. Second, in both of the private sectors, the racial and ethnic composition of the group shifting (column 3) includes more minorities than does the current composition of these schools. Fourth, among those shifting into the Catholic sector, there is a higher proportion of minorities (column 3, .11 + .11 = .22) than in U.S. schools as a whole (column 5, .12 + .07 = .19); but this is not true in the other private sector (.02 + .06 = .08).

Altogether, what can be said in response to the questions posed is that the direction of change in racial segregation between the public and the private schools is toward less segregation, because the proportion of minorities among those coming into the private schools would be somewhat greater than the proportion already in these schools—and that this would come about primarily through the shifts of minorities (especially Hispanics and higher income blacks) into the Catholic schools. The magnitude of the impact of this small income is, of course, small, but it is the direction which is of interest here. Thus the common belief that changes which brought increased attendance at private schools would necessarily increase racial and ethnic segregation is not supported by these data, since the data indicate that for Catholic schools, which constitute two-thirds of the private sector, both blacks and Hispanics would respond to these additional financial resources to as great an extent as, or to a greater extent than, whites, and that both parts of the private sector would come to have higher proportions of minorities than they now do.

Using the same hypothetical income change, we can calculate the number of students not from each racial or ethnic group but from each income level that could be expected to shift from the public to the private schools as a result of such a change. The figures needed for this calcula-

TABLE 3–18

Predicted Numbers of Hispanics, Non-Hispanic Blacks, and
Non-Hispanic Whites Shifting to Catholic and Other Private
Schools with $1,000-Increase in Family Income[a]: Spring 1980

Group	Predicted Number	Proportion of Total Population	Proportion of those Shifting[b]	Present Composition[c] Sector	Present Composition[c] U.S.
To Catholic Schools					
Total	11,901	.0021	1.00	1.00	1.00
Non-Hispanic whites	8,913	.0020	.75	.85	.77
Non-Hispanic blacks	1,262	.0018	.11	.06	.12
Hispanics	1,290	.0032	.11	.07	.07
Other	436	.0022	.04	.02	.04
To Other Private Schools					
Total	7,144	.0012	1.00	1.00	1.00
Non-Hispanic whites	6,371	.0014	.89	.90	.77
Non-Hispanic blacks	178	.0003	.02	.03	.12
Hispanics	396	.0010	.06	.04	.07
Other	199	.0010	.03	.03	.04
Total					
Total	19,045	.0033	1.00	1.00	1.00
Non-Hispanic whites	15,284	.0034	.82	.86	.77
Non-Hispanic blacks	1,440	.0020	.08	.05	.12
Hispanics	1,686	.0042	.09	.06	.07
Other	635	.0032	.03	.03	.04

[a] In the calculations, each of the seven income ranges is identified with its midpoint. For the "below $7,000" category, the midpoint is set at $3,500; for the "above $38,000" category, the midpoint is assigned at $45,000. In order to approximate the percentages of whites, blacks, and Hispanics at each $1,000 increment, the differences between the percentages at the seven income levels are divided by the number of $1,000 increments that are between the midpoints of adjacent levels. The calculation is carried out as follows: $N_{ij} \times S_{ij}$, where N_{ij} is the total number from racial or ethnic group i in income level j (sophomores and seniors combined) and S_{ij} is, for racial or ethnic group i at income level j, the estimated change in proportion in Catholic or other private schools with increment of $1,000 in income. S_{ij} is calculated for each income level as described below. For each of the seven levels, this is:

level 1 (below $7,000)	$(P_2-P_1)/6$
level 2 ($7–12,000)	$\frac{1}{2}[(P_2-P_1)/6+(P_3-P_2)/4.5]$
level 3 ($12–16,000)	$\frac{1}{2}[(P_3-P_2)/4.5+(P_4-P_3)/4.0]$
level 4 ($16–20,000)	$\frac{1}{2}[(P_4-P_3)/4+(P_5-P_4)/4.5]$
level 5 ($20–25,000)	$\frac{1}{2}[(P_5-P_4)/4.5+(P_6-P_5)/9]$
level 6 ($25–38,000)	$\frac{1}{2}[(P_6-P_5)/9+(P_7-P_6)/13.5]$
level 7 (above $38,000)	$(P_7-P_6)/13.5$

The second column, proportion of those in public school, is obtained by taking the total number of sophomores and seniors, subtracting out the number who did not report family income (and thus were not used in the above calculations), and dividing this into the predicted number shifting.

[b] "Proportion of those shifting" may not add to 1.00 because of rounding.

[c] The proportions in these two columns are based on numbers of whites, blacks, and Hispanics who gave a usable response to the question about family income (BB101) and will thus differ somewhat from other figures in this section.

tion are given in table 3–17 in the rows labeled "Total," and the method is the same as that described in the note to table 3–18.

Table 3–19 gives the results of this exercise. In order to simplify the presentation, the seven-category income variable (BB101) is collapsed into three categories. The figures under the "Total" heading show the combined shifts into both private sectors. Column 2 shows that this income change would lead about equal proportions of students from the three income levels to shift. This would mean, as shown in column 3, that the income composition of those shifting would be .181 in the lowest income category, .358 in the middle category, and .462 in the highest category. This distribution is much less skewed than that currently in the private schools and is approximately the same as the overall U.S. distribution. The conclusion, then, is that an increase in economic resources of this sort would function to decrease the between-sector economic segregation.

The patterns for Catholic schools and the other private schools reveal some interesting differences. Students from low- and middle-income families would constitute a far larger proportion of the incoming students in the Catholic schools than in the other private schools (.221 + .431 = .652 versus .118 + .244 = .362). When the proportions shifting are compared to the proportions currently enrolled, it is clear that in Catholic sector and private sector as a whole the income distribution would move in the direction of the overall U.S. distribution. It appears that this change in income would have little effect on the income distribution in the other private sector, though.

Though this hypothetical experiment is suggestive, it is important to recognize that it does not predict the results of a policy change, such as a tuition tax credit. To make such a prediction, we would need information on the price elasticity of private schooling for each of these groups, rather than on income elasticity, and that information is not available.

It is useful to also point out that paradoxically, a general increase in the standard of living would be expected to have effects in the opposite direction to those described in this section—that is, toward making private school attendance more highly dependent on income. The reason is that schooling is labor intensive, and thus the price of private schooling increases approximately at the same rate as incomes generally. It thus becomes more expensive relative to other goods. This is a special case of general phenomenon which also accounts for why the performing arts become less and less self-supporting as affluence of a society increases (Baumol and Bowen, 1968).

One could thus expect private school enrollments to decline if the standard of living increases and the relative attractiveness of public and pri-

The Student Composition of Public and Private Schools

TABLE 3-19

Predicted Numbers of Students at Different Income Levels Shifting
to Catholic and Other Private Schools with $1,000-Increase
in Family Income: Spring 1980

Income Level[a]	Predicted Number[b]	Proportion of Total Population	Proportion of Those Shifting[c]	Present Composition	
				Sector	U.S.
To Catholic Schools					
Total	12,890	.0023	1.000	1.000	1.000
Below $12,000	2,848	.0026	.221	.087	.191
$12,000–19,000	5,549	.0027	.431	.301	.354
$20,000 or more	4,493	.0017	.349	.612	.455
To Other Private Schools					
Total	8,313	.0014	1.000	1.000	1.000
Below $12,000	981	.0009	.118	.091	.191
$12,000–19,000	2,032	.0010	.244	.267	.354
$20,000 or more	5,300	.0020	.638	.641	.455
Total					
Total	21,203	.0037	1.000	1.000	1.000
Below $12,000	3,829	.0035	.181	.089	.191
$12,000–19,000	7,581	.0037	.358	.290	.354
$20,000 or more	9,793	.0037	.462	.622	.458

[a] The seven-income categories of variable BB101 are collapsed into these three levels in order to simplify presentation.

[b] The method of calculation used to obtain the predicted numbers at each income level shifting is the same as that described in footnote "a" to table 3-14, except that the N_{ij} and S_{ij} terms reduce here to N_j and S_j—the total number of students in income level j (from table 3-17), and the estimated change in proportion in Catholic or other private schools for the group of students at income level j, respectively.

[c] "Proportion of those shifting" may not add to 1.000 because of rounding.

vate schools remains unchanged. The fact that the fraction of children in private schools has remained approximately constant over a long period of increasing standard of living implies that the relative attractiveness of public schools to private schools has declined over this period.

4

School Resources

BY school resources, we refer to course offerings provided to students, physical facilities available to students, special and federally funded programs, and the quantity, quality, and breadth of teaching and professional support personnel. These physical and human resources available in a school constitute boundaries of opportunity for students within a given school. Only, for instance, if calculus is taught at a school should one anticipate that students at that school may master certain mathematical principles.

The debate concerning the relative merits of private and public secondary schools incorporates some presumed resource differences between these two sectors. For example, some argue that public schools, because of their size and school district linkages, can provide a wider range of course offerings to students. And, insofar as size continues to distinguish public schools from other types, they will provide a broader range more efficiently. Others have argued that the limitations of private schools in this area are more than compensated for by the greater attention that students receive in the private sector. This chapter provides information relevant to this aspect of the public-versus-private debate.

In comparing school resources, we include the two special subgroups of schools referred to in chapter 1: high-performance public schools and high-performance private schools. Although the selection of these schools was based not on representativeness but on the proportion of high-performing seniors, the resources available to students in them show

72

something about what exists in public and private schools where academic performance is especially high. For simplicity of exposition, we sometimes refer to these subgroups of schools as "sectors," but when we speak of the "three school sectors," the reference is always to the public, Catholic, and other private sectors.

The school questionnaire provides information on a number of resources provided by the school, but our analysis will be limited in certain areas. The most important omission is the general level of school expenditure. Principals were informed that they need not respond to an item about per-pupil expenditure if they had recently provided this information in an NCES survey. Since this information had been provided by many schools in the preceding year, the item remained unanswered for a large number of schools. Until the data from these earlier surveys are added, per-pupil expenditure is unavailable for analysis.

For certain resources (those that varied according to school enrollment), two tables will be presented: one that reports the percentage of schools within each sector having a particular resource and one that reports the percentage of sophomore students within each sector attending a school where a particular resource exists (referred to as student access).[1] This manner of presentation allows examination of both the resource variability among sectors and, through a comparison of the two tables, the extent to which certain resources are disproportionately found at larger schools. Most of the analysis, however, focuses on the accessibility of various resources within each sector.

Course Offerings

Table 4–1 shows the percentage of schools within each sector offering a selected sample of academic, technical, and vocational courses. The items

[1] To determine the percentage of sophomores in each sector having access to a given resource, the response on each item was weighted by the sum of sophomore weights attached to that school. The proportion of sophomores in the total student population represented by a given school is slightly different from the proportion of seniors, primarily because of differential dropout between the sophomore and senior years. However, in the analysis we assume that this weighted sophomore estimate is sufficiently close to that for the high school student body as a whole that we can simply make reference to "students" within various sectors.

Obviously, our term "access" cannot be strictly correct for those courses with prerequisites. A student must have had second-year French to be eligible for (and therefore have access to) third-year French. The use of the term "access" has been chosen to reduce the number of convoluted phrases required in describing the variation among sectors from a student's perspective.

TABLE 4–1

Percentage of Public and Private Schools Offering Specific Courses: Spring 1980

Course	U.S. Total	Major Sectors			High-Performance Schools	
		Public	Catholic	Other Private	Public	Private
Total Number of Schools	20,316	15,766	1,571	2,966	12	11
Mathematics						
Geometry	97	96	100	95	100	100
Algebra 2	96	97	98	95	100	100
Trigonometry[a]	76	76	91	69	96	70
Calculus	47	47	60	38	94	100
Science						
Chemistry	94	96	100	79	100	100
Physics	89	90	95	79	100	100
Language						
Third-year Spanish	45	46	86	19	100	60
Third-year French	39	39	76	22	81	100
Third-year German	20	20	27	16	76	40
Other						
Auto mechanics	41	50	8	12	68	10
Driver training	82	89	63	52	81	20
Economics	63	63	71	58	80	90
Ethnic or black studies	16	16	16	12	41	20
Family life or sex education	65	69	63	45	66	30
Home economics	84	97	50	33	100	10
Psychology	59	58	56	66	89	80
Wood or machine shop	74	89	4	32	100	50

[a] Trigonometry may be incorporated into another subject, such as analytical geometry, and not reported here. Thus the figures presented here may underestimate coverage of the topic.

were taken from a larger list in the school questionnaire (see appendix B). The percentage of students within each type of school having access to these courses is reported in table 4–2. Our analysis will begin with mathematics and science, those courses presumed to be the most demanding, as well as especially important to the successful pursuit of many branches of postsecondary education.

MATHEMATICS AND SCIENCE COURSES

Nationally, nearly all schools offer algebra 2 and geometry (95 to 100 percent). A smaller percentage of schools offer trigonometry (76 percent) and calculus (47 percent), but table 4–2 shows that student access to these subjects is better than these percentages suggest: 84 percent of students

TABLE 4-2

*Percentage of Sophomore Students in Public and Private Schools Attending
Schools Where Specific Courses Are Offered: Spring 1980*

Course	U.S. Total	Major Sectors			High-Performance Schools	
		Public	Catholic	Other Private	Public	Private
Mathematics						
Geometry	99	99	100	98	100	100
Algebra 2	98	98	97	98	100	100
Trigonometry[a]	84	84	91	90	93	74
Calculus	63	62	71	61	94	100
Science						
Chemistry	98	98	100	92	100	100
Physics	96	96	96	91	100	100
Language						
Third-year Spanish	72	72	94	44	100	68
Third-year French	65	64	82	48	91	100
Third-year German	39	40	40	31	82	44
Other						
Auto mechanics	61	66	11	18	65	14
Driver training	86	87	68	74	78	25
Economics	72	71	79	73	79	86
Ethnic or black studies	28	29	17	9	45	25
Family life or sex education	76	76	67	67	79	32
Home economics	93	96	61	45	100	11
Psychology	71	71	72	69	88	82
Wood or machine shop	87	94	9	50	100	47

[a] Trigonometry may be incorporated into another subject, such as analytical geometry, and not reported here.
Thus the figures presented here may underestimate coverage of the topic.

have access to trigonometry and 63 percent to calculus. However, variations do exist among sectors for some mathematics and science course offerings. For example, nearly all students in high-performance public and private schools have access to a calculus course, as compared with 62 percent in public schools, 71 percent in Catholic schools, and 61 percent in other private schools. For the country as a whole, nearly all students have access to physics and chemistry (96 percent and 98 percent, respectively) and there are only slight differences among sectors. In every sector, over 90 percent of the students have access to these basic science courses.

Thus, there is only one substantial difference in science and mathematics course accessibility among these sectors—calculus—and it arises in the high-performance schools, in both the public and private sectors. Among the three sectors, Catholic schools show slightly higher accessibility rates for science and mathematics courses than do public or other private schools.

LANGUAGE COURSES

Language course offerings, in addition to their assumed value in augmenting one's mastery of English, provide the skills relevant to several aspects of adult life. For instance, German has traditionally been considered the second language of serious academic pursuits, French the language of culture, and Spanish the practical second language for Americans. Although one should be cautious in making inferences from such a typology, it may provide some orientation to the differences in language learning opportunities among public, Catholic, and other private schools.

In order to assess the degree to which students have an opportunity to acquire mastery of these languages, school administrators were asked to report whether their schools offered third-year Spanish, French, and German. Nationally, 45 percent of the schools offer third-year Spanish, 39 percent third-year French, and 20 percent third-year German. Overall, this suggests relatively little attention to foreign languages in an era in which there is more international mobility and communication than ever before.

But the different sectors vary considerably in their offerings. Among the three sectors, Catholic schools provide the most extensive language offerings: More than three quarters offer third-year French and even more offer third-year Spanish; less than half of the public schools and less than a quarter of the other private schools offer these courses. In all three sectors, only about a quarter or less of schools offer third-year German. Both public and private high-performance schools offer more extensive language opportunities than the schools in any of the three major sectors, but German is available less often than the other two languages even in these schools.

Student access to these courses provides a different view on the question, revealing more clearly the differences in opportunities among the sectors. The other private and public sectors show the largest shift, indicating the great variation in language course offerings between large and small schools in these two sectors. In general, it is in the smaller schools that these courses are not offered, so that the percentage of students having access to the courses is greater than the percentage of schools offering them.

In addition to the variation in language course offerings with school size in the public and other private sectors, patterns not shown in the tables appear noteworthy. Third-year courses in one language appear to be offered at the expense of similarly advanced courses in other languages in both the public and other private sectors. Moreover, 73 percent of the other private schools offer no third-year language courses, leaving 44 percent of the students without access to any third-year language. In contrast, the majority of Catholic schools offer third-year courses for at least two languages.

Returning to the initial typology, it can be said that both Catholic and public schools emphasize Spanish, the "practical language"; that Catholic schools, as well as the high-performance schools, tend to emphasize French, the "language of culture"; and that high-performance public schools provide German, the "language of scholarship", more often than any other type of school. In terms of inaccessibility of advanced language courses, German is least often available in all sectors, and students in the other private sector are least likely to have access to a third year of study in each of the languages.

SOCIAL STUDIES COURSES

In the area of social studies, four courses are available for analysis: economics, ethnic or black studies, family life or sex education, and psychology. We will only attempt to highlight some of the initial findings here. Extra caution should be taken in the interpretation of accessibility to these courses, since the subject-matter boundaries are more fluid than any of those we have yet considered.

Economics and psychology are available to comparable proportions of students: between 69 percent and 86 percent of the students in each of the sectors have access to these courses. Ethnic or black studies are available to substantially fewer students in any sector. The greatest accessibility is found in the public sector, where 29 percent of the students in public schools as a whole and 45 percent in the high-performance schools are offered such a course. Lowest accessibility to such courses is found in the other private schools. Family life or sex education courses are available to the majority of students in all sectors (except the high-performance private). Again, the greatest accessibility to these courses is found in the public sector.

TECHNICAL, VOCATIONAL, AND PRACTICAL COURSES

The last series of courses we will consider are those that are technical, vocational, or practical in nature: auto mechanics, wood or machine shop, driver training, and home economics. Here there are extensive differences between the public and private sectors. In the public sector, well over half (66 percent) of the students have access to an auto mechanics course, 94 percent to a wood or machine shop course, 87 percent to a driver's training course, and 96 percent to a home economics course. Only in the case of driver's training do the private sectors offer these courses at comparable rates, although home economics is available to about half the students in private schools. The lowest accessibility to technical or vocational courses is to be found in the Catholic sector, where wood or machine shop courses and courses in auto mechanics are each available to only about 10 percent of the students.

It is in this area of technical and vocational courses that high-performance private and public schools differ the most in course offerings. Well over half of the students in the high-performance public schools have access to these courses, whereas less than half of those in high-performance private schools have such access. This suggests the difference in character of these two sets of high-performance schools: The public schools are large and comprehensive; the smaller private schools, specializing as college preparatory schools, seldom offer the more practical courses.

More generally, students in public schools have much greater access to technical and vocational courses than those in private schools. (The degree to which access translates into course enrollment will be examined in chapter 5.) Although we cannot investigate the sources of these differences in course offerings, one possible source can be suggested. Technical and vocational courses are more costly than others. The low availability of these courses in Catholic and other private schools may be due in part to their cost relative to their perceived value by parents.

Staffing Patterns

Staffing patterns represent another set of boundaries to the capacities of schools to foster students' intellectual and emotional growth and to provide an environment in which these can take place. To assess the degree to which private and public schools differ in their staffing patterns, and thereby in their capacities to provide resources for intellectual and emotional growth, we report simple student-to-staff ratios within each sector.[2]

[2] The formula used in calculating these ratios is shown at the bottom of table 4–3.

TABLE 4–3

Staffing Ratios for Public and Private Schools: Spring 1980
(Average number of students per staff type[a])

Staff	Major Sectors			High-Performance Schools	
	Public	Catholic	Other Private	Public	Private
Total Number of Schools	16,051	1,572	3,123	12	11
Mean Enrollment	757	546	153	1,386	310
General Professional Staff					
Overall Ratio	15	16	6	15	7
A. Teachers	16	18	7	18	8
B. Assistant principals, deans	503	410	120	433	163
C. Counselors	323	235	55	284	182
D. Librarians and media specialists	597	340	212	696	163
E. Remedial specialists	504	891	382	563	0
F. Psychologists	2,025	4,579	1,177	2,064	1,033
Other Staff					
A. Teacher aides	349	2,549	124	380	1,033
B. Volunteers	839	385	101	312	344
C. Security guards	1,824	17,055	780	1,868	1,395

[a] $\text{Ratio} = \dfrac{\text{weighted enrollment}}{\text{weighted number of full-time equivalent staff}}$

As the first line of table 4–3 shows, Catholic and public schools have much larger ratios of students to staff members than do other private schools. Catholic and public schools have a student-professional staff ratio of sixteen and fifteen respectively; the other private schools have, on average, six students for each full-time professional staff person.

Nearly all of this difference is attributable, of course, to the student-teacher ratio, shown in line 2 of table 4–3. Among the three sectors, Catholic schools have the highest student-teacher ratio (eigtheen), followed closely by public schools, while the other private schools have less than half as many students per teacher. Comparison of the high-performance schools shows a similar public-private difference, with the private schools having less than half as many students per teacher.

Other staffing ratios associated with intellectual stimulation and growth include those for librarians and media specialists, remedial specialists, and teacher aides. Among the three sectors, the greatest difference in these staffing patterns is the lower ratio of students to remedial specialists and teacher aides in other private schools. It is possible that this is attributable to the higher incidence of special education schools in the other private sector (as shown in table 2–6). High-performance private schools have the lowest ratio of librarians and media specialists to students of any of the sectors. Of course, some of this variation is attributable to school size (to be discussed later).

In the areas of emotional growth and control of the school environment, we examined three student-to-staff ratios: assistant principals and deans, counselors, and security guards. Again, among the three major sectors, the other private schools have the lowest student-to-staff ratios. Of particular note is the low student-to-counselor ratio in the other private schools (55, as compared with 324 in the public schools and 235 in Catholic schools). Catholic schools show the highest student-to-security-guard ratio, indicating that there are very few Catholic schools with security guards. The ratio of full-time security guards to schools is approximately 1 for every 2.4 public schools, 1 for every 31 Catholic schools, and 1 for every 5 other private schools.

Finally, it is interesting to note the incidence of volunteers within each school type. Volunteers, relative to student enrollment, provide the least service to public schools, where there is on the average 1 full-time volunteer for every 841 students. By contrast, other private schools have the greatest relative number of volunteer services—approximately 1 full-time volunteer for every 100 students.

These comparisions on staffing patterns can be misleading, given the different sizes of the schools in each sector. That the public schools tend to be large and the other private schools very small means that if there were 1 staff member per 757 students in both of these sectors there would be 1 per school in the public sector and only 1 for every 5 schools in the other private sector. Thus, the ratios of students to remedial specialists of 382 to 1 in the other private sector and 504 to 1 in the public sector work out to be 1.5 per school in the public sector, but only .4 per school in the other private sector. And although the number of students per assistant principal and dean is only 120 in other private schools compared to 503 in public schools, the number per school (1.3 and 1.5, respectively) is approximately equal.

In addition to the quantity of personnel available to students, the quality or training of personnel is also relevant to a student's intellectual growth. The proportion of teachers holding master's or doctor's degrees is one indicator of staff quality. The three sectors do not differ markedly in the proportion of teachers holding advanced degrees: The average public school has 39 percent of its teachers holding master's or doctor's degrees, the average Catholic school 42 percent, and the average other private school 34 percent. The high-performance schools, however, do differ from the others in this respect. In the public high-performance schools, 67 percent of the teachers hold advanced degrees, and in the private high-performance schools 54 percent hold advanced degrees.

Regarding staff resources, then, one can draw several conclusions. There is a striking contrast between the student-teacher ratios in the public and Catholic schools and that in the other private schools. For specialized staff, the comparison is more difficult: the student-staff ratios are in many cases lower in the other private schools, but the fact that the other private schools tend to be small means that there are fewer of them with at least one such specialist than there are public or Catholic schools. The three sectors are similar in the proportions of their teaching staff with advanced degrees, but high-performance public and private schools have higher percentages of teachers with advanced degrees.

Special Programs

Financial resources translate not only into staff and curriculum, but also into programs serving the special needs and interests of students. Table 4–4 shows for each sector the percentages of students having access to selected

TABLE 4–4

Percentage of Sophomores in Public and Private Schools Having Access to Selected Special Programs: Spring 1980[a]

| | | Major Sectors | | | High-Performance Schools | |
Program	U.S. Total	Public	Catholic	Other Private	Public	Private
Work experience or occupational training credit	83	88	42	30	89	25
Credit by contract	30	31	24	18	50	11
Travel for credit	13	13	14	8	56	24
College board advanced placement courses	47	47	49	42	85	100
Program for gifted or talented	56	58	37	36	56	73
Bilingual program	28	31	5	6	50	0
Alternative school program	47	51	8	11	50	0
Program for pregnant girls (or mothers)	41	43	22	15	24	0
Student exchange program	55	57	37	44	67	78

[a] Sophomore access was estimated by weighting the school response by the sum of sophomore weights in that school. These weighted responses for each sector were used to determine the proportion of sophomores in a given sector having access to a program. (See footnote on p. 73 for further discussion.)

special programs. We examine three classes of special programs: alternative credit programs, programs for the talented, and programs for students with special interests or needs.

Alternative means of earning high school credits provide students with a broader range of learning-experience options. This survey inquired about three alternative ways of earning credit: work experience or occupational training credit, travel for credit, and credit by contract. Public and private schools differ most in the proportion of students having access to work experience or occupational training credit: 88 percent of the students in public schools have access to this as compared with 42 percent in Catholic schools and 30 percent in other private schools. Substantially fewer students in all types of schools have access to travel for credit or credit by contract. Nationally, 13 percent of all schools have travel for credit, and 30 percent have credit-by-contract programs. Travel for credit is more often found in high-performance schools, both public and private. Credit by contract, while in evidence within all school types, is more often available to public school students.

Programs oriented toward high-achieving students are available in all types of schools with a few substantial, but not surprising, differences. Programs for the gifted or talented appear in relatively low proportions in all but the high-performance schools. The similarity among the public, Catholic, and other private sectors is greatest in the area of college board advanced placement courses (between 42 and 49 percent of the students in each of these sectors have access to such courses), and this similarity is in sharp contrast to the high-performance public and private schools, where nearly all students have access.

Programs for students with special needs or interests include bilingual programs, alternative-school programs, programs for pregnant girls, and student-exchange programs. Generally, more public schools than private schools have these programs. In particular, bilingual programs are offered with substantially greater frequency in public schools. Approximately a third of the students in all public schools have access to such a program, as do half the students in high-performance public schools.

Alternative-school programs and those for pregnant girls appear most frequently in public schools. Alternative schools began in the 1960s outside the public school system, and table 2–6 shows that in the total universe of schools there is a higher percentage of alternative schools in some types of private schools than in the public sector. However, this question asked about alternative *programs* in the school. Although very few public schools are alternative schools (1.4 percent; table 2–6), many have an alternative-school program for a subset of students within the school. It is this which accounts for the relatively high percentages for public schools in table 4–4.

The major differences among the three sectors in the availability of special programs appear to be two: First, public schools have more programs emphasizing concrete career preparatory experience; second, public schools generally have more programs designed for students with special needs or interests than does either of the private sectors.

Physical Facilities

The physical facilities of a school do more than provide space for traditional classroom activity. For instance, subject-area resource centers may provide a way for students to pursue the activity of learning more informally, student lounges and cafeterias provide arenas for student culture to emerge, and areas allocated for remedial assistance provide space for specialized equipment and resources.

Table 4–5 shows the frequency that various facilities are available to students in each sector. The accessibility of career-related facilities in the public sector points again to its stronger orientation toward career preparation: 85 percent of the public school students attend a school where

TABLE 4–5

*Percentage of Sophomores in Public and Private Schools Having
Access to Certain Physical Facilities: Spring 1980*[a]

| Facility | U.S. Total | Major Sectors | | | High-Performance Schools | |
		Public	Catholic	Other Private	Public	Private
Subject area resource center (not library)	26	25	42	27	56	70
Career information center	85	85	92	51	89	49
Occupational training center	27	30	1	0	18	0
Remedial reading or mathematics laboratory	67	69	50	27	69	11
Media production facilities	56	56	51	63	51	64
Indoor lounge	22	21	26	63	45	93
Cafeteria	96	97	92	82	100	82

[a] Sophomore access was estimated by weighting the school response by the sum of the weights in that school. These weighted responses for each sector were used to determine the proportion of sophomores in a given sector having access to each facility. (See footnote on p. 73 for further discussion.)

there is a career information center, and 30 percent attend a school where there is an occupational training center. Only Catholic schools exceed public schools in the availability of career information centers.

The provision of special laboratories for remedial reading and mathematics work are most in evidence in public schools: About two-thirds of the students in this sector are in schools with at least one of these facilities. In the Catholic sector, about half of the students are in schools with such a laboratory, while only about one quarter of the students in the other private sector are in schools with such a laboratory.

Over half of the students in every school type attend schools with media production facilities. Without greater detail on their utilization and capacities, few inferences can be made. One may assume that these facilities permit teachers to prepare audio and/or video learning materials as well as to develop learning activities involving student originated productions.

Among the three major sectors, student lounges appear most frequently in other private schools, and almost all high-performance private schools have student lounges. It is possible that the small enrollments of other private schools makes it more feasible to provide this facility. Nearly all schools of all types have student cafeterias.

This comparison of facilities indicates again the general similarities between Catholic and public schools as compared to the other private schools. These measures of physical facilities are of course superficial; a comprehensive comparison of physical facilities in different sectors would require a different kind of survey.

Federal Programs

One set of resources for which we expect to find differences between public and private schools is federally-financed programs. For instance, given that some of the federal funds under the Elementary and Secondary Education Act (ESEA) are targeted to groups with special needs, we might expect private schools to participate less frequently. Yet private schools are eligible for federal funds, and some participate in federal programs. It is instructive, in this context, to review the current participation in federal programs of public and private schools.

Federal programs for education maintain certain eligibility criteria for schools, usually compensatory or vocational in nature, which may limit the number of schools eligible for funding.[3] Also, in some areas, funding is not automatic but depends on proposals from the school or school district, and schools differ in their initiative in obtaining federal funds. The differences in federally-funded programs at different schools are a result of all of these factors.[4] Furthermore, in this survey a positive response by a school administrator does not always mean that a school participates as a school. The question was worded so that a positive response could also imply participation in the program by some students in the school.

ESEA provides a broad range of resources and program opportunities to school districts and schools. While eligibility varies among programs, private schools participate in most of the ESEA programs that the survey covers. The participation rate of private schools is highest in the library program (Title IVB), in which nearly all of the Catholic schools, 43 percent of the other private schools, and 50 percent of the high-performance private schools participate (see table 4–6). Catholic schools participate in this program at a higher rate than public schools. In other ESEA programs, considered all together, Catholic schools generally participate less than public schools, but their participation is not negligible; other private schools participate hardly at all.

Among vocationally-oriented programs, the differential participation of public schools is even more evident. Participation in the programs associated with CETA and VEA is almost exclusively in public schools. Catholic schools have low participation rates, and other private schools participate almost not at all. At the other extreme, high-performance public schools

---

[3] Eligibility for funding under these federal programs differs somewhat for public and private schools. ESEA Title I funds are allocated through state education agencies to local educational agencies (LEAs). Although private schools that meet the Title I criteria are eligible, participation depends upon arrangements with the LEA. Probably in part as a result of the method of allocation, private secondary institutions seldom participate in Title I programs. For this and some of the other federal programs, some of the positive responses by school administrators may be in error. Funds authorized by Titles IVB, IVC, IVD, VII, and IX in ESEA explicitly permit funding to private secondary schools, provided, of course, that other eligibility and use criteria are met. Federal legislation also permits Vocational Education Act (VEA) funds to be given to private secondary schools, but it appears that most state plans for VEA funds do not include private secondary schools. (See Galladay and Wulfsberg, 1980.)

Guidelines for Talent Search and Upward Bound programs indicate that this money goes almost exclusively to higher education institutions, with high school students participating individually in the programs. Comprehensive Employment and Training Act (CETA) programs are administered by the Department of Labor, and the prime sponsor is seldom not an educational institution. Thus, high school students participate in these three programs, while high schools themselves do not.

[4] For discussion of the status of federal programs in private schools, see *Summary and Evaluation Report* and *How to Service Students with Federal Education Program Benefits*, both published in 1980 under the auspices of the Technical Assistance Institutes at the National Catholic Educational Association.

TABLE 4–6

Percentage of Public and Private Schools Reporting That the School or Its Students Participated in Selected Federal Programs[a]: Spring 1980

Program	U.S. Total	Major Sectors			High-Performance Schools	
		Public	Catholic	Other Private	Public	Private
Elementary and Secondary Education Act (ESEA)						
Title I: Economic disadvantaged	56	69	24	1	21	20
IVB: Library	81	86	99	43	76	50
IVC: Educational innovation	31	38	22	0	42	20
IVD: Supplementary centers	22	23	31	12	17	0
VII: Bilingual education	10	12	0	4	33	0
IX: Ethnic heritage series	7	8	13	0	4	0
Vocational Education Act 63 (VEA)						
Consumer and homemaking	60	77	8	1	69	0
Basic program	53	67	5	1	20	0
Persons with special needs	38	48	5	1	80	0
Cooperative education	45	55	14	6	91	0
High school work study	44	55	6	6	94	0
Comprehensive Employment and Training Act (CETA)	65	81	17	5	84	0
Upward Bound	17	21	8	2	23	10
Talent Search	13	16	4	1	1	20

[a] Participation is usually by school for ESEA and VEA programs; the remaining programs generally involve student-level participation at the secondary level.

show almost universal participation in federal work-related programs (particularly Cooperative Education and Work Study).

In general, federally-funded, vocationally-oriented programs are largely the domain of public schools. In ESEA programs, Catholic schools participate at levels comparable to schools in the public sector for some titles, while other private schools seldom participate, except in the library program.

Conclusion

A number of patterns distinguishing the school resources of the different sectors can be seen in the findings shown in this chapter.

School Resources

First, there is the effect of size differences, which lead the other private schools, smallest in size on the average, and, to a lesser extent, the Catholic schools to have a narrower range of courses than do the public schools and to have relatively fewer special programs and physical facilities (such as remedial reading laboratories).

Second, there is a difference in orientation, which means that the courses and programs less frequently found in private schools are of certain types: vocational and technical courses, work-related programs, and, in general, nonacademic courses and programs. The one traditional academic subject in which courses are least often found in other private schools is foreign languages. Other differences are found in the high-performance schools. These schools, public and private, differ from other schools in more uniformly providing advanced academic resources. The high-performance schools differ from one another, however, in the context in which these resources are offered: The high-performance private schools are more narrowly specialized in academic directions, while their public-sector counterparts superimpose more advanced academic courses and programs on an even more comprehensive range of courses and programs than is found in the public sector as a whole.

Third, the other private schools have a much lower student to professional staff ratio than the public and Catholic schools. In particular, the other private schools operate with many fewer students per teacher than do the public or Catholic schools—a difference so great that the low student-teacher ratio might be considered a hallmark characteristic of non-Catholic private schools. The low ratio probably arises in part from the small size of the other private schools and in part from conscious policy.

Fourth, private schools overall show lower participation in federally-funded programs, but this is selective, with Catholic schools participating as frequently as public schools in a few of the programs.

5

The Functioning of
Public and Private Schools

THE functioning of a school depends both on its student resources and on its own resources, such as those examined in the preceding chapter. In ways that neither educators nor sociologists understand perfectly, and in which the accident of specific personalities plays some role, the various components result in a school that functions in a particular way. In this chapter, we examine that functioning in sufficient depth to see some of the similarities and differences in the ways schools in the different sectors function.

The functioning of these types of schools will be examined in five areas:

1. Student coursework.
2. Levels of participation in extracurricular activities.
3. The standards of discipline set by the school.
4. Student behavior, including involvement in schoolwork and discipline-related behavior.
5. Student attitudes.

The last two aspects of the functioning of these schools—behavior and attitudes on the part of students—could be treated equally well as outcomes of schooling, which are covered in the next chapter. Student responses about their interest and involvement in school, the behavior that causes disciplinary problems in the school, and the attitudes of students, all play a part in the functioning of the school, but they are in part shaped by the school as well. Thus, their inclusion in this chapter rather than the next is somewhat arbitrary. Because we examine these behaviors and attitudes descriptively, as aspects of the functioning of each type of school, the question of just how much the type of school is reponsible for these differences in behavior and attitudes remains unanswered. In the next chapter, we return to differences in behavior and discipline and provide some answers to this question.

Student Coursework

Chapter 4 reported the courses and programs offered in each school sector, but it showed only student access, not exposure to coursework of different kinds. This section examines what courses students say they plan to take or have taken. Several items in the student questionnaire provide information about this.

One question asked sophomores the number of semesters in major subject-matter areas they had taken in the 10th grade; another item asked them to report the number of semesters in these same areas they planned to take in grades 11 and 12. A similar question asked seniors about their coursework in grades 10, 11, and 12. By combining sophomores' responses to the two questions, the plans of sophomores can be compared to the actual actions taken by seniors. Table 5–1 shows the average number of semesters planned by sophomores and taken by seniors in grades 10, 11, and 12. These three years translate into six semesters of coursework, but the total number of semesters taken in a subject can exceed six, since students can enroll in more than one course in a subject per semester.

The table reveals interesting comparisons among types of schools, among subjects, and between sophomores' plans and seniors' actions. What is perhaps most striking is the similarity of the sophomores' plans to what seniors actually did. Overall, there are small differences between the two in both directions, but the only uniform increases among all sectors are in English, history, and business courses, and the only uniform decrease is in other vocational courses. Thus, sophomores seem to know with reasonable accuracy what they will take in the next two years—assuming, of course, that the sophomores will in two years show a profile similar to that of 1980 seniors.

Not shown in the table are the variabilities in sophomore expectations

TABLE 5-1

Average Number of Semesters in Various Subjects, Planned by Sophomores and Taken by Seniors, in Public and Private Schools: Spring 1980

Subject	Major Sectors						High-Performance Schools			
	Public		Catholic		Other Private		Public		Private	
	Grade		Grade		Grade		Grade		Grade	
	10	12	10	12	10	12	10	12	10	12
Mathematics	4.0	4.0	4.9	4.9	4.5	4.7	5.1	4.9	5.6	6.0
Science	3.3	3.4	4.1	4.0	4.0	4.0	4.4	4.6	4.6	4.9
English	5.3	5.8	5.7	6.2	5.4	6.1	5.7	6.0	5.8	6.2
History	4.0	4.6	4.3	4.9	4.2	4.7	4.5	4.8	3.9	4.6
Spanish	1.0	.9	1.9	1.8	1.3	1.4	1.7	1.6	1.3	1.8
French	.6	.5	1.1	1.0	1.4	1.4	1.3	1.2	2.7	2.2
German	.2	.2	.2	.2	.3	.4	.5	.4	.5	.4
Business	1.7	2.1	1.5	2.1	1.2	1.5	1.3	1.6	.3	.3
Trade, technical	1.7	1.8	.7	.5	.8	.8	1.4	1.2	.6	.4
Other vocational	1.4	1.3	1.2	.9	1.1	.9	1.2	.8	.6	.3
Total	23.2	24.6	25.6	26.5	24.1	25.9	27.2	27.0	25.8	27.1

[a] Responses taken from EB004 in senior questionnaire.

and senior realizations. For the academic subjects, the variation among seniors in what they have actually taken is less than the variation among sophomores in what they think they will take. That is, while sophomores, on the average, have accurate expectations about the number of semesters of each of these academic subjects they will take, there are more extremes in the expectations of sophomores than in the actions of seniors. The reverse is true for the nonacademic subjects (business courses, trade, technical, and other vocational courses). In the public schools (and to a lesser extent in the private schools), the seniors are more extreme in the amount of coursework they have completed than are the sophomores in their expectations. This, of course, is related to the way high schools are structured, with academic subjects more or less standard fare for all students (though at differing levels of difficulty) and vocational courses taken primarily by those students who go into (or are directed toward) a vocational program. Some students who will never take a technical or vocational course expect to take a few such courses, while others who will take many of these courses underestimate that number as sophomores.

Table 5-1 also allows comparison of sectors according to the average amount of coursework completed in academic and nonacademic courses. The average amount of academic coursework completed by public school seniors provides a basis for comparing students in other sectors. On the average, these students complete two years of mathematics, one and a half years of science, two and a half years of history, three years of English, and one and a half years in foreign languages. Of course, this list does not include all academic coursework, but it does indicate the exposure of U.S. public high school students to basic academic courses.

Students in the private sector vary somewhat from this modal picture of public school students. On the average, students in Catholic schools and other private schools take three to four more semesters of academic coursework (the first seven courses shown in table 5–1) than do students in public schools. A smaller difference is found between high-performance private and public schools (although students in the latter schools take slightly more academic coursework than do students in the Catholic or other private sectors). Considering each academic subject separately, the differences among the public, Catholic, and other private sectors are rather small. The students in high-performance private schools stand out in two subjects: The average senior completes more than a semester of mathmatics and of French beyond that completed by students in other sectors.

The differences between the public and private sectors are reversed for business, trade, technical, and other vocational courses. These courses are less frequently taken by private school students, with the differences especially great for the high-performance private schools.

German has nearly vanished as a subject studied by students in all types of schools. French is also infrequently taken in the public schools, but it remains the primary foreign language studied by students in the high-performance private schools and occupies an equal position with Spanish in the non-Catholic private schools.

Altogether, the comparison of specific subjects taken in public and private schools indicates no sharp divergence between the two. Perhaps the greatest areas of divergence are foreign languages, of which the private school students take more, and nonacademic occupational courses, of which the public school students take more. Other than this, one can say only that the private school students take, on the average, slightly more courses, and that these are generally in academic subjects.

Looking at specific academic courses, such as calculus or physics, however, there are greater differences between the types of schools. Seniors were asked about each of nine academic courses: four mathematics courses, two science courses, and third-year courses in each of three foreign languages. Table 5–2 shows the percentage of seniors in each school type taking these courses—within each area, the courses are ordered by the percentage of students taking each.

In mathematics courses, ranging from geometry to calculus, about half to two-thirds as many public school students take these courses as do

TABLE 5–2

*Percentage of Seniors in Public and Private Schools Reporting They
Have Completed Selected Academic Courses[a]: Spring 1980*

Course	U.S. Total	Major Sectors			High-Performance Schools	
		Public	Catholic	Other Private	Public	Private
Geometry	56	53	84	77	87	100
Algebra 2	49	42	70	66	76	99
Trigonometry	24	22	44	42	57	70
Calculus	6	6	11	10	22	63
Chemistry	38	37	53	51	68	79
Physics	20	18	23	28	46	67
Third-year Spanish	4	3	7	8	11	11
Third-year French	3	2	6	10	8	18
Third-year German	1	1	1	2	5	2

[a] Responses taken from items EB004 C–E and EB005 in senior questionnaire.

Catholic or other private school students. Comparing Catholic schools
with other private schools in each of the mathematics courses, a slightly
higher percentage of Catholic school students than other private school
students take these courses. An exceptionally high proportion of students
in high-performance private schools take these advanced mathematics
courses, with 63 percent taking calculus, the most advanced. The percentages for the high-performance public schools lie between those of the
private sector as a whole and those of the high-performance private
schools. Generally, the more advanced the course, the smaller the ratio of
public school enrollment to private school enrollment.

Neither of the two science courses, chemistry and physics, is taken by a
large proportion of students, except in the high-performance schools.
Chemistry is taken less often in all types of schools than algebra 2 but
more often than trigonometry. Physics is taken less frequently, only about
half as often as chemistry (except in the high-performance schools). It is
taken by fewer students than take trigonometry but by more students
than take calculus. In these sciences, the public schools are somewhat closer to the private schools than is true for mathematics.

The third year of a foreign language is taken by only a few students in
any type of school. We have no direct comparisons with earlier cohorts or
other developed countries, but both of these comparisons would undoubtedly emphasize the relative lack of advanced foreign language training
among contemporary American high school students in public and private
schools. In the public schools, attended by about 90 percent of the students, the highest enrollment for a third-year language course is 3 per-

TABLE 5–3

Percentage of Seniors in Public and Private Schools Where
Selected Academic Courses Are Offered Who Have Taken
These Courses[a]: Spring 1980

| Course | U.S. Total | Major Sectors | | | High-Performance Schools | |
		Public	Catholic	Other Private	Public	Private
Geometry	57.3	54.4	84.5	79.0	86.1	99.8
Algebra 2	50.2	47.8	72.3	67.1	75.5	98.8
Trigonometry	28.0	25.5	48.1	46.8	52.5	94.2
Calculus	10.4	9.5	14.7	24.6	23.5	62.2
Chemistry	39.2	37.6	52.8	54.6	68.5	78.9
Physics	21.3	20.4	24.4	30.6	45.8	66.6
Third-year Spanish	5.0	4.4	7.5	16.7	11.5	17.2
Third-year French	3.8	3.1	6.4	18.9	9.5	20.8
Third-year German	2.3	2.2	1.2	7.0	5.3	4.5

[a] Responses taken from items EB004 C–E and EB005 in senior questionnaire.

cent, in Spanish. The percentage of students in public schools enrolled in any third year language course is 6 percent, compared with 14 percent in Catholic schools and 20 percent in other private schools. It is not the case that the lower percentage of students taking each of these courses in the public schools is due to lack of opportunity. Table 4–2 in the preceding chapter showed that the percentage of private school students in schools where such a course is available is smaller than, or at most equal to, the percentage of public school students in such schools. That is, these courses are generally more available in the public sector, but are taken by fewer students.

If we look at the percentages of students in those schools where the course is available who take the course, the differences in table 5–2 are slightly magnified. Table 5–3 shows these percentages, and the differences between public and private are slightly greater. This is due, at least in part, to the small sizes of private schools. In such schools, the percentage of students interested in a given course must be fairly high for the absolute number to be great enough to warrant the teaching of the course. Therefore, the percentages taking a course where it is offered tend to be especially high in the other private sector where school size is quite small.

The public-private school differences are, however, reduced if, in the schools where the courses are offered, we look only at those students who say they expect to get a four-year college degree. Table 5–4 shows these comparisons. The course profiles in mathematics and physics in public schools are much closer to those in Catholic and other private schools. In

TABLE 5–4

Percentage of Seniors in Public and Private Schools Expecting to Finish Four-Year College Who Have Taken Selected Academic Courses Where These Courses Are Offered[a]: *Spring 1980*

| Course | U.S. Total | Major Sectors | | | High-Performance Schools | |
		Public	Catholic	Other Private	Public	Private
Geometry	82.1	80.1	94.3	90.5	94.2	99.8
Algebra 2	74.4	73.0	83.6	81.4	86.4	98.8
Trigonometry	49.6	47.3	62.9	59.5	67.1	94.5
Calculus	19.7	18.7	20.8	33.1	29.9	63.5
Chemistry	63.0	62.3	67.0	66.7	79.8	79.6
Physics	35.4	35.2	34.0	40.0	58.4	66.9
Third-year Spanish	7.7	7.1	8.4	19.9	13.6	14.2
Third-year French	6.6	5.6	8.7	23.4	12.1	21.1
Third-year German	3.5	3.4	1.9	7.1	5.0	4.6

[a] Items used in this analysis include EB004, EB005, and BB065.

languages, however, the differences between the other private schools on the one hand and public and Catholic schools on the other remain great.

Altogether, comparing coursework taken in the public and private schools, we can say that a superficial look at the number of semesters in general subjects shows a great similarity between public and private; but, when we examine specific advanced courses in these schools, a far greater percentage of private school students take these courses. If we control for students' higher education plans, these differences are reduced, and, presumably, statistical controls on family background would reduce the differences even more. Thus, while the student bodies of public and private schools as a whole differ considerably in their taking of these advanced courses, students with similar college plans (and similar in other respects) have similar course profiles. This leaves open the question whether these college plans are brought to the school wholly from the outside or are in part generated by the different school environments. We examine that question in the next chapter.

Extracurricular Activities

In addition to the academic courses students take in each of these types of schools, they also participate in extracurricular activities. And, because the schools are organized quite differently from one another, we might expect the extracurricular activity profiles of students to differ according to the type of school they attend. Table 5–5 shows the percentage of students in each sector participating in each of thirteen types of school activities listed in the student questionnaire. The activities are grouped into four loosely related areas.

Few major differences exist between the participation profiles of sophomores and seniors. The only major difference in the public schools is the 10-percent increase in senior participation in vocational education clubs. Among the smaller differences, however, some are consistent across sectors. Band and orchestra participation appears to decline slightly, as does participation in subject matter clubs. In contrast, participation in hobby clubs and cheerleading appears to increase (the athletics questions are not quite comparable at the sophomore and senior levels, and cannot be directly compared), as does participation in debate or drama. Participation in chorus or dance appears to decline slightly in the public and Catholic schools, but to increase in the other private and high-performance private schools.

Among school sectors, the public schools and the Catholic schools seem similar, and somewhat different from the other private schools. The high-performance private schools differ from public and Catholic in the same direction as do the other private schools, but more substantially. The principal difference between the public and Catholic schools on the one hand and the other private and high-performance private on the other is that in the latter a number of activities appear to increase over time, with seniors participating considerably more than sophomores. In the public and Catholic schools, where levels of participation are, in general, slightly lower at the sophomore level, this growth does not occur. The differences between school types at the senior level in the last two activities, school newspaper and student government, suggest that the same generalization would hold for these activities if they had been included at the sophomore level.

Regardless of the reason, the result is that participation in extracurricular activities in the other private and high-performance private schools is considerably higher by the senior year than that found in public and Catholic schools at the sophomore level. This can be seen in a slightly different way by looking at two measures of sophomore-senior differences for the seven activities that are directly comparable (lines 3 through 9 in table 5–5): the number of activities in which seniors show a higher participation rate than sophomores, and the sum of senior-sophomore difference in percentage participating. These are shown in table 5–6. The table

TABLE 5-5

Percentage of Sophomores and Seniors in Public and Private Schools Participating in Various Extracurricular Activities[a]: Spring 1980

	Major Sectors						High-Performance Schools			
	Public		Catholic		Other Private		Public		Private	
	Grade		Grade		Grade		Grade		Grade	
Activity	10	12	10	12	10	12	10	12	10	12
Varsity athletics (seniors only)	NA[b]	35	NA	37	NA	58	NA	39	NA	73
Athletics (sophomores) or other athletics (seniors)	53	41	62	47	69	55	20	26	84	65
Cheerleading and pep club	14	15	16	15	13	17	17	13	11	17
Debate, drama	10	14	14	18	18	33	18	15	24	36
Chorus, dance	22	21	23	20	28	31	20	19	24	27
Band, orchestra	17	15	10	9	15	14	18	15	11	12
Subject matter clubs	26	24	28	25	27	25	24	21	30	23
Vocational education clubs	15	25	4	7	7	9	6	8	3	0
Hobby clubs	21	23	21	22	24	27	21	26	34	43
Honorary society	NA	17	NA	20	NA	17	NA	17	NA	13
School newspaper	NA	18	NA	28	NA	45	NA	24	NA	57
Student government	NA	18	NA	20	NA	30	NA	19	NA	29

[a] Responses taken from items BB032 A–L.
[b] NA = not applicable; sophomores not asked about participation.

TABLE 5–6

Differences in Sophomore and Senior Participation in Extracurricular Activities in Public and Private Schools: Spring 1980

Differences	Major Sectors			High-Performance Schools	
	Public	Catholic	Other Private	Public	Private
Sum of senior-sophomore differences[a]	12	0	24	−17	21
Fraction of activities in which senior participation is higher	4/7	3/7	5/7	2/7	5/7

[a] Sum of percentage differences in sophomore and senior participation excluding athletics.

shows that, by both measures, the other private and high-performance private schools are distinguishable from the other types of schools. Participation grows over time in these schools, but declines or grows less in the others.

One might conjecture that extracurricular activities are organized differently in the Catholic and public schools than in the other private schools. In particular, there are two approaches a school may take to the organization of extracurricular activities. One is a selective orientation which recruits younger students into, say, less selective choruses, with subsequent narrowing down for the more selective chorus, or into junior varsity athletics with only the best going on to the varsity. Another approach, the intramural orientation, holds the philosophy that everyone ought to try everything. This latter approach may be seen in elite English schools that aspire to develop a "well-rounded" individual.

If the public and Catholic schools have the selective orientation to extracurricular activities, and the other private schools more often have the intramural orientation, this would explain the participation decline from sophomore to senior in public and Catholic schools and the growth in the other private schools.

Disciplinary Standards

Discipline in schools is regarded by many as the most important problem in American education. In a yearly Gallup Poll concerning education, the general public has for a number of years ranked discipline as the most important problem in schools. And superintendents, principals, and teachers complain bitterly about constraints on them, legal and otherwise, which they regard as preventing them from imposing and maintaining order in their schools.

Discipline is also one of the areas in which public and private schools are believed to differ most. Catholic schools in particular are frequently regarded as highly disciplined in comparison with public schools. It is of special interest, then, to see the similarities and differences in disciplinary standards and in student behavior in public schools and the private school sectors. In this section, we examine disciplinary standards; in the next, we examine student behavior.

Several questions were asked, in the school questionnaire and the student questionnaire, about rules and enforcement of rules. Table 5–7 shows how the responses to two of those questions compare for the different sectors, and how the students' and administrators' responses compare.

There is not a great difference among the sectors, according to both administrators and students, in responsibility for property damage. Virtually all administrators in all sectors indicate that students are held responsible. Sophomore responses are also similar across types of schools, although the percentage is somewhat lower in public schools. In all sectors, a substantial minority of sophomores say no such rule is enforced. The difference between administrators and students, of course, might be in interpretation of what "enforced" means: For some of the students, "enforced" might include finding the student who is responsible, and their responses may reflect the opinion that the student is often not found. The difference between administrators and sophomores is greatest in the public schools and least in the Catholic schools, consistent with the general

TABLE 5–7

Percentage of Sophomores and Administrators Reporting That Certain Rules Are Enforced at Their School[a]: Spring 1980

Item and Group	U.S. Total	Major Sectors			High-Performance Schools	
		Public	Catholic	Other Private	Public	Private
Students Responsible to School for Property Damage						
Sophomores	65	64	77	71	66	71
Administrators	97	96	95	100	100	100
Rules About Student Dress						
Sophomores	46	42	97	69	14	93
Administrators	58	51	100	70	44	90

[a] Response taken from items 4B020 and SB054.

perception that discipline is most stringently enforced in Catholic schools and least enforced in public schools.

Rules about student dress distinguish the sectors sharply—and there is little disagreement between sophomores and administrators. In virtually all of the Catholic schools, about two-thirds of the other private schools, and perhaps half of the public schools there are enforced rules regarding student dress. Thus the greater strictness in this area of the Catholic schools, as well as the intermediate position of the other private schools, is evident.

Table 5–8 shows responses of seniors and sophomores to general questions about the effectiveness and the fairness of discipline in the school. Among the three sectors, students in Catholic schools are the most likely to rate their school as "excellent" or "good" in effectiveness of discipline, and public school students are least likely to do so. On fairness of discipline, again the private schools are more often rated by their students as good or excellent than are the public schools; but this time the Catholic schools and the other private schools are approximately alike. It is in effectiveness of discipline, as perceived by their students, that the private schools (and especially the Catholic schools) depart most sharply from the public schools.

The two sets of high-performance schools differ sharply on both of these aspects of discipline. The high-performance private schools are the highest of all sectors in both aspects, while the high-performance public schools are hardly distinguishable from the public schools as a whole.

TABLE 5–8

Percentage of Sophomores and Seniors in Public and Private Schools Rating Their Schools' Effectiveness and Fairness of Discipline as "Excellent" or "Good" [a]: *Spring 1980*

Item	U.S. Total	Major Sectors			High-Performance Schools	
		Public	Catholic	Other Private	Public	Private
Effectiveness						
Strictness of Discipline [b]						
Seniors	44	42	72	58	52	79
Sophomores	44	41	76	65	40	79
Fairness of Discipline						
Seniors	37	36	47	46	40	62
Sophomores	40	39	52	50	41	68

[a] Responses taken from items BB053 F–G.

[b] Sophomores were asked to rate the strictness of discipline in their schools; seniors, the effectiveness of discipline.

The lower rating of public schools by their students in fairness of discipline is somewhat ironic. In the past decade and a half, legal strictures to ensure fairness of discipline, such as requirements for due process before suspension, elaborate review processes, and statistical comparisons of disciplinary actions by race to ensure racial fairness, have been imposed by the courts or the federal government on public schools. These strictures are much less fully imposed on private schools (in part, of course, simply because attendance at these schools is by choice rather than assignment). Yet, it is the private schools, less bound by the strictures designed to ensure fairness, that are more often regarded as fair by their students. This suggests that the legalistic approach to ensuring fairness in discipline may be less effective than other approaches in bringing about fairness—and the upper panel of the table suggests that it may indeed be counterproductive for effectiveness of discipline. Of course, the effectiveness of discipline is also dependent on other factors. In particular, private schools have more control over the entrance and exit of their students than do public schools.

One other question somewhat related to the disciplinary climate of a school asked the students about teachers' interest in students. The responses to that question are shown in table 5–9. The table shows that among the three sectors it is the teachers in other private schools who are most often regarded as interested in their students. Teachers in the public schools are, by far, least often viewed as interested in students. Again, the high-performance private schools are highest in perceived interest of teachers, while the high-performance public schools are similar to the public schools as a whole. Here, and to a lesser degree in other aspects of discipline, the smaller average size of the private schools (and especially the other private schools) may be responsible for some of the differences.

Another way to examine the difference in disciplinary standards in each type of school is to aggregate the student response in each school and

TABLE 5–9

*Percentage of Sophomores and Seniors in Public and
Private Schools Rating Their Teachers' Interest
in Students as "Excellent"* [a]: *Spring 1980*

Class	U.S. Total	Major Sectors			High-Performance Schools	
		Public	Catholic	Other Private	Public	Private
Seniors	14	12	25	41	15	64
Sophomores	11	9	25	34	16	55

[a] Responses taken from item BB053E.

then compare the school averages and variations within each sector. This procedure gives us a way to compare general school climates among sectors. Such an aggregation of responses was done for the discipline and climate items discussed previously—teacher interest in students, effectiveness of discipline, and fairness of discipline—as well as for an item on school spirit. The responses were aggregated across both grades, and the school was characterized according to the average student response. Figure 5–1 shows the mean of the school rating for each sector, and an indication of the variation among schools obtained by adding and subtracting two standard deviations. (About 5 percent of schools would fall outside of two standard deviations.) Thus, one can compare both the average school climate for each sector, and the degree of similarity for schools within each sector.

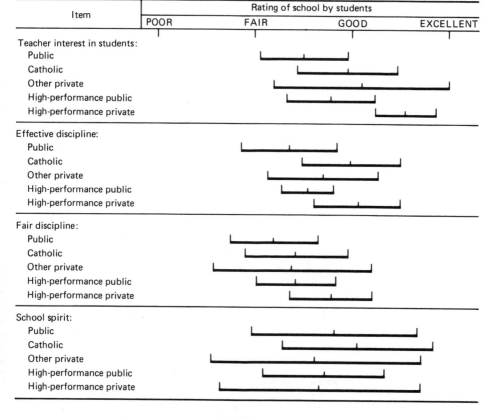

FIGURE 5–1

School Aggregate Ratings of Discipline, Teacher Interest, and School Spirit by Students in the Public and Private Sectors: Mean and Variation Within Each School Sector: Spring 1980

Some general differences in variation hold across at least three of the four measures: the very broad distributions among the other private schools, and the tight distributions of high-performance private and public schools. The breadth of the distributions for the other private schools implies that these schools differ considerably among themselves in fairness and effectiveness of discipline. For instance, although they are higher than the public schools in average perceived fairness, a few are seen as worse than nearly any public school in fairness of discipline. Teacher interest in other private schools shows a similarly broad distribution. Finally, there is high variability in school discipline climates in other private schools, and high consistency among both public and private high-performance schools.[1]

When we compare the average school in each sector, we find that the high-performance private schools are highest in teacher interest, effectiveness of discipline, and fairness of discipline, and low only in school spirit (though they show a wide variation). Conversely, the public schools are lowest in teacher interest and in effective and fair discipline; in school spirit they are relatively high, exceeded only by the Catholic schools. High-performance public schools tend to be rated slightly higher on these aspects of school environment than the public schools, except in school spirit.

Comparing Catholic and other private schools, the Catholic schools are higher in effectiveness of discipline and in school spirit, the other private schools are higher in teacher interest, and the two are about equal in fairness of discipline.

These results at the school level are consistent with the individual-level results, except that the inclusion of the variation among schools within each of the sectors on measures of discipline reveals the great variation within the other private schools.

Altogether, the indicators of disciplinary standards and disciplinary climate indicate that the standard stereotypes are by and large true. The Catholic schools are strictest in discipline; the other private schools are somewhat less strict and appear to nurture the student to a greater degree (as evidenced by perceived teacher interest). The public schools, taken as a whole, are neither strict nor do they nurture the student. In addition,

---

[1] Some part of the variability in all sectors is due to sampling variability, since only a sample of students in each grade level was included in the study. For most sectors, this sampling variability is small, since, if all sampled students responded, the school average is based on seventy-two student responses. But some schools, especially in the other private sector, were so small that the total of the sophomore and senior classes was considerably below seventy-two. Thus a part of the broader variability for other private schools is due to this sampling variability.

they are least often regarded by their students as fair in their exercise of discipline. The comparisons are not encouraging ones for American public schools.

Student Behavior

In this section, we compare the obverse of disciplinary standards, that is, student behavior in different sectors, including involvement in school, attendance, tardiness, and cutting classes. Student behavior is in part the consequence of the way a school is organized and administered and in part the cause. We know that students attend school with different degrees of regularity, making teaching more or less difficult; that students spend varying amounts of time on homework; and that, when in school, students exhibit varying amounts of behavior problems. The question of interest here is just how the various sectors of education compare in student behavior.

INVOLVEMENT IN SCHOOL

Involvement in school is one aspect of student behavior. There are several measures of this in the student questionnaires. One is the amount of time spent on homework; a second is the true-false response to a statement that the student is interested in school; a third is another true-false response to a statement that the student likes to work hard in school.

The average amount of time spent on homework differs considerably among the sectors. The averages for sophomores are: less than four hours a week in the public schools; over five and one-half in Catholic schools, other private schools, and high-performance public schools; and over nine hours in the high-performance private schools. Again, the other private schools show a greater diversity than the Catholic schools, with more students at each extreme. Most homogeneous are high-performance private schools, where nearly all of the sophomores spend over three hours per week and almost half spend over ten hours (table 5–10).

Seniors spend less time on homework than do sophomores, except in the high-performance private and public schools, where, on the average, slightly more time is spent. From this evidence, seniors appear slightly less involved in schoolwork than are sophomores. One other point in the table is noteworthy: In both the Catholic schools and the high-performance pri-

TABLE 5–10

Average Time Spent on Homework by Sophomores and Seniors in Public and Private Schools: Spring 1980

Time Spent on Homework Each Week[a]	U.S. Total		Major Sectors						High-Performance Schools			
			Public		Catholic		Other Private		Public		Private	
	Grade		Grade		Grade		Grade		Grade		Grade	
	10	12	10	12	10	12	10	12	10	12	10	12
No homework assigned	2.3	3.6	2.4	4.0	0.0	0.6	1.7	1.0	1.3	0.7	0.0	0.0
None	4.5	4.0	4.7	4.2	2.3	2.3	2.4	3.8	2.2	2.3	0.6	1.9
Less than one hour	14.1	16.3	14.9	17.1	6.3	9.9	6.3	8.0	7.5	8.0	0.9	2.2
One to three hours	28.3	30.3	29.2	31.2	20.3	24.8	17.6	17.8	16.3	19.5	3.5	4.5
Three to five hours	24.0	21.3	24.0	21.0	24.9	25.1	22.5	22.8	23.2	22.8	12.0	6.8
Five to ten hours	20.5	18.0	19.4	17.0	32.8	27.1	29.8	27.3	36.8	27.2	35.2	29.0
More than ten hours	6.4	6.4	5.4	5.6	13.3	10.2	19.8	19.3	12.7	19.6	47.9	55.6
Average[b]	3.9	3.7	3.7	3.5	5.6	4.9	6.0	5.8	5.6	5.7	9.1	9.5

[a] Responses are taken from item BB015 in student questionnaire.

[b] Calculated by assigning 0.5, 2.0, 4.0, 7.5, and 12.5 to the last five categories in the table, and 0 to the first two.

vate schools, no sophomore, and almost no senior, reports not having homework assigned; in the public schools, 2.4 percent of sophomores and 4 percent of seniors report that none is assigned.

Although watching television is not part of school functioning, it stands as a kind of alternative time expenditure for high school students, and it is useful to see how students from the different types of schools balance their time between television and homework. Table 5–11 shows the amount of time during the week that all students spend watching television, and these results can be compared to the amount of time spent on homework. Comparison of tables 5–10 and 5–11 reveals that the lesser time spent on homework by the average public school student is matched by a greater amount of time spent in watching television. Because of the different time categories used for the two items, and because of a general normative pressure to overreport time spent in homework and underreport time spent watching television, the absolute numbers of hours in the two activities cannot be directly compared.

But the direction of the differences among the sectors is exactly reversed for television watching and for homework. The public school students are lowest in homework, highest in television watching; the students in high-performance private schools are highest in homework, lowest in television. These two time expenditure reports suggest the differing levels of demands imposed on students in the different types of schools.

In addition to comparisons by school type, comparison of seniors and sophomores is of interest. Seniors watch less television than sophomores and are also less occupied by homework. This suggests that seniors have undertaken activities outside the home and school: Another report from this study (Lewin-Epstein 1981), indicates that employment is often one of these activities.

Student reports of interest in school and liking to work hard in school give another view of the capacity of these schools as constituted to capture the attention of their students (see table 5–12). These items, however, show considerably fewer differences among students by sector than does the item concerning time spent on homework. It is true that fewer of the students in public schools and more of the students in high-performance private schools report being interested in school, but the differences between the public and private schools as a whole are very small. The same can be said for responses to the question about liking to work hard: There are only small differences among the schools, and the public schools are not consistently the lowest.

In general, for both of these questions, the seniors show, as already suggested by their spending less time on homework, slightly less interest

TABLE 5–11

Average Time Spent Watching Television by Sophomores and Seniors in Public and Private Schools: Spring 1980

Number of Hours per Day[a]	U.S. Total		Major Sectors						High-Performance Schools			
			Public		Catholic		Other Private		Public		Private	
	Grade		Grade		Grade		Grade		Grade		Grade	
	10	12	10	12	10	12	10	12	10	12	10	12
None	2.6	3.6	2.4	3.4	2.8	4.0	7.6	9.7	4.0	4.1	7.6	11.0
Less than one	6.5	10.9	6.0	10.5	8.3	11.5	17.3	18.8	11.6	17.3	24.7	25.2
One to two	13.2	18.0	12.9	17.7	16.4	21.2	15.6	21.6	20.3	23.6	28.2	24.7
Two to three	19.5	22.1	19.6	22.2	20.4	23.8	16.1	18.0	24.4	23.2	16.8	20.7
Three to four	18.0	17.3	18.0	17.4	18.7	17.5	18.3	13.3	14.2	15.6	9.7	8.2
Four to five	12.8	11.0	13.0	11.3	12.3	9.1	8.3	7.1	8.7	6.8	4.3	3.3
Five or more	27.4	17.1	28.1	17.6	21.3	13.0	18.8	11.4	18.8	9.5	8.6	7.0
Mean[b]	4.1	3.3	4.2	3.4	3.7	3.0	3.2	2.6	3.2	2.6	2.2	2.0

[a] Responses taken from item BB048 in student questionnaire.
[b] Calculated by assigning 0, .5, 1.5, 2.5, 3.5, and 4.5 to each of the categories, respectively.

TABLE 5–12

Percentage Distributions in Public and Private Schools of Students Interested in School and of Students Liking to Work Hard in School: Spring 1980

Item[a]	U.S. Total		Major Sectors						High-Performance Schools			
			Public		Catholic		Other Private		Public		Private	
	Grade		Grade		Grade		Grade		Grade		Grade	
	10	12	10	12	10	12	10	12	10	12	10	12
Interested in School?												
Yes	76.4	73.7	76.2	73.2	78.7	76.3	78.1	82.1	80.9	76.1	88.4	88.7
No	23.6	26.3	23.8	26.8	21.3	23.7	21.9	12.9	19.1	23.9	12.6	11.3
Like Working Hard in School?												
Yes	54.0	52.3	54.0	52.2	52.8	52.3	56.4	54.2	53.8	57.8	63.6	56.7
No	46.0	47.7	46.0	47.8	47.2	47.7	43.6	45.8	46.2	42.2	36.4	43.3

[a] Responses taken from items BB059C and BB061E in student questionnaire.

in school than do the sophomores. Thus, again, there is indication that in all sectors the interest and involvement of seniors in high school is somewhat lower than that of sophomores.

SCHOOL ATTENDANCE

Another area of student behavior is attendance. We examine three potential problems in this area: absence from school for reasons other than illness, class cutting, and tardiness. Student behavior in these categories differs according to type of school. Table 5–13 shows that the school sectors are ordered alike for all of these types of attendance problems for both seniors and sophomores: Students in Catholic schools show the highest consistency of attendance, students in other private schools are next, and students in public schools are lowest. Curiously, students in high-performance public schools have the poorest attendance records.

This table includes, in addition, evidence that seniors are less well disciplined in attendance than are sophomores. In all types of schools, and by all three measures, seniors show less consistency in their attendance than do sophomores. This is especially noteworthy because the seniors are a more select group, excluding those students—on the whole, less well disciplined—who have dropped out between the sophomore and senior years. Thus, students' reports on attendance provide further indication that seniors are less involved in high school than are sophomores.

REPORTS ABOUT DISCIPLINE FROM ADMINISTRATORS AND STUDENTS

In addition to these reports by students concerning their own behavior, there is information about the school's behavioral climate from two other sources: The school questionnaire included questions, answered by the school's administrative staff, regarding the seriousness of various types of behavioral problems among students; and sophomores were asked about how often certain behavior problems, in some of the same areas as well as some others, arise in the school. Responses to these questions offer two additional views of the school's behavioral climate. In two of the areas, student absenteeism and class cutting, it is possible to examine the same behavior from three perspectives: the students' reports of their own behavior, the school administrators' reports about what happens in the school, and the students' reports about what happens in the school. In the area of verbal abuse of teachers, it is possible to get two perspectives: reports from the administrative staff and from the students about what happens in the school.

TABLE 5-13

Percentage of Sophomores and Seniors in Public and Private Schools Reporting Good Attendance Practices: Spring 1980

Attendance Item[a]	U.S. Total		Major Sectors						High-Performance Schools			
			Public		Catholic		Other Private		Public		Private	
	Grade		Grade		Grade		Grade		Grade		Grade	
	10	12	10	12	10	12	10	12	10	12	10	12
Never absent except when ill	34.7	25.6	33.7	24.8	48.8	34.0	37.0	30.8	32.2	19.4	50.3	34.5
Never cut classes	69.9	55.2	68.6	53.6	88.7	74.6	71.0	59.3	56.8	41.6	81.4	64.4
Never late to school	42.2	36.0	42.0	35.9	47.7	41.2	35.6	28.2	33.5	32.8	40.3	28.0

[a] Responses taken from items BB016, BB017, BB059E in student questionnaire.

Table 5–14 presents the administrators' and the sophomores' responses concerning behavioral problems. Comparing the two areas in which there are three perspectives, we find some interesting differences. First, two of the three assessments show Catholic schools to have the best attendance and public schools to have the worst. But the perspectives differ: Students' reports of their own behavior show less difference among school types than do administrators' and sophomores' reports about the school. There is a logical basis for the difference between students' reports of their own behavior and reports on a "school problem." If 5 percent of students are chronically absent in one school and 15 percent are absent in another, it is logically consistent for no one in the first school to report that this "often happens" or is a "serious problem," and for all students and administrators in the second school to report that it often happens or is a serious problem. Such reports on a school can show greater extremes than the actual behavioral averages.

Table 5–14 also includes data on areas of behavior not related to attendance; these have to do with disorderly and disobedient behavior while in school, and in some cases directed toward the school. The difference between public and private schools stands out just as strongly here as in attendance. The incidence of problems of all sorts is high in public schools, however reported and by whomever reported. There is, however, a reversal between the two sectors of private schools. In most of these areas of behavior—specifically verbal abuse of teachers, fighting, drug and alcohol use, and vandalism—Catholic schools show slightly higher rates of incidence than do other private schools.[2] The students' reports and the administrators' reports are reasonably consistent in this (except that administrators report much lower levels of verbal abuse of teachers than do sophomores, suggesting that the responses of the two may be referring to somewhat different behavior—"verbal abuse" versus "talking back"). In absenteeism and cutting classes, as indicated earlier, the other private schools are higher than the Catholic schools. It seems likely that the reason for the somewhat poorer attendance in the other private schools is that these schools are somewhat less strict about enforcement of attendance or disciplinary action for absence than are Catholic schools. This conjecture is reinforced by the fact that while absenteeism and cutting classes, as reported by students of themselves and of other students, are more prevalent in other private schools than in Catholic schools, the principals less often define this as a "problem."

[2] The reason for this difference is not readily apparent, but two factors suggest themselves: the greater proportion of other private schools in rural areas may allow them some isolation from drug and alcohol abuse problems. Or the substantially lower pupil-teacher ratio in the other private schools may allow for better control of student behavior.

The Functioning of Public and Private Schools

As indicated by earlier data, the high-performance public schools resemble the public schools as a whole more than they resemble any of the private sectors, while the high-performance private schools tend to show fewer disciplinary problems than either the Catholic or other private schools.

In the area of use of alcohol or drugs, however, administrators in both sets of high-performance schools more often report a behavior problem than do administrators in any other sector. Administrators in three-fifths of the high-performance schools report a "serious" or "moderate" problem in this area. In the absence of further information (students were not asked about alcohol or drug use), we can merely note this.

It is possible not only to characterize each of the sectors by the distribution of student behavior, but also to characterize each school according to the level of discipline problems students perceive in the school. In addition to the items concerning attendance, cutting classes, and verbal abuse, sophomores were asked about three areas of student behavior problems in their school—not obeying, getting in fights, and threatening or harming teachers. For each school, the students' responses to these six items were averaged, so that the school is characterized by the level of discipline problems as perceived by all sophomores.

As in the analysis of disciplinary standards, where a similar aggregation was done for each sector, the results are tabulated as the mean and the variation. (That is, plus and minus two standard deviations. In some cases, this exceeds the upper limits of 3.0 or goes below the lower limit of 1.0, but this can still serve as a measure of the variation among schools. On the graph, the bars are truncated at the limits.) About 5 percent of schools lie outside of a range of two standard deviations. The results are shown in figure 5–2.

Several general results hold over all areas of student behavior. Again, the high-performance private schools show a tight distribution, just as they did earlier in the case of disciplinary standards. And, again, the other private schools show the largest variation in most areas, though in the area of threatening or attacking teachers it is only the public schools that show much variation.

In all areas of behavior, without exception, the public schools have greater student behavior problems than schools in any other sector. In some areas, such as attendance, cutting classes, fighting, and threatening teachers, the *average* public school is outside the whole range of Catholic schools in the direction of more behavior problems (that is, at a point beyond which we would find less than 2.5 percent of the Catholic schools). The difference between the schools in these two sectors in student behavior problems is clearly very great. The difference between

TABLE 5-14

Assessments of Disciplinary Problems by Administrators and Students
in Public and Private Schools: Spring 1980

Item and Group[a]	U.S. Total	Major Sectors			High-Performance Schools	
		Public	Catholic	Other Private	Public	Private
Student Absenteeism						
Administrators: percentage reporting it is a "serious or moderate problem"	47.2	56.6	15.2	13.8	58.1	0
Sophomores: percentage reporting "students often don't attend school"	42.9	46.2	8.1	16.1	28.2	2.8
Sophomore and senior behavior: absent five or more days, not ill	19.0	20.2	8.5	13.5	14.2	7.9
Cutting Classes						
Administrators: percentage reporting it is a "serious or moderate problem"	29.1	37.0	4.6	0	39.2	0
Sophomores: percentage reporting "students often cut classes"	58.4	62.4	15.9	25.9	67.0	6.5
Sophomore and senior behavior: cut classes now and then	36.8	39.0	18.4	34.3	50.7	26.7

Verbal Abuse of Teachers						
Administrators: percentage reporting "verbal abuse is a serious or moderate problem"	8.6	9.6	4.7	5.3	22.6	0
Sophomores: percentage reporting "students often talk back to teachers"	39.8	41.6	22.8	21.7	25.7	9.2
Fighting and Disobedience						
Sophomores: percentage reporting "students often fight"	25.1	26.8	9.4	5.8	14.7	2.5
Sophomores: percentage reporting "students often don't obey"	28.7	30.2	14.6	13.0	18.8	4.6
Drug and Alcohol Use						
Administrators: percentage reporting it is a "serious or moderate problem"	42.3	48.5	26.2	18.0	61.3	60.0
Vandalism of School Property						
Administrators: percentage reporting it is a "serious or moderate problem"	21.8	24.5	13.8	11.7	27.1	20.0

[a] Responses taken from BB016, BB059E, and YB019A in student questionnaire and SB056 in school questionnaire.

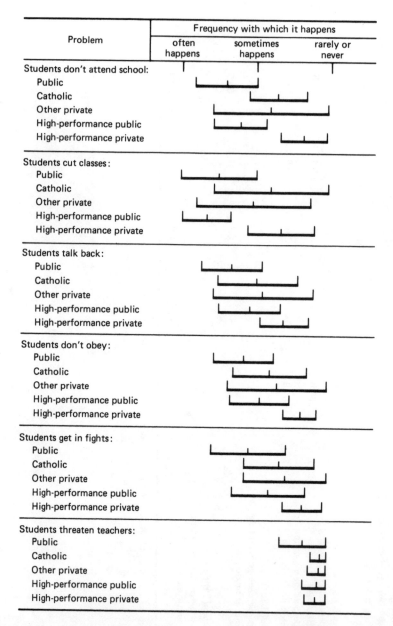

Figure 5–2. *School Aggregate Assessment of Discipline Problems by Sophomore Students in Public and Private Schools: Mean and Variation Within Each School Sector: Spring 1980*

public schools and other private schools is also great. In every area except cutting classes and threatening teachers, the average for other private schools is beyond the range of public schools in the direction of fewer behavior problems (that is, at a point beyond which we would find less than 2.5 percent of the public schools).

These characterizations of behavior problems in the schools show extremely great differences between the public schools and the private schools. In sum, although the distributions of schools do overlap, in some areas the majority of public schools are beyond the limits of the distribution of private schools.

Students' Attitudes

Students' attitudes toward themselves and their environments were elicited in the student questionnaire. Several questions related to what is ordinarily termed "self-concept"—just how good one feels about oneself—were asked, using a five-point agree/disagree scale. Another set of questions, using the same scale, tapped what is ordinarily termed "internal control" or "fate control," that is, the degree to which one feels in control of those things one regards as important.

By examination of these questions it is possible to see how students in each type of school feel about themselves. Information about such feelings or attitudes gives a sense of the psychic state of a school's student body, and thus adds to our sense of just how the schools function as social systems.

The proportion of students within each sector expressing a strong sense of fate control is shown in table 5–15. Six items intended to elicit these feelings are listed there. The differences among sectors are not large, but they are consistent. For nearly all items, public school students are lowest, Catholic school students are next, students in other private schools and high-performance public schools are only slightly higher, and students in high-performance private schools are somewhat higher than the rest. Averages are shown at the bottom of table 5–15, indicating the differences. As these figures show, seniors in all types of schools have a somewhat higher belief in their control of their own fates than do sophomores, with the magnitude of the differences being about equal to that between the public and private school students at the same grade level. However, the seniors in other private and high-performance private schools exceed

TABLE 5-15

Percentage of Sophomores and Seniors in Public and Private Schools Expressing a Strong Sense of Fate Control: Spring 1980

	U.S. Total		Major Sectors						High-Performance Schools			
			Public		Catholic		Other Private		Public		Private	
	Grade		Grade		Grade		Grade		Grade		Grade	
Fate Items[a]	10	12	10	12	10	12	10	12	10	12	10	12
Good luck important (disagree strongly)	24.8	32.4	24.4	32.0	29.9	35.6	27.4	36.8	26.6	38.8	33.2	38.2
Someone stops me (disagree strongly)	9.6	13.8	9.3	13.4	12.6	15.8	11.3	20.1	15.5	22.5	16.4	31.8
Plans don't work out (disagree strongly)	22.6	27.9	22.3	27.5	25.6	29.6	24.3	34.7	26.2	36.8	37.7	43.2
Should accept conditions (disagree strongly)	9.9	16.2	9.6	15.7	12.2	19.8	12.8	23.1	14.2	21.0	22.6	33.1
What happens is my doing (agree strongly)	19.3	22.6	19.4	22.6	18.7	21.7	17.7	24.7	19.7	18.6	16.9	32.8
My plans work out (agree strongly)	13.6	16.5	13.7	16.5	12.4	15.7	12.5	18.8	15.5	14.9	14.4	23.4
Average	16.6	21.6	16.5	21.3	18.6	23.0	17.7	26.4	19.6	25.4	23.5	33.8

[a] Responses taken from BB058 in student questionnaire.

the sophomores in their sense of fate control somewhat more than is true in the other sectors.

A variety of experiences, both within the school and outside it, give some people more self-confidence about themselves than others. Academic achievement and leadership experience are two of the in-school experiences that can foster the growth of self-esteem. Table 5–16 shows the variation in high self-esteem responses for students in various types of schools. Again, senior responses indicate higher self-esteem than do those of sophomores regardless of sector. Generally, the magnitude of the differences is approximately the same for Catholic and both types of public schools. The senior-sophomore difference is greater in the other private and high-performance private schools, as it is for fate control. Although it is beyond the scope of the present study, future researchers may want to focus attention on those characteristics in which these two sectors are especially different from the other sectors: teacher interest (table 5–9), involvement in extracurricular activities (table 5–6), and number of teachers relative to students (table 4–3). These factors, as well as school size, may play a role in the greater change between the sophomore and senior years in these schools. However, a cautionary note is necessary. Although there is consistency between tables 5–15 and 5–16 in the greater sophomore to senior difference in other private and high performance private schools, the results are not statistically significant, and may be due to sampling variations. In addition, there may be a bias due to school nonresponse in the other private sector. For these reasons, the results shown here should be regarded as merely suggestive.

Finally, we examine student concern for social and economic inequalities. Students were asked about the importance of a variety of factors in their lives, and "working to correct social and economic inequalities" was among the items. We report only the responses of non-Hispanic whites for two reasons. First, because we are interested in capturing a concern for the social welfare of others, we wished to study the responses of those who are less often the victims of inequality. Second, because minority students are disproportionately represented in the public sector, their inclusion would have distorted the between-sector comparison. Table 5–17 shows that among the three major sectors there are only slight differences in the proportion of non-Hispanic white students who consider it "very important" to work toward correcting social and economic inequalities, and in all cases the proportion is relatively small (between 9 and 13 percent). Among sophomores, public school students are slightly more concerned than students in the private sector. In both the Catholic and public sectors, the proportion of seniors who consider working to correct inequalities

TABLE 5-16

Percentage of Sophomores and Seniors in Public and Private Schools Giving High Self-Esteem Responses[a]: Spring 1980

Self-Esteem Item	U.S. Total		Major Sectors						High-Performance Schools			
			Public		Catholic		Other Private		Public		Private	
	Grade		Grade		Grade		Grade		Grade		Grade	
	10	12	10	12	10	12	10	12	10	12	10	12
Take positive attitude toward myself (agree strongly)	26.9	32.7	26.9	32.7	26.4	30.9	26.7	33.5	24.8	35.2	35.4	46.0
I'm a person of worth (agree strongly)	26.9	33.5	26.6	33.1	29.5	36.1	29.7	38.6	35.4	36.8	41.1	55.0
Able to do things as well as others (agree strongly)	26.7	33.6	26.5	33.5	28.3	33.3	31.2	37.4	29.0	35.2	41.0	52.4
On the whole, satisfied with myself (agree strongly)	18.9	22.6	18.9	22.4	19.2	22.8	20.0	25.8	21.2	24.7	25.6	32.7
I'm not good at all (disagree strongly)	11.0	14.4	11.0	14.3	10.4	14.0	10.0	15.2	7.9	13.1	13.6	20.7
Not much to be proud of (disagree strongly)	32.6	39.9	32.3	39.4	35.5	43.9	35.0	43.9	37.8	43.6	43.9	58.7
Average	23.8	29.5	23.7	29.2	24.9	30.2	25.4	32.4	26.0	31.4	33.4	44.3

[a] Responses taken from BB058 in student questionnaire.

TABLE 5-17

Percentage Distribution by Grade and School Type of the Perceived Importance Among Non-Hispanic-White
Students of Working to Correct Social and Economic Inequalities[a]: Spring 1980

| Perceived Importance | U.S. Total | | Public | | Catholic | | Other Private | | High-Performance Sector | | | |
| | | | | | | | | | Public | | Private | |
	10	12	10	12	10	12	10	12	10	12	10	12
Total percent	100.0	100.0	100.0	100.0	100.0	100.0	100.0	100.0	100.0	100.0	100.0	100.0
Very important	12.0	11.1	12.1	11.1	11.5	9.8	11.1	13.2	15.0	12.6	13.6	15.0
Somewhat important	49.6	46.5	49.6	46.8	49.3	46.0	52.1	40.5	47.3	44.9	46.0	38.2
Not important	38.4	42.4	38.4	42.1	39.2	44.2	36.8	46.3	37.7	42.5	40.4	46.8

NOTE: Details may not add to totals because of rounding.
[a] Responses taken from BB057 in student questionnaire.

"very important" is slightly lower than that of sophomores, while more other private school seniors than sophomores consider it "very important." All of these differences, however, are small. Perhaps more important is that for all sectors more seniors than sophomores consider this issue "not important." However, the increase in the private sector appears to be greatest, especially in the other private sector. Overall, the data suggest that among non-Hispanic white students there may be less loss of concern for social and economic inequalities in the public sector than in the private sector between the sophomore and senior years.

Conclusion

It should be said that the majority of high school students appear to enjoy working hard in school and report that they are interested in school, regardless of the type of school they attend. Also, student exposure to coursework does not differ greatly by type of school. But schools in the different sectors appear to differ sharply in some respects: the number of advanced courses students take, the disciplinary standards established for students, and the general behavior patterns of students.

Catholic schools are distinguished from others in the relatively tight disciplinary standards established, their reported effectiveness, and the high attendance patterns of their students. Furthermore, the reports of students in Catholic schools concerning discipline tend to match better with principals' reports than do those of students in other types of schools. In terms of extracurricular involvement, Catholic school students appear to have experiences comparable to those of public school students.

In all of the private sectors, students take more academic subjects, and more advanced academic subjects, than students in the public sector (except for the high-performance public schools). Other private schools, as well as high-performance private schools, are distinguished by the growth in participation in extracurricular activities between the sophomore and senior years. The standards of discipline in other private schools are similar to those in the Catholic schools, though somewhat less strict, and the climate appears to involve closer teacher-student relations than in either Catholic or public schools.

Public schools, in general, are distinguished by their discipline problems, the lower average number of academic courses completed by their students, and the lower number of hours spent on homework. However, for public school students planning to complete four years of college, exposure to advanced science courses is not much below that of students in the private schools, though these students take substantially fewer advanced mathematics courses than do students in private schools.

Students in high-performance public schools are more likely to complete advanced mathematics courses than students in other private or Catholic schools but are less likely to do so than students in high-performance private schools. Students in high-performance public schools also spend about the same amount of time on homework as do students in Catholic and other private schools. But students in high-performance public schools are distinguished by their consistently higher rate of absenteeism and class cutting. In other areas of discipline, they differ less from other private and Catholic schools, though they show somewhat greater discipline problems.

The types and amounts of courses completed, as well as the disciplinary climate, appear, then, to be important differences in the functioning of these schools. In the next chapter, we discuss how these schools differ in outcomes for their students.

6

Outcomes of Education

A central question in any consideration of policy concerning public and private schools is the outcomes of these differing forms of schooling for the students they undertake to educate. This is not, however, a single question: There are two dominant, as well as several subsidiary questions. The two dominant questions are "What are the results achieved by public and private schools as they currently function?" and "What would be the different outcomes of public and private schooling for the same boy or girl going through the two different kinds of schools?" The first is useful for purely descriptive purposes, to see just what the students completing public and private schools in the U.S. are like, how they are similar and how they differ. It is the second, however, that is more central for parents, and central to policy arguments about the relative merits of public and private schools.

The first of the questions is simple and straightforward, and can be answered directly by comparing seniors in public and private schools on various measures: test scores, post-high-school plans, interest in school, adherence to discipline, effort expended on schoolwork, attitudes toward oneself and others, and so on. Some of these measures, which show differences in the way the schools function, were examined in chapter 5; others, which are purely outcomes of schooling, are examined here.

The second question is more difficult: it requires an experiment that can never be precisely carried out, but is approximated every day. What would be the difference in outcome for a given boy or girl in the different school settings? It is impossible to have the same person in two different schools, but we can observe the results when, for instance, a brother goes to a public school, while his sister goes to a private school; or two boys who have grown up as neighbors and friends are sent, one to a private school and the other to a public school.

In answering the second of these questions with data of the sort contained in High School and Beyond, statistical controls are used as substitutes for the ideal but unattainable experiment. The quality of the answer to the question depends on the statistical controls that are used. In attempting to answer the question, we will use a kind of triangulation, obtaining evidence through different types of analyses in order to get a more secure fix on the results.[1]

Yet whatever the statistical controls, and despite the differing kinds of analysis, some measure of uncertainty must remain. When the sophomores are retested two years hence, the existence of measures at two points in time will help remove some of the uncertainty; but even then, uncertainty will remain. This uncertainty, however, is the situation with all questions of cause and effect. Our task will be to use the evidence at hand to cast as much light on the causal questions as possible.

In addition to these two major questions, there are subsidiary questions as well: What would be the outcome differences between public and private schools if some input resource other than students were the same? For example, how would public and private schools differ in outcomes if they were, on average, the same size, or if the per-pupil expenditures in each were the same? Some of these hypothetical questions are relevant to policy issues, because some policies would equalize these schools on certain resource inputs. A voucher plan, for example, such as that which has been proposed in California, would nearly equalize per-pupil expenditures among public and private schools in the state.[2]

As in the case of the questions about outcomes for students who are alike, these questions about outcomes when various input resources or characteristics are made similar cannot be answered with certainty. The answers, nevertheless, are valuable, not only for policy purposes, but also

---

[1] The analyses in this chapter are those that were done for the draft report, with only minor additions including standard errors. Results of some further analyses appear in footnotes throughout the charter. Additional analyses have been done to pursue further selection bias questions; those are discussed in the addendum.

[2] This plan has been developed by John Coons, Professor of Law at the University of California, Berkeley. There was an initial attempt, later withdrawn, to put the voucher proposal on the California ballot for referendum.

because they give some insight into the sources of any different effects that public and private schools have on students. They offer ideas about what policies may be valuable, both in public schools and in private schools, to increase the school's effectiveness.

Descriptive Differences in Outcomes Between Public and Private Schools

From one point of view, the products of a school are its graduates, and we should therefore look only at seniors to discover the differences in these products. From another point of view, however, the school's products are its students at every stage of their schooling, so that it is reasonable to view the performance, behavior, and attitudes of sophomores as the school's products as well. We take the second view, examining these attributes of sophomores as well as seniors.

Some of these descriptive differences in outcomes (that is, certain behavior of students in schools and certain attitudes about self and school) have been examined in the preceding chapter and will not be reexamined here. In this chapter, we focus on two outcomes: scores on standardized tests and plans beyond high school.

COGNITIVE ACHIEVEMENT IN EACH SECTOR

Tests were given to sophomores and seniors in each of the schools studied. The tests differed somewhat for sophomores and seniors, but three of the tests had a number of items in common. The vocabulary tests had eight words in common, the reading tests had eight questions in common, and the mathematics tests had eighteen items in common. The results are given separately for the sophomore tests (in table 6–1), for the senior tests (in table 6–2), and for the common subtests taken by both seniors and sophomores (in table 6–3).

The sophomore test scores in table 6–1 show that the average student in public schools scores below the average student in either the Catholic or other private schools in every area tested. Students from Catholic schools and from other private schools have similar averages, and the high-performance schools, both private and public, show averages above those of students in the other sectors. The high-performance private schools, more selective and more homogeneous, show averages considerably above

TABLE 6–1
Means and Standard Deviations for Sophomore Test Scores in Public and Private Schools: Spring 1980

Test	U.S. Total	Major Sectors			High-Performance Schools	
		Public	Catholic	Other Private	Public	Private
Means						
Reading (19)[a]	9.1	8.9	10.5	10.5	11.7	14.5
Vocabulary (21)	10.9	10.7	12.9	13.1	14.1	17.6
Mathematics (38)	18.6	18.3	21.5	22.3	24.9	30.2
Science (20)	10.9	10.8	11.9	12.4	13.2	15.1
Civics (10)	5.8	5.8	6.5	6.4	7.1	7.8
Writing (17)	10.3	10.1	11.9	11.5	12.8	14.7
Standard Deviations[b]						
Reading	3.9	3.8	3.6	3.9	4.1	2.8
Vocabulary	4.4	4.3	3.9	4.5	4.2	2.6
Mathematics	7.4	7.4	6.6	7.8	7.5	4.8
Science	3.8	3.8	3.3	3.5	3.5	2.4
Civics	2.0	2.0	1.9	1.9	1.9	1.4
Writing	4.0	4.0	3.5	3.8	3.4	2.0

[a] Numbers in parentheses refer to total number of test items.

[b] Standard deviations shown are standard deviations of individual test scores. Standard errors for sector mean achievement may be found by multiplying the standard deviations shown by the following numbers:

	U.S. Total	Public	Catholic	Other Private	High-Performance Public	High-Performance Private
Sophomores	.006	.006	.019	.044	.054	.055
Seniors	.006	.007	.020	.048	.062	.058

TABLE 6–2
Means and Standard Deviations for Senior Test Scores in Public and Private Schools: Spring 1980

Test	U.S. Total	Major Sectors			High-Performance Schools	
		Public	Catholic	Other Private	Public	Private
Means						
Reading (20)[a]	10.9	10.8	11.9	13.0	13.5	16.0
Vocabulary (27)	13.1	12.9	15.1	15.9	18.0	21.6
Mathematics (32)	19.1	18.9	21.1	22.4	23.9	28.1
Picture Number (15)	11.3	11.3	12.1	11.9	11.6	13.0
Mosaic (89)	45.3	45.2	47.3	51.0	54.2	55.3
Visual (16)	7.7	7.7	7.5	8.6	8.8	9.8
Standard Deviations[b]						
Reading	4.2	4.2	3.8	4.2	4.0	2.6
Vocabulary	5.4	5.3	5.1	6.0	5.7	3.7
Mathematics	6.3	6.3	5.6	6.1	5.7	2.7
Picture number	3.7	3.7	3.3	3.5	3.5	2.8
Mosaic	14.6	14.6	12.6	14.7	16.0	14.5
Visual	3.1	3.1	3.0	3.2	3.2	3.3

[a] Numbers in parentheses refer to total number of test items.

[b] See footnote b, table 6–1 for calculating standard errors for sector means.

TABLE 6–3

Mean Scores on Subtests That Are Identical for Seniors and Sophomores in Public and Private Schools: Spring 1980

Subtest	U.S. Total		Major Sectors						High-Performance Schools			
			Public		Catholic		Other Private		Public		Private	
	Grade		Grade		Grade		Grade		Grade		Grade	
	10	12	10	12	10	12	10	12	10	12	10	12
Means												
Reading (8)[a]	3.67	4.54	3.60	4.48	4.34	5.00	4.32	5.34	4.85	5.77	6.06	6.71
Vocabulary (8)	3.78	4.58	3.69	4.48	4.59	5.35	4.78	5.56	5.11	6.24	6.65	7.22
Mathematics (18)	9.56	10.80	9.40	10.63	11.05	12.10	11.28	12.74	12.53	13.76	15.09	16.38
Standard Deviations												
Reading	2.01	2.10	2.00	2.10	1.92	1.96	2.05	2.04	2.12	1.94	1.49	1.18
Vocabulary	1.90	1.97	1.88	1.97	1.84	1.74	2.00	1.94	1.86	1.65	1.24	.97
Mathematics	4.04	4.24	4.04	4.24	3.56	3.82	4.17	4.14	3.80	3.62	2.33	1.70

[a] Numbers in parentheses refer to total number of items on subtests.

those for the high-performance public schools. These differences in average test scores and in standard deviations illustrate again the differences between the two sets of high-performance schools. The high-performance public schools are generally large upper-middle-class suburban schools with student bodies that perform well above those of the average public school, yet they contain much more diversity in performance than the high-performance private schools, as comparison of the standard deviations shows.

Some subject-matter variations exist between the sectors. The Catholic schools are about half a standard deviation above the public schools in vocabulary (using the U.S. total standard deviation); a little less than half above in reading, mathematics, and writing (English composition); and about a third above in civics and science. The other private schools are slightly higher than the Catholic schools in mathematics and science; slightly lower in civics and writing.

It is also useful to look at the standard deviations of the test scores in each of the school types. The standard deviations are smaller on every test in the Catholic schools than they are in the public schools, showing a greater homogeneity of student performance in Catholic schools. In the other private sector, they are larger than those of public school students for about half of the twelve tests for both sophomores and seniors and smaller for about half.

The standard deviations can be thought of as test score variations consisting of two parts: the variation among students within a school and the variation among schools within the same school sector. The public schools, Catholic schools, and other private schools differ greatly in the fraction of the variance that is between schools. Over all twelve tests in the sophomore and senior years, the fraction between schools is .11 for Catholic schools, .18 for public schools, and .28 for other private schools. This, taken together with the smaller overall variances for Catholic school students and the roughly equal overall variances for public and other private school students, means:

1. The school-to-school variation in average test scores is considerably less in Catholic schools than in public schools;
2. The school-to-school variation in average test scores is considerably greater in other private schools than in public schools.

The high school-to-school variation in the other private schools shows the extreme heterogeneity among these other private schools. They include the prestigious schools that are often thought of as *the* private schools in America, schools that roughly coincide with membership in the

National Association of Independent Schools. They include a wide range of church-related schools, as shown in chapter 2, some of which operate on a shoestring; and they include, as well, schools that have sprung up in response to school desegregation policies and other unpopular policies in the public schools. These schools vary, too, in the kinds of students served. Some children are in private schools because their parents feel the local public school offers too little challenge. But others are marginal students, in private schools because they have done poorly in public school. Some private schools cater to low achievers, others to high. Altogether, the large variations in test scores in the "other private" category of schools indicates the wide range of levels at which these schools operate and the wide range of functions they serve for different types of students.

Both the lower overall variations in Catholic sector test scores and the less school-to-school variation are as one might expect. Students in these schools come from backgrounds that are more homogeneous in education and income level than those of students in either the public schools or the other private schools.[3] In addition, the schools themselves are more homogeneous, all operating under the same church, and with some common practices.

The schools that show the least variation in test scores among their students are the high-performance private schools. Because they are within the prestigious segment of the private schools they, too, draw students from rather homogeneous backgrounds. In addition, they were selected for inclusion in this study on the basis of their similarity in performance on a standardized test, the National Merit Scholarship Test. Thus, on both these grounds, they can be expected to show, as they do, considerably lower variation in test score performance by their students.

In contrast, the high-performance public schools show about the same diversity of performance as do the public schools as a whole, though the average level of performance ranges from about two-thirds of a standard deviation to nearly a full standard deviation above that in the public schools as a whole.

The senior test scores show a pattern similar to those for the sophomore tests. Again, on the six tests, the public schools are lower than the Catholic and other private schools, with only one exception among the twelve comparisons between public schools and the two private school sectors. The other private schools are slightly higher than the Catholic schools on five of the six tests. The high-performance public schools are (except for the

---

[3] Table 3–9 shows the lesser variation in income among parents of children in Catholic schools than among parents of children in other schools.

picture number test) higher than the other private schools, and the high-performance private schools are in turn considerably above the high-performance public schools.

It is tempting to compare the senior and sophomore scores for the three tests with comparable content (vocabulary, reading, mathematics) in order to draw some inference from the scores of the two cohorts about "gains" or "growth" in achievement. However, there are difficulties in doing so. One principal difficulty is that the tests are not the same at the two grade levels. Another difficulty is that the students in the two grades cannot be considered as representative samples of the same population, largely because of dropouts between the sophomore and senior years.

The first of these difficulties can be overcome by examining subtests consisting of the items that are identical in the two years. These subtest scores are presented in table 6–3. The table shows the same differences between school sectors seen in tables 6–1 and 6–2. The public school students' averages are lowest, Catholic school students are somewhat higher, and the other private schools are highest among the three major sectors. Students in the high-performance public schools are somewhat higher still, and the students in high-performance private schools are considerably higher than all.

When we look at differences between grades 10 and 12, for the purpose of inferring something about growth in achievement over the two years, the first striking point is that the growth seems rather small everywhere. Out of eight questions on reading comprehension, the average sophomore answers about four correctly, and the senior answers, on the average, less than one additional question correctly. Similarly, for the eight vocabulary items, the average sophomore answers about half correctly, while the average senior has learned less than one more. In mathematics, of the eighteen problems, the average sophomore answers only a little more than half, and the average senior only a little over one additional item.

The differences between sophomores and seniors, which could, with some caveats, be regarded as growth, seem very much the same among the different sectors, except for the high-performance private schools, in which the growth is less in vocabulary and reading. This result for the high-performance private schools is almost certainly due to a ceiling effect. The average number of correct answers among sophomores was only 1.9 less than the total number of items in reading and 1.3 less in vocabulary. This means that many sophomore students had all items correct: 16 percent of the sophomores in these schools had all items in the reading test correct, and 35 percent had all items in the vocabulary test correct. These students' scores could not be bettered by their senior counterparts.

The only gains could come in that fraction of the student body with less-than-perfect scores, and, even then, the opportunity for gain was small, since only one or two items were missed. For other schools, these data show no strikingly different degree of growth from the sophomore to the senior year.

It might be argued that the lack of growth from the sophomore to the senior year can be explained by the fact that these tests do not cover subject matter that is an explicit part of the curriculum in the later years of high school. The mathematics items are all rather elementary, involving basic arithmetic operations, fractions, and only a few hints of algebra and geometry. Explicit attention to reading comprehension and to vocabulary expansion is not part of standard curricula in the 10th through 12th grades. We would, thus, not expect the variation in intensity and scope of the academic courses taken during these years—as examined in chapter 5—to have a direct impact on the variations in the sophomore to senior test score gains. Two or three of the tests given to sophomores (science, civics, writing composition skills) should reflect such curriculum variations when they are administered again in 1982 to these same students as seniors.[4] Yet the academic courses that are taken in grades 10, 11, and 12 should provide the kind of practice and experience that would lead to somewhat greater growth than the one item per test. Few sophomores in public and private schools, with the exception of those in high performance private schools, get all items correct, therefore there is great room for learning. Thus the small rates of growth are rather surprising.

There are difficulties in inferring differential growth among school sectors (or, as appears to be the case, lack of differential growth) on the basis of these comparisons. First, there may have been differential growth that occurred prior to the testing date in grade 10. That is, the spring of grade 10 is not the entry point into high school for these students, and thus differences between grades 10 and 12 capture only part of the growth that occurs during the students' high school careers.

Second, these are two cohorts, and differential dropout rates among the sectors may result in the seniors being a differently-selected group than the sophomores in each of the sectors. (We return to the question of differential dropout later in this chapter.)

Third, entirely apart from different dropout rates, the two cohorts are samples from the population of sophomores and seniors in each type of school, and normal sampling variation, particularly in the private sectors, where the samples are not large, can lead to differences.

---

[4] These science, civics, and writing composition tests were not given to the 1980 seniors. Instead, the senior test battery replicated the tests given to 1972 seniors surveyed in NCES's earlier longitudinal study, to allow for 1972 to 1980 comparisons.

Fourth, it may be that average growth rates obscure differences in growth among segments of the student population. For example, it could be, because of the great diversity among the other private schools, that there is high growth among some (for example, the prestigious "independent" schools) and low growth among others. These differences would be masked by the overall 10-to-12 comparisons made in table 6–3.

An attempt is made in subsequent sections on private school effects to examine the question of differential growth. At this point, all that can be said is that there are differences at grade 10, which are certainly due in part to differential selection of students into different types of schools, and that similar differences are found at grade 12.

POST-HIGH-SCHOOL PLANS IN EACH SECTOR

Sophomores and seniors were asked about their plans after high school. One question asked only about schooling: "As things stand now, how far in school do you think you will get?" Across sectors, students differed considerably in their responses to this question. Table 6–4 shows the results.

For sophomores, the mode was less than four years of college for public school students and college graduate for Catholic and other private school students. For both the public and private high-performance schools, it was an M.A. or Ph.D. Almost 30 percent of public school sophomores expected not to go beyond high school, while 12.4 percent among the students in other private schools, was the next highest percentage. Altogether, the distributions of sophomore schooling expectations were very similar in the Catholic and other private schools.

Seniors in all sectors except Catholic schools show higher educational expectations than sophomores. The differences are not large for public school students, but are rather large for students in other private schools and in the high-performance private schools, where the seniors show about a 10-percent increase saying they expect to get an M.A. or Ph.D.

The immediacy and concreteness of college plans are shown by responses to another question which asks when, if ever, the student plans to attend college (either two-year or four-year). Responses to this question are shown in table 6–5. As with expectations about ultimate level of schooling, there are differences in the immediacy of college plans, differences in which the sectors are ordered in the same way as before.

Public school sophomores show the greatest percentage deferring college or undecided (nearly 40 percent taken altogether) while in these uncertain categories, the Catholic and other private schools show percentages in the 20-to-30 range. At the other extreme, only about 5 percent of

TABLE 6-4

Percentage Distributions by Grade of Expected Educational Attainments in Public and Private Schools[a]: Spring 1980

	Major Sectors								High-Performance Schools			
	U.S. Total		Public		Catholic		Other Private		Public		Private	
	Grade		Grade		Grade		Grade		Grade		Grade	
Expected Level	10	12	10	12	10	12	10	12	10	12	10	12
Total	100.0	100.0	100.0	100.0	100.0	100.0	100.0	100.0	100.0	100.0	100.0	100.0
High school or less	26.5	19.8	28.2	21.1	9.8	8.2	12.4	8.9	8.6	4.6	1.0	1.0
More than high school but less than four-year college	33.0	34.6	33.5	35.6	27.2	27.3	27.3	22.1	19.0	16.1	1.3	0.6
Four-year college	22.7	25.4	21.6	24.4	33.2	36.2	32.2	30.7	30.5	30.6	32.3	22.8
M.A. or Ph.D. or other advanced professional degree	17.8	20.1	16.6	18.8	29.8	28.2	28.2	38.3	41.9	48.7	65.4	75.6

NOTE: Details may not add to totals because of rounding.
[a] Responses taken from item BB065 in student questionnaire.

TABLE 6–5
Percentage Distributions by Grade for Time of Entry to College in Public and Private Schools[a]: Spring 1980

Planned Time of Entry	U.S. Total		Major Sectors						High-Performance Schools			
			Public		Catholic		Other Private		Public		Private	
	Grade		Grade		Grade		Grade		Grade		Grade	
	10	12	10	12	10	12	10	12	10	12	10	12
Total	100.0	100.0	100.0	100.0	100.0	100.0	100.0	100.0	100.0	100.0	100.0	100.0
In the year after high school	48.5	59.3	41.8	57.4	71.2	77.0	64.9	73.2	74.8	84.6	94.7	95.1
Later	15.8	10.6	16.2	11.0	10.8	6.9	13.7	8.0	16.2	6.5	3.6	3.0
Don't know	21.2	10.5	22.1	10.8	13.0	7.1	14.1	8.4	5.2	2.7	1.5	.6
No plans to enter	14.5	19.6	15.4	20.8	5.1	9.0	7.4	10.4	3.8	6.1	.4	1.4

NOTE: Details may not add to totals because of rounding.
[a] Responses taken from item BB115 in student questionnaire.

the sophomores from high-performance private schools show this uncertainty.

In every sector, the seniors show a higher percentage planning to go immediately to college, with the differences greatest by far in the public schools. But there is also, in every sector, an increase in the percentage who are definitely not going to college. The number who say they plan to defer college decreases in all sectors, and the number who say they don't know decreases even more sharply. Thus, post-high-school plans, whether for college or for something else, have crystallized considerably by the senior year among students in all school sectors. The percentage of seniors who still don't know, or plan to defer college, remains greatest in the public schools, as it was for the sophomores, but the crystallization appears to have been greatest in the public schools.

Plans for higher education constitute one type of post-high-school plan; another is plans for a job. We ask, for those seniors who are planning to work in the year after high school, just how concrete their plans are: Do they have a job "lined up" before they finish school? Table 6–6 shows responses to this question among seniors from the different types of schools.

Here it is the public school seniors whose plans are most fully implemented. Of those who plan to work full time after high school, a higher percentage in the public schools already have a definite job lined up. The sectors are ordered in approximately the reverse of their order with respect to concreteness of college plans. Just as college plans are less concrete and less fully implemented among public school seniors who expect to attend college than among their counterparts in private schools, job plans are less concrete and less fully implemented among those private school seniors who do plan to go to work after they finish high school. This suggests that the private schools—perhaps because most do not have vocational programs, perhaps because of less tangible factors—do less than the public schools in aiding the job placement of their graduates who are not going on to college.

Effects of Private Schools on Outcomes of Schooling

It is evident from the preceding section that students in different sectors vary in their achievement on standardized tests and in their post-high-school plans. What is not clear is whether going to a public school, a Catholic school, or another type of private school makes a difference in

TABLE 6–6
Percentage Distributions of Job Status for Those Seniors in Public and Private Schools Who Plan to Work Full Time Next Year[a]: Spring 1980

Definite Job Lined Up	U.S. Total	Major Sectors			High-Performance Schools	
		Public	Catholic	Other Private	Public	Private
Total						
Number	1,776,998	1,648,034	84,193	44,580	13,164	191
Percentage	100.0	100.0	100.0	100.0	100.0	100.0
Yes	53.5	53.9	50.1	45.1	50.3	30.0
No, but looked	22.0	22.0	24.4	17.0	18.6	18.9
No	24.4	24.0	25.4	37.8	31.1	51.0

NOTE: Details may not add to totals because of rounding.
[a] Responses taken from item EB073 in student questionnaire.

either of these outcomes. For not only did seniors in these different sectors vary in test performance and in plans for further education, sophomores did as well. Thus the differences may well be due merely to the student selection factors associated with each of the sectors. In this section, we will try to answer that fundamental question: Are the differences across sectors entirely due to selection, or are there also different effects on basic cognitive skills and on plans for further education? That is, what would be the outcomes for the same student in each of those sectors? This is a central question both for policies that affect the fortunes of public and private schools and for parental decisions about where to send children to school.

There are two classical methods of answering this question with data from ongoing (that is, nonexperimental) schools. Both have some defects. One method is to use multivariate analysis to statistically control family background characteristics. It is hoped that by comparing outcomes for students with the same parents' education, the same income, the same parental interest in the child's education, and so on, the students in different schools will be "equated" in terms of their backgrounds, and any differences found in outcomes can then be attributed to something about the school. The other method is to measure the outcome variable early in the student's school career and again later. Differential change in the outcome variable is then attributed to something about the school. This method in effect uses the students' own prior responses as a control for the later ones, using the prior responses to control for differential selection into different schools.

The principal defect of the first of these methods is that it is seldom possible to control on *all* relevant background characteristics. Thus the possibility always remains that the differences attributed to differences in schools are instead due to some unmeasured aspect of the student's background. This defect is particularly important here, for one known difference between parents of children in public schools and parents of children in private schools is that the latter have chosen their child's school and are paying tuition to implement this choice. It seems probable that this behavior is an indicator of additional differences in the parents' behavior toward the child's education, differences that could well affect the very outcomes that are of interest. Yet this difference between parents, by its very nature, is not something on which students in public and private schools can be equated.[5] This approach therefore is particularly defective in comparing public and private schools.

The second approach, use of the same student's earlier response on the same outcome variable, is free from some of the defects of the first approach, but it has defects of its own. For example, it may be that the rate of change in an outcome variable such as achievement is different among students at different levels of performance, even if they are subject to the same school environment. If this is the case, then differential changes in schools that had students who were initially different can be mistakenly attributed to effects of the school.

But the virtues and defects of this second method of discovering effects of different types of school are irrelevant to the present inquiry because the data do not include prior measures of these outcome variables for the same students. For the sophomores, such analysis will be possible two years hence, when they are seniors, but not at present.

The fact that measures of the outcome variable are available for sophomores and seniors in the same schools does, however, give some additional ways of obtaining evidence about possible differential effects of the dif-

[5] It is possible that some analysis could be carried out comparing aggregate outcomes in geographic areas where private schools are widely available with outcomes in those areas where private schools are largely unavailable. If there is an effect of private schools, then the overall achievement in the former areas, after statistically controlling on family background characteristics, should be different from that in the latter areas. If s is the average outcome score for public schools, standardized for family background, and $s + c$ is the average standardized score for students in private schools (where c, either positive or negative, is the private school effect), then c can be estimated as follows: If p_1 is the proportion of students in private school in area 1, and p_2 is the proportion in area 2, the overall student average in area 1 should be $(1-p_1) s + p_1 (s + c)$, or $s + p_1 c$. In area 2, the average should be $(1-p_2) s + p_2 (s+c)$, or $s + p_2 c$. The difference between these averages is $(p_1 - p_2) c$. Thus, if there are areas in which p_1 and p_2 are considerably different, it is possible to estimate c, the private school effect, by this method. The method assumes, of course, that s, the background-standardized outcome score, is the same in both areas; an assumption that may not be true. Because of the necessity of this assumption, and because p_i is rather small in all areas i (see table 2–2), we have not used this method here. We have, however, done so in the addendum.

ferent types of schools. In the remaining parts of this chapter, we attempt to use several methods to determine whether there are differential effects. The greatest attention is paid to cognitive achievement as an outcome of schooling. This is followed by an examination of plans for higher education as a second type of outcome. Throughout this section, we examine only the three major sectors, leaving aside the two high-performance sectors.[6]

EFFECTS ON COGNITIVE ACHIEVEMENT

Table 6–7 shows, for sophomore scores on the reading, the vocabulary, and the mathematics subtests, the estimated addition to sophomore scores that is due to being in a Catholic or other private school rather than a public school—for students with the same measured background characteristics.[7]

In order to minimize the effects of differences in initial selection masquerading as effects of differences in the sectors themselves, achievement subtests were regressed, by sector and grade, on a large number of background variables that measure both objective and subjective differences in the home. Some of these subjective differences may not be prior to the student's achievement, but may in part be consequences of it, so that there may be an overcompensation for background differences. It was felt desirable to do this so as to compensate for possible unmeasured differences in family background; but of course the result may be to artificially depress the resulting levels of background-controlled achievement in Catholic and other private schools. (A few additional background variables were initially included; those that showed no effects beyond the ones listed in the following paragraph were eliminated from the analysis.)

---

[6] The two high-performance sectors present several problems of different importance in different parts of this chapter. One is the small number of schools and students in these sectors: 12 schools, 311 seniors, and 370 sophomores in the high-performance public schools and 11 schools, 326 seniors, and 353 sophomores in the high-performance private schools. A second is the fact that, especially in the private schools, the average number of items correct among sophomores is close to the upper limit. Most important for the next section is that they have been selected on the basis of achievement levels.

[7] The background characteristics used as controls are described in the text that follows. The regression analyses on which these two tables are based are separate regressions for each school sector at each grade level. This was done, rather than use of a single regression equation with dummy variables for sectors, to allow for different effects of background characteristics in different sectors. The estimated increment at the sophomore level due to each of the two private sectors is obtained by first calculating the predicted test score in each sector for a student with background characteristics standardized to that of the average public school sophomore, and then finding the difference between the private sector and the public sector. Regression equations used in this table and in table 6–8 are given in appendix tables A–6 through A–9.

TABLE 6–7

Estimated Increments to Test Scores in Public and Private Schools With Family Background Standardized: Spring 1980[a]
(Standard errors in parentheses)[b]

	Reading	Vocabulary	Mathematics
Public School Sophomores	3.60	3.69	9.40
Standardized Increments for:			
Catholic schools	.32	.36	.58
	(.048)	(.045)	(.091)
Other private schools	.14	.33	.56
	(.064)	(.060)	(.121)
Senior increment in public schools	.73	.63	.88
	(.018)	(.018)	(.037)
Raw increments (from table 6–3)			
Sophomore Increments for:			
Catholic schools	.74	.90	1.65
Other private schools	.72	1.09	1.88
Senior increment in public schools	.88	.79	1.23

[a] Family background refers to seventeen subjective and objective background characteristics which are listed in the text. The relevant regression coefficients and sector means are reported in appendix A, tables A–5, A–6, A–7, A–8, and A–9.

[b] Standard errors for the differences are obtained by pooling variances for the predicted achievement in each sector for a student with the family background characteristics of the average public school sophomore. Variances for an estimated $\hat{Y}$ are calculated as follows: $X'_k (\Sigma_{bb} X_k)$ where X_k is the vector of means for the family background variables of the public school sophomores and Σ_{bb} is the variance-covariance matrix of the regression coefficients (see Draper and Smith, 1966:56).

These calculated standard errors do not include a design effect, but assume a simple random sample. With a stratified probability sample of the sort used in this study, a direct empirical estimate of standard errors of a statistic can be made, though it is expensive to do so. For one critical set of statistics, the Catholic and other private increments for sophomores (shown in table 6–7) and for seniors (obtainable from tables 6–7 and 6–8), empirical standard errors were estimated. They are:

	Reading	Vocabulary	Mathematics
Sophomore Catholic	.049	.091	.088
Other private	.135	.174	.119
Senior Catholic	.110	.063	.112
Other private	.222	.061	.129

See Coleman, Hoffer, Kilgore (1981a) Appendix A, pages A–6 through A–7 for further details.

The background characteristics used in the analysis include the following, classified as clearly prior to (that is, unaffected by) the student's achievement level and not clearly prior to the student's achievement level.

Clearly prior
Family income
Mother's education
Father's education
Race
Hispanic-non-Hispanic

Number of siblings
Number of rooms in the home
Both parents present
Mother's working before child was in elementary school
Mother's working when child was in elementary school

Not clearly prior (in rough order of likelihood of being prior)
Encyclopedia or other reference books in home
More than fifty books in home
Typewriter in home
Owns pocket calculator
Frequency of talking with mother or father about personal experiences
Mother thinks student should go to college after high school
Father thinks student should go to college after high school

These variables were used to account for student achievement in twelve regression equations: public sophomores, public seniors, private sophomores, and private seniors for each of the three areas of achievement.[8] Then, in order to control or standardize on student background, the expected achievement for a student with the average background characteristics of the public school sophomore students was calculated for each grade level within each of the three sectors (public school seniors, Catholic and other private sophomores, and Catholic and other private seniors). These expected achievement levels can then be compared to find the difference between sectors and between grades, having standardized for family background. The results of all of this are given in table 6–7.[9]

The increments for each type of private school are positive, showing

---

[8] The total variance explained by these background factors in each of these equations is listed in appendix A, tables A–6 through A–9. In the private school regressions, dummy variables were used for other private and high-performance private schools. The latter, however, are not included in the results discussed in this section.

[9] Throughout this section, the subtests consisting of common items for sophomores and seniors are used in the analysis. This is done to facilitate sophomore-senior comparisons, which are made in many of the analyses and are central to the analysis of tables 6–7 and 6–8. However, it is useful to indicate at this point that the basic inference drawn from table 6–7 would be unchanged if the full tests were used. Rows 1, 2, and 3 of the table would become:

	Reading	*Vocabulary*	*Mathematics*
Public school sophomores	8.92	10.67	18.39
Catholic increment	.67	.99	1.17
	(.085)	(.091)	(.159)
Other private increment	.37	.73	1.50
	(.030)	(.185)	(.321)

Standard errors of the increments, obtained by the method described in the footnote to table 6–7, are in parentheses. The private school increments are larger for the full tests, but

that students of the same background characteristics have generally higher achievement in both of these types of private schools than in the public schools. However, the differences are reduced compared to the raw differences from table 6–3 (shown in the lower half of table 6–7), because of the statistical control of family background. They are slightly higher for Catholic schools than for other private schools.

Comparing the Catholic and other private schools background-controlled increments to the raw increments shows that for Catholic schools, between half and two-thirds of the raw increments are eliminated when background differences are statistically controlled, and for other private schools, over two-thirds of the raw increments are eliminated. The greater reduction for students in the other private schools is due to the fact that their backgrounds differ more from public school students than do the backgrounds of Catholic school students. Thus, in general, with these background characteristics controlled, Catholic school sophomores perform at the highest level, sophomores in other private schools next, and sophomores in the public schools lowest.[10]

The background-standardized senior public school increment, shown in the fourth line of table 6–7, provides additional information. First, the estimated sophomore-to-senior growth rates are below the raw increments (shown in the lower half of table 6–7), indicating that the family backgrounds of seniors are slightly higher than those of sophomores—a differ-

---

expressed as fractions of the total number of items in the test (18, 21, and 38 rather than 8, 8, and 18) they are very close to the same.

Another point concerning this comparison involves standardizing to the "average public school sophomore" rather than the "average U.S. sophomore." This was done for convenience, since the means for the former were at hand, and the public school sophomores are very close to the total population means. Another alternative would have been to standardize for the "average private school sophomore," but, because this is such a small fraction of the total, it is ten times as far from the national average as is the public school average, and we originally considered it too atypical to estimate. But the results of such a private school standardization can be calculated from tables A–5, A–6, A–7. They tend to show a smaller effect for these higher-status students:

	Reading	Vocabulary	Mathematics
Catholic increment	.24	.40	.38
Other private increment	.07	.38	.36

This smaller effect for higher-status persons is another expression of the "common school effect" of Catholic schools which we discuss in the next section. (The apparently lower other private increment here is misleading; the equation in which the other private schools appear is dominated by the Catholic school effects. See table 6–9.)

[10] These results would be generally the same if one used a single regression equation for all students with dummy variables for attendance at a Catholic school and at an other private school, but the measured effects would generally be smaller.

Coefficients and standard errors (in parentheses) for the sophomore single equation are

ence that is attributable to greater dropout rates between grades 10 and 12 for students from lower backgrounds. Thus, the estimated growth from sophomore to senior, which appears low in table 6–3, is even less than what appears there.

Second, comparing the increments in Catholic and other private schools with the senior increments in public schools indicates that the Catholic school increments are about half as large, that is, about one grade level, while the other private increments are about half as large in vocabulary and mathematics, but only about a fifth as large in reading. Thus, except for reading comprehension in the other private schools, which is almost negligible, the estimated increments due to attendance at Catholic or other private schools are about one grade level.

Another way to examine differential growth in public and private schools is suggested by table 6–3, which compares sophomores and seniors in each sector on identical subtests. That table compares raw scores, uncontrolled for family background differences; it is possible to do something like this, but controlling on family background differences. In effect, this is an extension of table 6–7, with increments calculated at the senior level for each of the private sectors, and then comparing the senior-level increments to the sophomore-level increments shown in table 6–7. Senior-level increments that are larger than sophomore-level increments indicate greater sophomore-to-senior growth in the private sector; smaller increments indicate greater growth in the public sector.

The excess of sophomore-to-senior increments in both private sectors beyond the increment (shown in table 6–7) in the public sector is shown in table 6–8. The table shows, overall, little or no evidence of extra growth in the Catholic schools beyond that in the public schools, but consistent extra growth in the other private schools. The amount of extra growth in the other private schools averages about a quarter of the sophomore-senior

---

shown below both for the subtests and for the full tests discussed in the preceding footnote. The coefficients may be directly compared to the Catholic and other private increments shown in table 6–7 and in the previous footnote. The sizes of the coefficients are in nearly all cases smaller than the values shown in table 6–7. In all cases, except three for other private schools (reading subtest and full test, and the mathematics subtest), the sizes of the coefficients are considerably greater than twice their standard errors (see appendix table A–12 for the full equation).

Coefficients:	Subtests			Full tests		
	Reading	Vocabulary	Mathematics	Reading	Vocabulary	Mathematics
Catholic	.26	.41	.46	.54	.92	.88
	(.04)	(.04)	(.09)	(.09)	(.09)	(.16)
Other private	.02	.31	.22	.06	.44	.75
	(.07)	(.06)	(.12)	(.11)	(.12)	(.21)

TABLE 6-8

Estimated Sophomore-to-Senior Achievement
Growth in Catholic and Other Private Schools
Beyond That in Public Schools for Students With
Average Public School Sophomore Background[a]:
Spring 1980
(Standard errors of differences in parentheses)

	Reading	Vocabulary	Mathematics
Catholic	−.07	.19	.01
	(.072)	(.066)	(.136)
Other private	.27	.17	.17
	(.095)	(.087)	(.180)

[a] Estimates are obtained from separate regressions for sophomores and seniors in each sector. Predicted achievement is standardized to the mean public school sophomore background characteristics for seventeen objective and subjective characteristics. "Extra growth" is obtained by comparing these standardized achievements between grades and then across sectors. Standard errors for the differences between Catholic and other private sophomore-to-senior growth and public sophomore-to-senior growth are calculated by taking the square root of the sum of variances of the sophomore-to-senior differences for the sectors under comparison. The variances of the sophomore-to-senior differences are obtained by the method described in the footnote to table 6–7. Regression coefficients, standard errors, and R^2s are given in tables A–6 through A–9 in appendix A.

If the full tests were used rather than the subtests, senior scores and increments comparable to those in table 6–7 would be as follows (standardized to public school sophomores):

	Reading	Vocabulary	Mathematics
Public school seniors	10.41	12.45	18.48
Catholic increment	.54	1.29	.90
	(.098)	(.132)	(.138)
Other private increment	1.18	1.32	1.34
	(.208)	(.280)	(.290)

Although comparison of these increments directly to those in footnote 9, page 139, is less meaningful because of the different items in the total tests for sophomores and seniors, a comparison may still be made. The comparison shows that inferences would not be changed if the full tests had been used.

As in the sophomore tests, an alternative method for investigating the effect of school types is to look at a single equation model. The Catholic or other private school dummy coefficients for the subtests and the full tests are given below, followed by their standard errors in parenthesis (see appendix table A–13 for the full equation).

Coefficients:	Subtests			Full Tests		
	Reading	Vocabulary	Mathematics	Reading	Vocabulary	Mathematics
Catholic	.13	.46	.46	.32	1.15	.64
	(.05)	(.04)	(.09)	(.09)	(.12)	(.14)
Other private	.23	.34	.51	.78	.99	.96
	(.06)	(.06)	(.13)	(.13)	(.17)	(.19)

The subtest coefficients may be compared to the sum of the relevant rows in tables 6–7 and 6–8, and the full test coefficients may be compared to the measures shown earlier in this footnote. These coefficients are all lower than the effects calculated by use of separate equations for the public and private sectors, and all are consistently greater than two standard errors.

growth in the public schools (.27 + .17 + .17 from table 6–8 divided by .73 + .63 + .88 from table 6–7).

Thus, for a student body standardized to the public-school-sophomore average in family background, the expected achievement of sophomores is highest in Catholic schools, next in other private schools. As for sophomore-to-senior growth, there is evidence of about 25 percent more growth in the other private schools than in either the Catholic or public schools.

However, both of these results must be regarded with caution. The background controls may either overcompensate for or not wholly eliminate the selectivity bias leading to higher scores among private sector sophomores, and if selectivity affects growth rates as well as levels, they may either overcompensate for or not wholly eliminate selectivity bias in higher private school growth rates.

Working in the opposite direction for the sophomore-senior comparison is a different selectivity bias, due to dropouts. As will be evident later in this section, the dropout rate is considerably greater in the public schools than in either private sector. Since dropouts score lower in standardized tests than those who continue to graduation, this means that a part of the apparent sophomore-to-senior growth—and a larger part in the public sector—is spurious, due to the absence of low achievers who have dropped out before reaching the senior year.

Later, we attempt to find a practical way around both of these difficulties. At present, however, we examine another question related to differential achievement across sectors: the performance of students from different family backgrounds.

Effects for Students from Different Backgrounds. We can examine the difference in expected achievement levels of sophomores in each sector that are considerably above average in parental education and those that are considerably below average in parental education, holding constant other background factors (income, race, Hispanic-non-Hispanic ethnicity). We can carry out a similar examination for seniors. The results of such a comparison will show how well each of these school sectors functions for students from different family backgrounds.

In calculating the difference in expected levels of achievement of students in each sector with parents of extreme educational levels, we will assume first students whose parents are both high school graduates only, and then students whose parents are both college graduates.

Similarly, for the public and Catholic sectors, we can examine the difference in expected achievement levels of blacks and whites at both grade levels, controlling on parental income, education, and (Hispanic) ethnicity. And we can examine, in these two sectors, the difference in expected achievement levels of non-Hispanic-whites and Hispanics, with the same background controls.[11] Thus, we are asking what is the difference in achievement that occurs for students with contrasting background characteristics within each of the school sectors. In carrying out this analysis, we chose to examine separately Catholic and other private schools, because of evidence that students from differing family backgrounds fare differently in these two sectors. Consequently, it was necessary to reduce the number of background characteristics that were controlled, in order to obtain stable estimates. We believe that this does not affect the inferences drawn in this section.[12]

Table 6–9 shows the results of calculating these expected achievement differences. The first and most striking result is the greater homogeneity of achievement of students with different parental education levels in Catholic schools than in public schools. Second is the greater difference in achievement among students with different parental education levels in the other private schools than in the public schools. That is, the performance of children from parents with differing educational levels is more similar in Catholic schools than in public schools (as well as being, in general, higher), while the performance of children of parents with differing educational backgrounds is less similar in other private schools than in public schools (as well as being, in general, higher).

Thus we have the paradoxical result that the Catholic schools come closer to the American ideal of the "common school," educating all alike, than do the public schools. Furthermore, as the lower panels of table 6–9 show, a similar result holds for race and ethnicity. The achievement of blacks is closer to that of whites, and the achievement of Hispanics is closer to that of non-Hispanics in Catholic schools than in public schools.

Two possible interpretations of this result, which we will not pursue here, remain. One is that within the same school there is greater diversity in performance between children of different family backgrounds in pub-

[11] These comparisons are carried out using the same type of analysis as in tables 6–7 and 6–8, but with fewer background variables, as described in the text. Regression coefficients are given in appendix A, table A–11. For the black-white and Hispanic-non-Hispanic comparisons, the regression coefficients themselves are used, since black and Hispanic were dummy variables in the equation. For parental education, the difference is calculated as the sum of regression coefficients for parental education, multiplied by 5 (=7−2 where 7 is the coding on variables BB039 and BB042 for parents with college education, and 2 is the coding on those variables for parents with only high school education). The black-white and Hispanic-non-Hispanic differences are not shown for other private schools, because the numbers of blacks and Hispanics in the sample of these schools is small enough to make estimates unstable.

[12] The qualitative inferences made here in comparing Catholic and public schools would be unchanged if all seventeen background characteristics were controlled (analysis not reported here).

TABLE 6-9

Estimated Achievement at Grades 10 and 12 for Students With Parents of Different Educational Levels, Different Race, and Different Ethnicity, Otherwise Standardized to Public Sophomore Background: Spring 1980
(Standard errors for differences in parentheses)[a]

Comparison Category	Public Sector						Catholic Sector						Other Private Sector					
	Reading		Vocabulary		Mathematics		Reading		Vocabulary		Mathematics		Reading		Vocabulary		Mathematics	
	10	12	10	12	10	12	10	12	10	12	10	12	10	12	10	12	10	12
Parental Education																		
High school graduation	3.1	3.9	3.1	4.3	8.3	9.3	3.8	4.7	4.0	4.9	10.1	10.9	3.3	4.0	3.4	4.2	8.6	9.4
College graduation	4.2	4.9	4.3	5.0	10.6	11.7	4.6	5.1	4.8	5.6	11.2	12.4	4.6	5.4	4.8	5.6	11.3	12.7
Race and Ethnicity																		
White/anglo	3.8	4.7	3.9	4.6	9.9	11.0	4.3	5.0	4.5	4.8	11.0	12.0	b	b	b	b	b	b
Hispanic	3.0	3.5	3.2	3.7	8.1	8.8	3.8	4.6	4.0	4.8	9.5	10.7	b	b	b	b	b	b
Black	2.7	3.3	2.8	3.4	7.2	8.1	3.7	4.4	3.5	4.5	9.1	10.3	b	b	b	b	b	b
Differences																		
College vs. high school parental education	1.1 (.03)	1.0 (.03)	1.2 (.03)	1.2 (.06)	2.3 (.06)	2.4 (.06)	.7 (.09)	.5 (.10)	.8 (.08)	.7 (.08)	1.0 (.16)	1.4 (.19)	1.4 (.22)	1.4 (.23)	1.5 (.20)	1.5 (.21)	2.7 (.44)	3.3 (.43)
Anglo vs. Hispanic	.8 (.05)	1.2 (.06)	.7 (.06)	.9 (.05)	1.8 (.07)	2.2 (.11)	.5 (.14)	.4 (.16)	.5 (.14)	.5 (.13)	1.6 (.26)	1.2 (.30)	b	b	b	b	b	b
White vs. black	1.2 (.04)	1.3 (.04)	1.1 (.03)	1.3 (.04)	2.7 (.09)	2.9 (.08)	.6 (.16)	.6 (.17)	1.0 (.15)	.8 (.15)	2.0 (.29)	1.7 (.33)	b		b	b	b	b

[a] Standard errors of the differences are computed by the method described in the footnote to table 6–7, with the following modifications: Public school sophomore means are used in vector **X** only for those variables to be held constant. Contrast variables (parental education, race, ethnicity) are set at values appropriate for each estimation. For example, with the contrast for students whose parents are high school graduates versus those whose parents are college graduates, the values for both mother's and father's education is set at 2 and 7, respectively.

[b] Sample size too small to estimate reliably.

lic and other private schools than in Catholic schools. The other is that the greater diversity of performance arises through a greater diversity of schools: in some schools, composed primarily of students from higher socioeconomic backgrounds, performance is high, higher than would be predicted on the basis of comparable students' performance in more heterogeneous schools; in other schools, composed primarily of students from lower socioeconomic backgrounds, performance is lower than would be predicted on the basis of comparable students' performance in heterogeneous schools.

There may be some difference between public and other private schools in this, for public high schools are large on the average (758), while other private schools are small (215). As a result, a considerably greater fraction of the other private diversity in achievement is between schools than is true for public schools. It is possible with the data from the present study to examine these alternative hypotheses; however, that work must remain for further analyses of this data.

There is another important aspect of table 6–9. This is the comparison of achievement differences among students from different backgrounds at the sophomore and senior levels in different sectors. In general, these differences are smaller at the senior level than at the sophomore level in the Catholic schools, while they are greater at the senior level in the public and other private schools. Among nine comparisons at the senior level, six are smaller, two are equal, and one is greater in the Catholic schools; one is smaller, one is equal, and seven are greater in the public schools; and two are equal and one is greater in the other private schools.

Thus, not only is the achievement more alike among students from different backgrounds in the Catholic schools than in the other sectors, it also becomes increasingly alike from the sophomore to the senior year. In the public and other private schools, the achievement of students from different backgrounds diverges.

Estimates of Growth Rates. At two points, we have examined differences between sophomores and seniors in achievement on identical subtests in the raw scores of table 6–3, and the background-controlled scores of tables 6–8. However, there has been no serious examination of growth rates from sophomore to senior year. Two problems have not been taken into account. First is the fact that the sophomores and seniors are not the same students, nor even samples from the same population, due primarily to dropouts between the sophomore and senior years. If there is sophomore-to-senior dropout, and dropouts achieve at lower levels, then the seniors represent a higher-achieving segment of the total cohort of all youth at their age level than the sophomores do of their cohort at their age level. This leads to an overestimate of growth rates (for example, from table 6–3, or table 6–8) and an underestimate of the increase in divergence of scores of students from different backgrounds (table 6–9). And the greater the dropout rate, the greater these over- and underestimates.

The second problem is the "ceiling effect." If the sophomores in one school know an average of six of eight vocabulary items, while those in another school know only three of eight, the sophomore-senior growth in this first school can be a maximum of two items, while the growth in the second school can be a maximum of five items. Yet we have compared "growth" in previous sections by examining only growth in number of items. This could be remedied by standardizing sophomore-senior differences, dividing the difference by the number of items not learned by the sophomore year. An equivalent, but somewhat more informative calculation would be the calculation of an explicit learning rate, unaffected by the existence of a ceiling. The calculation is as follows. If q is a learning rate expressed as the probability per unit time of learning what remains to be learned, and p is the probability of knowing an item at a given time, then the equation for learning is $dp/dt = q(1-p)$. Solving for q, the learning rate, in terms of p_0 (the probability of knowing the item as a sophomore) and p_1 (the probability of knowing it as a senior), gives $q = -t^{-1} \log ((1-p_1)/(1-p_0))$. Estimates of p_0 and p_1 are given as the proportion of items correct as sophomores and seniors, respectively. The time difference is two years, so $t = 2$. The learning rate calculated in this way will be an instantaneous rate expressed as items learned per year per item not already learned.

Of these two problems, dropout and ceiling effect, the latter can be solved by calculating learning rates as indicated. The dropout problem (or more generally the problem that the sophomores and seniors are samples from different populations) cannot be solved with present data, but some gain in understanding is possible. In particular, it is possible to calculate different learning rates in each type of school, using different assumptions. Some of these assumptions almost certainly overestimate learning rates by not taking dropouts into account; some very possibly underestimate learning rates by overcorrection for dropouts. Thus, rates calculated under some assumptions favor schools in which dropout is high; others favor schools in which dropout is low. These estimates of learning rates under different assumptions can, therefore, give some bounds, not only to learning rates but also to the public-private differences.

The value of doing all of this, of course, is that estimates of growth provide a different and more effective way of correcting for bias due to selection into the private sector. In effect, they use the sophomore test score as a control for the senior test score, thus controlling for any selective factors which show up in high sophomore scores, and not only those which are related to measured background characteristics.

We will provide three estimates of growth rates in reading, vocabulary, and mathematics achievement, arrived at in different ways, and described as follows.

1. *Raw scores.* In table 6–3 are given raw test scores for sophomores and seniors in the three subtests. These test scores are not corrected for dropout. Thus learning rates calculated from them will overestimate learning rates and will overestimate them most for the public schools, where the dropout rate is highest (as will be indicated below).
2. *Background-standardized scores.* From tables 6–7 and 6–8 may be obtained growth rates in each sector for students with the measured background characteristics of public school sophomores. In the public sector as well as the private sector this means that there is a correction for dropouts by use of the background standardization which adjusts seniors' scores to those of the average public school sophomore. However, insofar as the lower scores of dropouts are not wholly accounted for by these background factors, there remains an uncorrected overestimate of learning rates. This will again be greatest in the public schools, where dropout rate is greatest. Here, then, any uncorrected selection bias operates against the private sectors.
3. *Dropout-adjusted senior scores.* It is possible to estimate the proportion of dropouts in each sector. Then by making assumptions about what part of the test score distribution they have come from, it is possible to recalculate senior scores by, in effect, adding back into the senior test score distribution their assumed sophomore scores. Our estimate of dropouts is obtained as follows. In each school, we know the total size of the senior roster and the total size of the sophomore roster. The difference between them is due to several factors, including the sizes of the total cohort for these two years, as well as the dropout rate between sophomore and senior years. Since all factors except the last are relatively minor, we may regard this difference as an estimate of the number of dropouts who are no longer present in the senior class.

Table 6–10 shows the total number of sophomores and seniors in the sampled schools in each sector, as well as the fraction this represents of the sophomore class and the fraction it represents of the senior class. The table shows that, according to this estimate, about 24 percent of the sophomore class in public schools has left school by the senior year, or a 24-percent dropout rate. The comparable rates in Catholic and other private schools are 12 percent and 13 percent, respectively.

The 24-percent dropout rate in public schools represents 31 percent of the senior class. This means that only about 76 percent (100/131) of the students who should be compared with sophomores to obtain a measure of

TABLE 6–10

*Total Rosters of Sophomores and Seniors in
Sampled Schools for Estimating Dropouts Between
Sophomore and Senior Years: Spring 1980*

Item	Public	Catholic	Other Private
Number of sophomores in sampled schools	369,942	16,030	2,009
Number of seniors in sampled schools	282,084	14,181	1,746
Difference	87,858	1,849	263
Proportion of sophomore class	.24	.12	.13
Proportion of senior class	.31	.13	.15

achievement growth have been included in the public school data—and it is likely that the missing 31 percent came primarily from the lower part of the distribution. Similar statements, though for smaller fractions of the class (13 to 15 percent), could be made about Catholic and other private schools. To adjust the senior test score distribution in each sector, we have assumed that the dropouts came from the lower 50 percent of the test score distribution on each test and were distributed in that lower half in the same way that remaining seniors in the lower half of the distribution are distributed. What this means in effect is that within the lower half of the senior test score distribution, and within the upper half, the distributions do not change; but the lower half, augmented by the dropouts, becomes a larger share of the total.

This assumption leads to modified senior test scores, giving the senior scores and estimated senior-sophomore gains shown in table 6–11. The

TABLE 6–11

*Estimated Sophomore-Senior Gains in Test Scores With Corrections for
Dropouts Missing From Senior Distribution: Spring 1980*

	Public			Catholic			Other Private		
Item	10	12	Est. Gain	10	12	Est. Gain	10	12	Est. Gain
Estimated Gains[a]									
Reading	3.57	4.05	.47	4.33	4.81	.47	4.30	5.11	.81
Vocabulary	3.68	4.09	.41	4.58	5.19	.61	4.73	5.35	.62
Mathematics	9.39	9.77	.38	11.04	11.73	.68	11.28	12.26	.98

[a] Numbers are rounded to two decimals independently so that some rounded "estimated gains" differ from the difference between rounded sophomore and senior scores.

estimated gain is reduced most in the public schools, because dropout is over twice as high as in either private sector.

The calculation of proportion of dropouts is probably high in all sectors, because the figures of 24 percent for public schools and 12 percent and 13 percent for Catholic and other private schools seems slightly higher than other data suggest. Also, the assumption about where the dropouts came from in the test score distribution may be unfavorable to those schools with high proportions of dropouts (in this case, the public schools), because dropouts may be less fully drawn from the lower part of the test score distribution than assumed. If there are errors in terms of numbers of dropouts and their locations in the achievement distribution, they probably lead to underestimates of learning rates—and the greatest underestimates where dropout is greatest, that is, the public schools.

Thus if we take learning rates calculated from each of these three sets of test scores raw, background-corrected, and dropout-corrected, we have learning rates which we can be fairly certain are overestimates in the first two cases and underestimates in the third; and are probably favorable to the public schools in the first two and to the private schools in the third.

Table 6–12 shows the estimated learning rates, calculated from (1) table 6–3; (2) tables 6–7 and 6–8; and (3) table 6–11. These rates provide a range for each test and each sector, within which the correct rate very likely falls. The rates are lowest for the mathematics items, and roughly comparable for the reading comprehension questions and the vocabulary

TABLE 6–12
Estimated Learning Rates From Three Sources:
Raw Scores, Background-Standardized to
Public School Sophomore, and Dropout-Adjusted

	Public	Catholic	Other Private
Reading			
Raw Scores	.11	.10	.16
Background-standardized	.09	.09	.13
Dropout-adjusted	.06	.07	.12
Vocabulary			
Raw Scores	.10	.13	.14
Background-standardized	.08	.12	.11
Dropout-adjusted	.05	.10	.10
Mathematics			
Raw Scores	.08	.08	.12
Background-standardized	.05	.06	.07
Dropout-adjusted	.02	.05	.08

words. For vocabulary and mathematics, there is no ambiguity: both rows 1 and 2, which are likely to be favorable to the public schools, and row 3, which is likely to be favorable to the private sector schools, show higher learning rates in both Catholic and other private sectors. In reading, however, there is a conflict: row 1 shows a lower rate in the Catholic sector than the public sector, while row 3 shows a higher rate in the Catholic sector.[13]

Thus, the overall evidence from calculation of ranges of learning rates strongly confirms the inference of somewhat greater achievement in the private sector for vocabulary and mathematics; the evidence is divided concerning the public-Catholic comparison in reading.[14]

EFFECTS OF SCHOOL SECTOR ON EDUCATIONAL PLANS

In the general description of outcomes it was evident that plans for further education are considerably different in the different sectors. What is not clear is just how much of this difference is a matter of selection and

---

[13] It should be pointed out that the apparent low sophomore-senior learning rate for reading in the Catholic schools is inconsistent with the raw and background-standardized sophomore rates, which are higher than in either of the other sectors. If a constant learning rate is assumed, and the public-school learning rate from row 2 is used to calculate the time when reading comprehension was zero, the time would be 6.8 years before the grade 10 test. If the same 6.8 years is used in conjunction with the background-standardized Catholic sophomore score of 3.92, this gives a learning rate of .10 during that period, greater than the .09 rate in the public sector.

[14] A problem not discussed in the text is the fact that some students in all sectors did not take the tests, and the proportion differs from sector to sector. For the mathematics test, it is 9.2 percent for sophomores and 13.0 percent for seniors in the public sector, 4.2 percent for sophomores and 8.8 percent for seniors in the Catholic sector, and 18.2 percent for sophomores and 19.0 percent for seniors in the other private sector. To take into account these differences, test scores were imputed for those with missing test scores, using a variety of predictor variables. For example, for the mathematics test for seniors, the following variables were included: grades in school; number of semesters of mathematics courses in grades 10 to 12; having taken algebra 2, calculus, remedial mathematics, advanced mathematics; reading the front page of the newspaper; interest in school; satisfaction with self; absences; tardiness; sex; father's education; mother's education; family income; race; and ethnicity. Separate regression equations were estimated for seniors and sophomores, and for public and private (the two private sectors together). R^2 were .37 and .50 for sophomores and seniors in public schools and .39 and .47 for sophomores and seniors in private schools. Recalculating the mean achievement in mathematics after values were imputed changes the means very little (sophomores: 9.2, 11.1, 11.2 in public, Catholic, and other private, and seniors: 10.4, 12.2, 12.7 in public, Catholic, and other private). Comparing these scores with those in table 6–3 shows little difference, with .2 decrease in both sophomores and seniors in public schools, .1 increase in both sophomores and seniors in Catholic schools, and .1 decrease in sophomores in other private schools, and no change in seniors. Consequently, imputed values were not included in making the calculations in the text. However, to fully test any effect of the missing values, dropout-adjusted rates were calculated for mathematics with imputed scores included. These were .02, .07, and .09 for public, Catholic, and other private schools respectively. These show slightly higher values for Catholic and other private schools, but do not change the qualitative inferences made in the text.

just how much is actually brought about by the type of high school attended. We will not be able to answer that question conclusively here, but it will be possible to understand more about the development of educational plans in each of the sectors.

First, controlling for the same seventeen family background characteristics used in table 6–7, it is possible to see the differences among the educational plans of students whose parents are similar in these respects. Table 6–13, comparable to the combined tables 6–7 and 6–8 for cognitive achievement, shows these differences. Table 6–13 is based, as in the case of cognitive achievement, on regressions of level of schooling expected at each grade level and in each sector.

The categories used in this analysis together with the value attached to each are given below. Thus, in examining table 6–13, the numbers should be interpreted in terms of these categories:

High school graduation or less	1
Some postsecondary education	2
Complete 4 years of college	3
M.A., Ph.D. or other professional degree	4

The table shows that, for the average public school sophomore, the level of education expected is 2.27, that is, slightly above "some postsecondary

TABLE 6–13

*Estimated Increments in Educational Expectations
for Students in Public and Private Schools With
Family Background Controlled[a]: Spring 1980
(Standard errors of differences in parentheses)[b]*

Expected level for public school sophomores	2.27
Sophomore increment in:	
Catholic schools	.25
	(.020)
Other private schools	.11
	(.041)
Senior increment in public schools	.08
	(.008)
Additional increment for seniors in:	
Catholic schools	−.11
	(.029)
Other private schools	.03
	(.060)

[a] Family background refers to seventeen variables used for table 6–7. Standardization procedures follow those used in tables 6–7 and 6–8.

[b] Standard errors for the increments are calculated by the method described in the footnotes to table 6–7.

education." The seniors in public schools are only .08 higher in expectations. Sophomores with comparable backgrounds in Catholic schools are almost one quarter of a level (.25) higher, while those in other private schools are about one-tenth of a level (.11) higher. The seniors in Catholic schools show .11 less gain than the seniors in public schools, or no gain relative to sophomores, while the seniors in other private schools show almost the same gain as the seniors in public schools. The lesser sophomore-senior gain in Catholic schools may, of course, be due to the higher levels for Catholic sophomores, which can produce a ceiling effect.

It is also difficult to estimate the differential sophomore-senior change in educational expectations in the different sectors, because of differential dropout in the different types of schools (as shown in table 6–10), although this is partially corrected by controlling on family background characteristics. It is possible, for example, that the estimated gain of .08 of an educational level in public schools is due solely to the fact that those with the lowest educational expectations, who are present in the sophomore class, are no longer present in the senior class.

This possible dropout effect can be eliminated by the use of retrospective accounts to learn whether or not the sophomores and seniors planned to attend college in earlier years of school. The seniors were asked whether they had expected to attend college when they were in grades 8, 9, 10, and 11. The sophomores were asked the same question about what their college expectations were when they were in grades 6, 7, 8, and 9. Although such retrospective accounts cannot be wholly reliable, they are the only source of such information for these students. And they do show changes over time, indicating that students did discriminate between years, and did not simply respond alike for all years. For the sample as a whole, table 6–14 shows in panel A that 49 percent of seniors indicated that they expected to go to college when they were in grade 8. This rose to 53 percent in grade 9, 58 percent in grade 10, and 63 percent in grade 11. For the sophomores shown in panel C, the figures are 41 percent at grade 6, 45 percent at grade 7, 53 percent at grade 8, and 60 percent at grade 9. Comparing the two cohorts for grades 8 and 9 shows that sophomores are 4 and 7 percent higher for these two grades, a difference that is probably due to the difference between a one- or two-year retrospection and a three- or four-year retrospection.[15] But we will ignore these differences here. The question, then, is whether there was a differential increase from grade 6 to grade 11 in different sectors.

[15] The true difference, if the sophomores and seniors were sampled from the same population (that is, if the senior sample did not exclude dropouts), would be greater than the 4 and 7 percent differences observed.

TABLE 6–14

Percentage of Seniors and Sophomores in Public and Private Schools Indicating Expectations to Attend College at Earlier Grades: Actual Percentage and Standardized Percentage[a]: Spring 1980

At Earlier Grade	U.S. Total	Public	Catholic	Other Private
Seniors				
A. Actual percentage				
At 8th grade	49	47	67	67
At 9th grade	53	51	71	69
At 10th grade	58	56	74	75
At 11th grade	63	62	79	78
B. Standardized percentage				
At 8th grade		44	55	48
At 9th grade		48	59	51
At 10th grade		54	62	57
At 11th grade		60	68	63
Sophomores				
C. Actual percentage				
At 6th grade	41	40	54	59
At 7th grade	45	43	60	61
At 8th grade	53	51	72	69
At 9th grade	60	58	78	73
D. Standardized percentage				
At 6th grade		40	42	43
At 7th grade		43	48	44
At 8th grade		51	59	54
At 9th grade		58	66	60

[a] Scores have been standardized to the average public school sophomore using the seventeen background variables identified on pages 138–139. Student questionnaire items BB068, EB068, and BB072 ask for college expectations in earlier grades.

Panel A in table 6–14 shows the actual percentage of seniors who reported expecting to go to college at each grade level in each sector, and panel B shows the expected percentage for students with family background at the public school sophomore average.[16] Panels C and D show comparable information for sophomores.

Looking at panels A and C, the actual responses, the data show that college expectations are higher in the private school sectors than in the public sectors. The differences between sectors in educational plans corre-

[16] The numbers in panels (b) and (d) are calculated using OLS equations to predict college plans. Given a dicotomous dependent variable, it would have been preferable to use a logit or probit analysis, but no computer program was available which allowed weighting for the large public school sample. Tables A-14 and A-15 show results using a logit analysis with unweighted data. The qualitative inferences do not differ.

spond to differences in family background in the different sectors, except that parental income and education are lower in Catholic schools than in other private schools, while college expectations in Catholic schools are about the same in both cohorts.

When backgrounds are standardized, in panels B and D of the table, the differences are in the same direction. The differences between public and private are reduced, though all private schools remain above the public schools. The Catholic schools become almost uniformly higher than the other private schools.

Apart from changes over the years, the differing levels of educational aspirations, when family background is controlled, show results similar to those in table 6–13. In both cases, students in Catholic schools show the highest educational aspirations when family background is controlled, students in other private schools the next highest, and public school students the lowest. Expectations are quite high in all sectors, however, and the differences between the sectors are not great.

However, the principal question at hand to which table 6–13 is relevant concerns the development or changes in expectations over years of school. What do these retrospective accounts show about such changes in different types of school? First, the expectations grow, and grow substantially. The difference in the sample as a whole is 14 percentage points between grades 8 and 11 for the seniors, and 19 points between grades 6 and 9 for the sophomores. For sophomores, there is very little difference among the sectors in their 6th grade expectations. Growth differs within each sector, but comparisons are difficult because varying amounts of growth are possible at different levels.

The most commonly accepted way of making comparisons in a case like this is by comparing not percentages, but the logarithm of the ratio of the percentage and its complement, $p/(1-p)$, called a logit. According to a reasonable model of the way effects take place to push proportions up or down, a measure of effects can be made by a comparison of logits for the background-standardized public school percentages and the background-standardized percentages for the two private school sectors, taken from panels B and D. The excess of the private school logit over the public school logit is a measure of the effect of being in the private school on the likelihood of planning to attend college. This "effect" of course includes both any actual effect of the type of school in bringing about college plans and any selection effect that is not captured by statistically controlling on family background.

Thus the fact of a positive value for the difference between private and public school logits is not evidence for an effect of being in that type of school on the development of college plans. What is evidence of such an effect is an increase over the years in school of the difference in logits.

Table 6–15 shows the difference in logits between each private school sector and the public schools, based on panels B and D of table 6–14. The results are very mixed. The data in panel A for the seniors shows a decline for the Catholic schools and a small increase for the other private schools. Thus the senior data suggest that being in a Catholic school has a lesser effect on increasing college plans than does being in a public school, and that being in an other private school has no greater effect.

But panel B for the sophomores presents evidence that conflicts with this. For the Catholic schools, the measure of effect does increase, suggesting that there is a greater effect of being in a Catholic school on growth in college plans than of being in a public school. The measure of effect does not increase for other private schools, suggesting no greater effect of being in such a school on college plans.

A somewhat more reliable indicator of growth in college plans over time by these students can be obtained by combining the senior and soph-

TABLE 6–15

Differences in Logits for College Expectations,
Standardized for Background, Between Each Type of
Private Schools and the Public Schools[a]:
Spring 1980

At Earlier Grade	Catholic	Other Private
A. *Seniors:*		
At 8th grade	.44	.16
At 9th grade	.44	.12
At 10th grade	.33	.12
At 11th grade	.35	.13
B. *Sophomores:*		
At 6th grade	.08	.12
At 7th grade	.20	.04
At 8th grade	.32	.12
At 9th grade	.34	.08
C. *Sophomores and Seniors:*		
At 6th grade (sophomores)	.08	.12
At 7th grade (sophomores)	.20	.04
At 8th grade (both)	.38	.14
At 9th grade (both)	.39	.10
At 10th grade (seniors)	.33	.12
At 11th grade (seniors)	.35	.13

[a] Logit of percentage expecting to attend college, minus comparable logit for public schools.

omore retrospective data to obtain a single series beginning at grade 8 and continuing through grade 11. To create such a series, the difference in senior logits shown in panel A for grades 8 and 9 is averaged with the difference in sophomore logits shown in panel B for grades 8 and 9. The result is shown in panel C. For the Catholic schools but not in the other private schools, there is a general increase in the gap between each sector and the public sector.

The end result of the analysis is that there is some evidence of the greater development of college plans in the Catholic sector than in the public sector, but little of greater development of college plans in the other private sector than in the public sector. The different sectors are consistently different in the proportions of students expecting to attend college, even after standardizing on parental education, family income, race, and ethnicity, and there is evidence from retrospective accounts by sophomores and seniors that these differences are not wholly due to initial selection.

Now we turn to the examination of different educational expectations for students with high or low parental education. As in the case of cognitive achievement, the differential educational expectations of students with especially high or low parental education in different sectors can be estimated, with a five-variable analysis, as in the case of cognitive achievement. As before, we examine the educational expectations of students whose parents both have only a high school education and students whose parents both have college degrees, in each type of school. The results of this analysis are shown in table 6–16. The numbers refer to the scale of educational levels described at the beginning of this section.

Table 6–16 shows that the educational expectations of students with parents of low education are lowest if the students are in public schools, and highest if they are in Catholic schools. The difference between Catholic and public schools is about .54 educational levels, and between other private and public schools it is about .25 of an educational level.

For children of parents with college degrees (row 2), expected education is higher in all sectors. But the difference between sectors is much less, only .23 educational levels between Catholic and public schools, and only .17 educational levels between other private and public schools.

The bottom part of the table shows the difference in educational expectations between children of high- and low-education parents in each type of school. Here, the differences are greatest in the public schools and least in the Catholic schools, with the other private schools in between. As in the case of cognitive achievement, the Catholic schools come closest to meeting the ideal of the "common school." The public schools are furthest

TABLE 6–16

Estimated Educational Expectations at Grades 10 and 12 for Students With Parents of Different Educational Levels, Different Race, and Different Ethnicity, Otherwise Standardized to Public Sophomore Background[a]: Spring 1980

(Standard errors in parentheses)

Comparison Category	Public Sector		Catholic Sector		Other Private Sector	
	10	12	10	12	10	12
Parental Education						
a. High school graduation	1.80	1.94	2.36	2.46	2.10	2.15
b. College graduation	2.80	2.89	3.05	3.09	2.90	3.12
Race and Ethnicity						
a. White/Anglo	2.23	2.34	2.63	2.66	b	b
b. Hispanic	2.31	2.38	2.72	3.01	b	b
c. Black	2.44	2.64	2.98	3.11	b	b
Differences						
a. College vs. High school parental education	.99 (.014)	.95 (.015)	.69 (.042)	.63 (.044)	.80 (.103)	.97 (.099)
b. Anglo vs. Hispanic	−.08 (.023)	.−04 (.026)	−.09 (.067)	−.34 (.071)	b	b
c. White vs. Black	−.21 (.018)	−.30 (.020)	−.35 (.076)	−.45 (.079)	b	b

[a] Standardization procedure follows those used in table 6–9.
[b] Sample size too small to estimate reliably.

from this ideal in educational expectations. Children from differing educational backgrounds in Catholic schools are most alike in their educational expectations, while children from differing educational backgrounds in public schools are least alike in educational expectations. In other words, in the public schools, the educational plans of children with college-educated parents diverge more sharply from those of children with high-school-educated parents than is true in any other type of school. And the divergence is least in Catholic schools.

The gains in educational expectations from the sophomores to the senior year are small in all sectors and for both levels of parental education. They are least in the Catholic schools. But, as indicated in previous analysis, the retrospective questions examined earlier probably give better information about the development of education plans than does the sophomore-to-senior comparison.

A similar comparison can be made for the public and Catholic sectors between blacks and whites and Hispanics and Anglos with comparable backgrounds. As is ordinarily found with plans or expectations for higher education, table 6–16 shows that blacks have higher expectations than whites of comparable backgrounds, and Hispanics have higher expectations than Anglos of comparable backgrounds (statistically significant in six of the eight cases). Here the estimates of the amount by which blacks exceed whites and Hispanics exceed Anglos are greater in the Catholic sector (though the difference is statistically significant only in one of four cases).

Factors Affecting Cognitive Achievement in the Schools

It is not sufficient to say that students are performing better in one sector of secondary education than another. The central question, for all schools, is why some produce better cognitive outcomes than others. We will treat that question here (though not comprehensively) by examining the degree to which, within each of the sectors, students in schools that differ from the average school in that sector—in ways that private schools differ from public schools—achieve more highly. This will allow us to identify school policies which increase achievement within each sector.

There is an additional value to such an analysis: it allows another test of the private school effects found earlier in this chapter. If it is true that the private sector is, on the average, more successful in increasing achievement, then within each of the sectors students should achieve more highly in schools that differ from the average school in ways that private schools differ from public schools—but only, of course, in those ways that make a difference for achievement. If the higher levels of homework that characterize private schools (chapter 5) are effective in leading to higher achievement, than in those schools that have high levels of homework—no matter whether they are Catholic, public, or other private—achievement should be higher than in other schools of that sector. If private schools are not more effective for cognitive achievement, or if some aspect of other private schools other than homework is the factor that makes for higher achievement, then achievement should not be higher, in such an analysis. If, for example, private schools are more effective, but it is their smaller size (as shown in chapter 2) that makes them so, then smaller schools in each sector, not schools with higher homework levels, should show higher achievement when student background is controlled.

Thus, this will be the general strategy: to examine the relations, within each of the sectors, of various factors that distinguish the Catholic and other private schools from the public schools. If certain of these factors consistently make a difference in cognitive achievement, whatever the sector, then this is rather strong evidence both that the different school sectors do bring about differing achievement, and that one way they do so is through their difference in the factors that in the analysis show effects on achievement. In addition, beyond confirming the differential effects on achievement of different school sectors, this approach will give some insight into the policies that, in any sector, affect achievement.

The first examination concerns discipline-related behavior. Analyses were carried out on the relation of attendance, being late to school and cutting classes, to achievement in each of the three sectors. Parental education, family income, race, and ethnicity were statistically controlled. The analyses were carried out for sophomores and seniors together, with a 0-1 variable for sophomore-senior grade level. Scores in the reading, vocabulary, and mathematics subjects with common items for seniors and sophomores were used as dependent variables.

Table 6–17 shows the regression coefficients for absenteeism, lateness, and cutting classes (all in the same equation) in each of the three types of schools. In addition, means on each of these variables are listed in the bottom panel. (Cutting classes is a 0-1 variable, so that the coefficient can be interpreted as an effect of "cutting classes now and then" versus not doing so. The other variables are scaled, with one unit being the difference in one category in the item responses.)

There is a high degree of consistency in the results. The coefficients are almost all negative, meaning that students who report missing school or class or being late achieve consistently less well, in all sectors, than those from the same types of family background who do not do these things.[17] Of the three types of behavior, lateness is least related to achievement.

Something about the magnitude of the effect of these types of behavior, at the levels at which they exist in the various types of schools, can be obtained by multiplying the regression coefficients shown in the upper

[17] This does not imply, of course, that public schools could easily establish and implement those policies. In chapter 5, we pointed out the much greater restrictions on the public schools in ability to carry out effective discipline.

It may well be that the variables used here are proxies for other policies or disciplinary differences among schools that are correlated with them. This will be examined in subsequent analysis (tables 6–20 to 6–22). There is also the possibility that variations in absence within a school are symptoms of individual factors that affect achievement, and it is these factors, rather than absence itself, which are responsible for the achievement differences. If this were the case, then, the measured effect of within-school variations in absence would be much greater than the measured between-school effect—a signal that school policies on absences would have little effect. This further analysis is not carried out here.

TABLE 6–17
Accounting for Reading, Vocabulary, and Mathematics
Scores: Regression Coefficients and Means for
Absenteeism, Lateness, and Cutting Classes, in
Analysis Which Includes Family Background and
Grade Level[a]: Spring 1980
(Standard errors in parentheses)

	Public	Catholic	Other Private
Reading			
Absenteeism	−.14 (.01)	−.14 (.03)	−.28 (.05)
Lateness	−.03 (.01)	−.07 (.03)	−.05 (.05)
Cutting classes	−.10 (.02)	−.20 (.08)	.01 (.14)
Vocabulary			
Absenteeism	−.09 (.01)	−.06 (.03)	−.21 (.05)
Lateness	−.02 (.01)	−.12 (.02)	.00 (.04)
Cutting classes	−.03 (.02)	−.19 (.08)	.15 (.12)
Mathematics			
Absenteeism	−.38 (.01)	−.33 (.05)	−.44 (.10)
Lateness	−.05 (.01)	−.13 (.04)	−.08 (.09)
Cutting classes	−.29 (.04)	−.43 (.14)	−.52 (.26)
Means			
Absenteeism	2.41	1.91	2.20
Lateness	2.21	2.00	2.43
Cutting classes	.36	.17	.33
R^2			
Reading	.173	.068	.214
Vocabulary	.203	.111	.248
Mathematics	.218	.089	.253

[a] Family background includes parental education, income, race, and ethnicity. Attendance variables include BB016, BB017, and BB059E.

three panels of table 6–17, by differences in the means of the variables between different sectors. The result shows the amount of extra achievement in one sector (the sector with the lower level of absences, lateness, or class-cutting) over that in another which is related to these three problems of discipline. For example, the difference between Catholic schools and public schools in cutting classes is a difference of 18 percent versus 38 percent. This difference (.18 − .38) multiplied by the regression coefficient of −.45 (effect of cutting classes on mathematics achievement in public schools) gives a value of .09. This means that, on the average, achievement was lower in the public schools by .09 of an item in the mathematics test because of disciplinary policies that allowed a level of 38 percent of students cutting classes rather than the 18 percent found in Catholic schools.[18]

Carrying out such an exercise over all tests, comparing the public schools with both private school sectors and summing over the three types of behavior, shows the loss in reading, vocabulary, and mathematics achievement in public schools that is due to the higher degree of absenteeism, lateness, and class-cutting found in these schools as compared to the levels found in both Catholic schools and other private schools (table 6–18). The public schools losses are highly consistent, are greater relative to the Catholic schools, and seem to be somewhat higher for mathematics. (The number of items on the mathematics test is eighteen, a little over twice that on the other two; consequently, its coefficients should be expected to be about twice as great as the others. But they are somewhat greater than this.) The achievement losses are not large, but this must be seen in perspective: The differences in mathematics due to Catholic-public behavior differences are about one-fourth of all the mathematics achievement gain from the sophomore to the senior year. In addition, the indicators we have used of different levels of discipline-related behavior are very likely pale reflections of the behavioral differences among these schools. Thus, the actual effects of all discipline-related behavioral differences between these schools may be considerably greater (as subsequent analysis indicates).

The suggestion that absenteeism, being late, and cutting classes may make more difference for mathematics than for reading or vocabulary is confirmed in another way. Regression analyses just like those described for tables 6–17 and 6–18 were carried out with these variables, but with logarithm of school size included. Then the same regression was carried out, but no longer including the three behavior variables. The question is: For which of the tests did the amount of explained variance go down most when the three behavior variables were not included? The answer is the mathematics test. In seven of eight comparisons of mathematics with other tests, the reduction is greater in mathematics. It thus appears that mathematics achievement is more sensitive to behavioral problems than is achievement in reading comprehension or vocabulary.

When we turn to size of school itself as a factor differentiating public and private schools, and possibly making for differential achievement, we

[18] When independent variables in a regression equation are correlated, as these three are, there is sometimes instability in individual coefficients, becoming extreme in opposite directions. This seems to be what has occurred for vocabulary in other private schools, for example. There are techniques, such as ridge regression, for restabilizing the coefficients. But if one is interested only in the combined effects, as we are here, then the approach we use in table 6–18 and subsequent analyses is ordinarily sufficient.

TABLE 6–18
*Achievement Losses in the Public Schools
Relative to Each Type of Private School
Due to Higher Levels of Absenteeism, Lateness,
and Cutting Classes in the Public Schools:
Spring 1980
(Standard errors of differences in parentheses)*

Test	Public Relative to	
	Catholic	Other Private
Losses (as fractions of an item) in:		
Reading	−.08	−.02
	(.01)	(.03)
Vocabulary	−.05	−.02
	(.01)	(.02)
Mathematics	−.26	−.08
	(.04)	(.05)

find that, when family background and grade in school are controlled, size of school is positively related to achievement in the Catholic and other private sectors for all three tests, and in the public sector for two of the three. Thus it appears that public schools have a gain in achievement relative to private schools as a consequence of their larger size. The amount of gain they experience can be calculated as was done in the case of the behavior problems: by multiplying the regression coefficient for the effect of size by the difference in average size between sectors.[19] Before presenting these results, however, it is useful to introduce another set of variables: the attendance variables whose effect was discussed previously. The relation of school size to achievement is positive, while the relation of absenteeism, lateness, and cutting classes to achievement is negative, but the latter are positively related to size. At least, this is the case in the public schools. The correlation of the three behavior problems with the logarithm of size is given below for each of three sectors.[20]

[19] The variable actually used in the regression is logarithm of size. In the calculation described in the text, regression coefficients for the school sector to which the size-related loss (or gain) will be attributed are used. This is because, as will be evident in the discussion, we want to distinguish the gain that private schools could expect through change in average size to that of public schools from the loss that public schools could expect through a change in average size to that of private schools.

[20] Because the number of private schools is 27, the number of Catholic schools is 84, and the number of public schools is 894, and because size is a school-level variable, sampling variation in correlations can be expected in other private schools, and, to a lesser degree, in Catholic schools.

	Public	Catholic	Other Private
Absenteeism	.02	−.02	.00
Lateness	.10	.00	−.20
Cutting class	.12	.00	.01

Controlling on the behavior problems in a regression of achievement on size is like a hypothetical experiment: What would be the effect of size on achievement if school staff were able to control the behavior problems that are correlated with size. The absence of correlation with size in the private schools (or, in the case of lateness, in other private schools, a negative relation to size) shows that the question is not a hypothetical one for staff in private schools. They apparently are able to control the behavior problems that in the public schools increase with size. This may be due to the greater degree of overall control that private schools are able to exercise, or to the smaller sizes of the schools.

Table 6–19 shows (in the upper three lines) the gains—or, in the case of reading, losses—that public schools experience in relation to Catholic and other private schools because of their large size. But comparing that to the next three lines shows that these gains are smaller than they would be—and the losses larger than they would be—with the behavior problems controlled. (It should be emphasized that the true effect of size might be less than indicated in this analysis because large schools in the public sector are positively associated with certain background variables that have not been statistically controlled, such as parental expectations and small family size, both of which are positively related to achievement. But, even if this is the case, it would merely reduce the measured effect of size by a constant amount.)

The positive effect of size, assuming that it is a true effect, might be due to any of several factors. It was once assumed, in fact, that larger schools meant better education, as in Conant's influential *The American High School Today* (1959). The arguments were that greater depth and breadth of program is possible in large schools, and that specialized classes dealing with advanced topics and better laboratory facilities are possible in larger schools. All these are true; but the data suggest that these virtues of size are largely cancelled out in public schools by the inability to manage behavior problems as school size increases—an inability that has very probably increased since Conant made his survey of high schools in 1958.

The analyses of tables 6–17 and 6–18 included only a small number of background variables, and did not include other possible school factors that might be responsible for some of the differences found. Initially our general strategy was to proceed in this way, examining sequentially the

TABLE 6–19

*Achievement Differences in Public Schools
Relative to Private Schools Due to the Larger
Size of Public Schools[a]: Spring 1980
(Standard errors of differences in parentheses)*

Item	Public Relative to	
	Catholic	Other Private
Family Background Controlled[b]		
Reading	−.01	−.03
	(.01)	(.02)
Vocabulary	.04	.11
	(.01)	(.02)
Mathematics	.04	.10
	(.03)	(.04)
Family Background and Attendance Controlled		
Reading	.00	.00
	(.01)	(.02)
Vocabulary	.05	.13
	(.01)	(.02)
Mathematics	.06	.17
	(.02)	(.04)

[a] Listed below are the coefficients for size, along with the R^2 for each equation, for each sector and achievement area (standard errors for coefficients are given in parentheses):

	With Family Background Controlled			With Family Background and Attendance Controlled		
	Reading	Vocabulary	Mathematics	Reading	Vocabulary	Mathematics
Public	−.02	.08	.07	.00	.09	.12
	(.01)	(.01)	(.02)	(.02)	(.02)	(.04)
R^2	.16	.20	.20	.17	.20	.22
Catholic	.02	.15	.21	.01	.15	.20
	(.04)	(.04)	(.08)	(.04)	(.04)	(.08)
R^2	.05	.10	.07	.07	.11	.09
Other	.15	.05	.23	.15	.06	.23
Private	(.05)	(.05)	(.10)	(.05)	(.05)	(.10)
R^2	.19	.23	.23	.22	.25	.26

[b] Family background variables include mother's education, father's education, family income, race, and Hispanic ethnicity. School size is the logrithm of school enrollment (SB002A).

effects of various school factors that differ between public and private schools, in separate regression equations. However, the correlations between these various school characteristics mean that such a procedure might easily lead to incorrect inferences, attributing effects to one factor in the schools that are due to a factor that is correlated with the first but not included in the equations.[21] Consequently, a single analysis is carried out for all of the factors to be examined. In addition, to reduce to the lowest level possible any spurious inferences due to differences in family background that are correlated with school factors, all of the family background factors used for the analysis reported in table 6–7 are included in subsequent analyses. For each of the characteristics of schools and of school functioning that is a source of possible differences in the effectiveness of public and private schools, we ask the following pair of questions:

1. What is the level of that characteristic in Catholic or other private schools, for students with the same subjective and objective background characteristics as the average sophomore public school student? For example, the overall average difference between Catholic school and public school sophomores in the amount of homework they do is the difference between 5.56 hours a week in the Catholic schools and 3.75 a week in the public schools. But for Catholic school sophomores with the same subjective and objective characteristics as the average public school sophomore, the 5.56 hours a week is reduced to 4.92 hours a week.[22] Thus, the difference in levels of homework for the same type of student between the public and Catholic schools is 4.92 − 3.75, or 1.2 hours a week of homework.
2. What difference in achievement would we expect to find in the public schools if the school factor were at the level at which it is found in Catholic or other private schools for students of a given background (that is, the background of the average public school sophomore)? For example, what increment in achievement would we expect to find in the public schools if the average public school student spent 1.2 more hours on homework? This is obtained by multiplying the 1.2 hours by the regression coefficient for the effect of homework on achievement in public schools, controlling for the effects of family background characteristics and other school factors.

Thus there are two questions of interest for each of the school factors that might contribute to the public-Catholic or public-other private difference in achievement: What is the difference between the level of that factor in the Catholic or other private schools and public schools, for students like the average public school sophomore? And what would be the

---

[21] We are indebted to Thomas DiPrete who first brought this matter to our attention. His analysis for another report from the High School and Beyond project, *Discipline and Order in American High Schools*, suggested that this might be the case.

[22] The standardized estimates of school functioning were calculated as follows: For each grade in the public and private sectors, we estimated separate regression equations for each of the school functioning variables using the seventeen family background characteristics. A background-standardized estimate for the level of school functioning in each grade and sector was calculated using the means of the public school sophomore characteristics and the effects of these background characteristics in the respective sector and grade.

expected difference in achievement in the public schools if that factor were at the level found in the Catholic or other private schools, controlling on family background and other school factors? We address these questions in turn.

DIFFERENCES IN SCHOOL FUNCTIONING FOR STUDENTS OF COMPARABLE BACKGROUNDS

Each of five areas related to the functioning of the school was examined as a potential means through which private schools obtain different levels of achievement from comparable students. These are:

1. *Different coursework.* This was measured in two ways. For the senior year, it was possible to measure coursework in mathematics, that is, the total number of courses that the student had taken among the following: algebra 1, algebra 2, geometry, trigometry, calculus. As chapter 5 showed, higher proportions of private school seniors than public school seniors have taken each of these courses. Unfortunately, for the reading and vocabulary tests, and for the mathematics test for sophomores, there is no comparable measure of coursework. Instead, for these tests, having taken an honors English course (for the reading and vocabulary tests) or an honors mathematics course (for the mathematics test) was used as the measure of coursework. This is a poor measure of coursework differences between public and private schools, both because the proportions of students having taken an honors course were very similar in the three sectors and because an "honors" course means very different things in different school contexts.
2. *Homework.* As chapter 5 showed, the amount of homework in the Catholic schools is greater than that in the public schools, and the amount in the other private sector is greater yet. For both sophomores and seniors it was possible to estimate the actual hours per week spent on homework.
3. *Attendance in school and class.* Chapter 5 showed that students in Catholic schools were much less often absent and much less likely to cut class than students in public schools. Students in other private schools were between the Catholic and public schools on these measures of behavior.
4. *Disciplinary climate.* Students were asked three questions related to the disciplinary climate of the school, as shown in chapter 5: how interested the teachers are in students, how effective the discipline is in the school, and how fair the discipline is in the school. Each school was characterized by the average of the responses for all the students in that school, and these averages were then used as measures of the school disciplinary climate. As chapter 5 showed, there were some differences in the average disciplinary climates in the three sectors.
5. *Student behavior in the school.* The behavior of all the students in the school may have some effect on what individual students learn, even controlling on the student's own behavior. The items used as a measure of the behavior in the school were the averages, over the school, of sophomore

responses to four questions asking the extent to which certain types of behavior occurred in the school: students absent from school, students cutting classes, students fighting, students threatening or attacking teachers.

Chapter 5 showed the differences in the levels of these school characteristics in public and private schools. The differences in these characteristics for students from the same family backgrounds are of interest here. More specifically, we are interested in the differences for students who have the family background characteristic of the average public school sophomore, so that the levels of the school characteristics are standardized to the public school sophomore population. The importance of this question lies in the fact that the family backgrounds of public, Catholic, and other private school students differ in both objective characteristics, such as parental education and income, and in subjective characteristics, such as the amount of student conversation with parents about schoolwork. In most of these ways, students in public schools have backgrounds that are less conducive to achievement than do students in private schools. Thus, the measures of school functioning, which are in part determined by the backgrounds from which the students come, must be adjusted or standardized for student background in order not to attribute to school policies those differences in achievement that are in fact due to student background effects on their school functioning.

The background-standardized measures of school functioning are shown in table 6–20. The table shows that with very few exceptions (all in the percentage taking honors mathematics or honors English) the Catholic and other private schools are higher in those characteristics that appear to be conducive to achievement (homework, teacher interest, fairness, or effectiveness[23]) and lower in those that appear inimical to achievement (absenteeism, cutting class, fighting, threatening teachers). The differences are generally reduced compared to those found in chapter 5 because standardization of family background brings the student behavior in the private schools closer to that in the public schools. Yet the differences remain in the same direction as those in chapter 5, when student background was not controlled.

DIFFERENCES IN ACHIEVEMENT ATTRIBUTABLE TO PARTICULAR SCHOOL CHARACTERISTICS AND STUDENT BEHAVIOR

Given these differences, it becomes possible to estimate the effect of being in a Catholic or other private school on achievement through school

[23] Sophomores were asked to evaluate the "strictness" of discipline; seniors, the "effectiveness."

TABLE 6-20

Differences Between Private and Public Schools in Student Behavior and School Climate,
Standardized to Family Background Characteristics of Public Sophomore Students[a]:
Spring 1980 (Standard error of difference in parentheses)

Item	Catholic and Public difference		Other Private and Public difference	
	Sophomore	Senior	Sophomore	Senior
A. Coursework Completed by Students				
Proportion taking honors English	−.02	.01	−.08	−.08
	(.011)	(.013)	(.014)	(.017)
Proportion taking honors Mathematics	.02	.02	−.07	−.03
	(.011)	(.012)	(.015)	(.017)
Average number of advanced mathematics	DNA	.71	DNA	.34
courses		(.034)		(.045)
B. Homework Completed by Students				
Average number of hours per week	1.17	0.78	1.31	1.27
	(.092)	(.100)	(.123)	(.133)
C. Attendance by Individual Students				
Absent from school	−.43	−.39	−.06	−.16
	(.028)	(.033)	(.037)	(.043)
Cut class now and then	−.20	−.21	−.04	−.08
	(.009)	(.013)	(.013)	(.017)
D. Disciplinary Climate as Perceived by Students[b]				
Teacher interest	.39	.40	.50	.51
	(.008)	(.009)	(.011)	(.012)
Fairness of discipline	.17	.18	.09	.12
	(.008)	(.007)	(.009)	(.010)
Effectiveness/strictness of discipline	.59	.59	.31	.31
	(.008)	(.008)	(.010)	(.011)
E. Student Behavior in School as Perceived by Sophomores[c]				
Absenteeism	.65	.66	.55	.56
	(.007)	(.008)	(.010)	(.010)
Cutting class	.79	.80	.54	.53
	(.010)	(.011)	(.014)	(.014)
Students fighting each other	.39	.38	.55	.56
	(.007)	(.007)	(.009)	(.010)
Students threatening teachers	.17	.16	.18	.17
	(.002)	(.002)	(.003)	(.003)

[a] The differences are obtained by estimating the level of a given school characteristic for a student with average background characteristics of a public school sophomore for each grade and sector. Thus, for each school characteristic Y in the ith sector and jth grade

$$\hat{Y}_{ij} = a_{ij} + \sum_{i=1}^{k} \bar{X}_k b_{ijk}$$

where a_{ij} is the intercept, b_{ijk} is the coefficient for the ith sector and jth grade for the kth background variable and $\bar{X}_k$ the public school sophomore mean on the kth background variable. Family background characteristics used in the analysis are the seventeen used in table 6–7.

[b] Difference in average of school level means.

[c] Difference in school means where a high value implies that students perceive it as happening rarely or never.

climate and student behavior. This will show, for example, the estimated gain in achievement if the amount of homework done by public school sophomores were the same as that done by Catholic school students with similar backgrounds (that is, an extra 1.2 hours a week), but other measured characteristics of the school remained the same.

In this way achievement differences between private and public schools shown in table 6–7 may be accounted for or explained. For example, in table 6–7, the reading achievement in Catholic schools of sophomores with backgrounds similar to those of public school sophomores is .32 times greater than that of the public schools sophomores. This difference of .32 items may be due in part to the 1.2 hours more homework in the Catholic schools. Carrying out the calculations, we can see that public school sophomores who are average in all the measured family background characteristics and in a school that is average in the measured school characteristics get .06 more items correct on the reading test if they do the same amount of homework as similar students (that is, background-standardized) do in the Catholic sector.

In carrying out this examination, the amount of achievement explained by the variables in each of the five areas of school functioning is added, to give a total explained by measured characteristics in that area.[24] Thus, in the area of coursework, homework, attendance, disciplinary climate, and student behavior, the analysis results in a number that is the amount of achievement difference between public and Catholic or other private schools that can be accounted for by the differences in the level at which that factor exists in each sector. If the number is positive, this means that the average public school student would gain in achievement if the public school operated at the same level as the average Catholic or other private school. If the number is negative, it means that the average public school student would have lower achievement if the public school operated at the same level as the average Catholic or other private school.

Table 6–21 shows the difference in achievement in reading, vocabulary, and mathematics between the average public school and public schools that function in specified ways like the average private school. The sum of these five differential achievements (labeled "total accounted for" in the table) is the amount of achievement difference explained by all these measures of school functioning. If that sum is less than the overall difference in achievement, controlling on background (taken from table 6–7) there remains an unexplained achievement difference between the

[24] In terms of calculations, this was estimated by multiplying the difference in the two levels of functioning (seen in table 6–20) by the relevant regression coefficient in the public sector (see appendix tables A–18 and A–19 for regression coefficients), and summing the products.

TABLE 6–21

Achievement Differences Between Private and Public Schools Due to Various Areas of School Functioning, for Students With Family Backgrounds Like That of the Average Sophomore in Public Schools[a]: Spring 1980

	Catholic			Other Private		
	Read-ing	Vocab-ulary	Mathe-matics	Read-ing	Vocab-ulary	Mathe-matics
Sophomores						
Coursework	.01	.01	.04	−.06	−.06	−.17
Homework	.05	.04	.13	.06	.04	.15
Attendance	.04	.03	.15	.00	.00	.02
Disciplinary climate	−.03	−.08	−.17	.06	−.01	.13
Student behavior	.33	.11	.46	.33	.19	.57
Total accounted for	.38	.09	.61	.39	.16	.70
Overall (from table 6–7)	.32	.36	.58	.14	.33	.56
Seniors						
Coursework	.01	.01	1.00	−.06	−.06	.47
Homework	.04	.03	.02	.07	.05	.03
Attendance	.02	.00	.04	.01	.00	.02
Disciplinary climate	.01	.00	.02	.10	.07	.01
Student behavior	.20	.01	.25	.18	.11	.41
Total accounted for	.28	.05	1.41	.30	.17	.94
Overall (from tables 6–7 and 6–8)	.24	.56	.60	.40	.51	.74

[a] Standard errors are not calculated for this table and table 6–22 because of the special complications in doing so. School-functioning differences used in calculating the achievement differences are sample estimates as are the regression coefficients also used in the calculation.

private and the public sector. If the total accounted for is greater than the overall difference (as, for example, with reading achievement for sophomores in the Catholic-public comparison—.32 overall differences and .38 accounted for), this suggests that there are other unmeasured school factors that partly compensate for the effects of these factors but are not included in the analysis. It is clear that the present analysis is imperfect, certainly excluding some factors that either augment or depress achievement in the public schools.[25]

Despite the existence of some puzzling differences between the overall differences and the total accounted for, the results shown in table 6–21 give an idea of the sources of the difference in achievement between the public and private sectors. Differences in the level of homework account for a small but consistent part of the differences in achievement; differ-

[25] This is especially true for advanced mathematics courses, where the regression coefficient is 1.40 in the private sector and 1.51 in the public sector.

ences in the student's own attendance patterns account for a smaller part. The effects of differences in the disciplinary climate are inconsistent in direction and size. The effects of coursework are difficult to assess, since the measurement is weak except in the senior year for mathematics, where the taking of specific courses was measured and where the effect of coursework on achievement was found to be great. The one area in which the effect of public-private differences is most consistently strong is student behavior (with one inconsistency, in the senior vocabulary test for the Catholic-public comparison).[26]

The effect of student behavior is considerably stronger at the sophomore level than at the senior level. This could reasonably be true for either of two reasons, one purely technical, the other substantive. The technical reason is that the measures of student behavior problems are based on sophomore perception of problems, and thus should reflect be-

[26] It is useful to examine a question similar to that examined in table 6–21 but for the functioning of private schools: How much loss in achievement would be expected in private schools that functioned like the average public school in the indicated ways? An answer to this both provides a partially independent check of the inferences made in the text on the basis of table 6–21 (since the calculations are made from a regression equation based on students in private schools) and gives some idea of the sensitivity of achievement in the private sector to each of these areas of school functioning. The comparable table for expected losses in private schools that function like the average public school in each of the five ways shown in this table (using private sector regression coefficients together with differences shown in table 6–20):

| | Sophomores | | | | | |
| | Catholic | | | Other Private | | |
	Reading	Vocabulary	Mathematics	Reading	Vocabulary	Mathematics
Coursework	.03	.03	−.05	.09	−.08	.18
Homework	−.02	−.01	−.10	−.02	−.01	−.12
Attendance	−.10	−.07	−.13	−.01	−.01	−.02
Disciplinary Climate	−.34	−.50	−.44	−.39	−.52	−.41
Student Behavior	−.33	−.44	−.57	−.33	−.57	−.61
TOTAL	−.76	−.99	−1.29	−.66	−1.03	−.98
	Seniors					
Coursework	−.01	−.01	−1.01	.06	.08	−.44
Homework	−.04	−.04	−.01	−.03	−.06	−.02
Attendance	−.06	−.03	−.15	−.68	−.01	−.06
Disciplinary Climate	−.62	−.72	−.63	−.06	−.71	−.45
Student Behavior	−.06	−.22	.40	.07	−.21	.44
TOTAL	−.79	−1.02	1.40	.64	−.91	−.53

Without going into detail the results are generally consistent with those of public school analysis shown in table 6–21. However, the total rows show that achievement in private schools is considerably more sensitive to the school's functioning than achievement in the public sector.

havior problems among sophomores more than among seniors. Insofar as these problems differ in the two grades of the same school, one would expect a lower relation of the perceived problems to senior achievement than to sophomore achievement. The substantive reason is that the sophomore year is before the end of compulsory education for many students. Thus in some schools there are a number of students who are uninterested in school, behave poorly, and perform poorly on tests such as those given as a part of the survey. By the senior year, many of these students have dropped out, and the remaining behavior problems may be less associated with achievement. Without further data, it is not possible to distinguish between these two possible reasons for the lower effects at the senior level.

These measures of student behavior are school-level measures and it is important to clarify exactly what they refer to. To some degree, the student's own behavior is statistically controlled through the two measures of the student's own attendance, which constitute area 3 in table 6–21. If the student's own behavior were fully controlled statistically, we could attribute this student behavior effect wholly to the effect of behavior problems among other students on the student's own achievement. As it is, such an inference is somewhat speculative, since the student's own behavior is not well controlled statistically. Yet the indication is that the effect may be not only through the interference of the student's misbehavior on that same student's achievement, but also through the general level of behavior disorder on the achievement of even those students whose behavior is good.[27]

A student's achievement may be affected by other students' behavior in several ways. Some of these are not completely understood, but the time a teacher must devote to disciplining students rather than teaching, how much repetition of material is required to have most of the students un-

[27] It is not fully clear just what is measured by these perceptions of student behavior. They are not direct measures of the actual rates of behavior problems, and they may be measures of some more subtle difference in the disciplinary character of the school. We conducted a partial test of this question for two of the four measures used in this analysis. Direct measures from the students are available for absenteeism and cutting classes. For each student, we calculated a measure of the average absenteeism and the percentage who cut classes among the surveyed students in that student's school, excluding the student's own responses. The effects of these two measures of attendance can be compared to the effects of the two measures obtained from sophomores' perceptions. Background-standardized differences between the public sector and the two private sectors on these two measures of attendance were calculated and the actual school-level behavior for each student was substituted in the general equation used in preparing table 6–21. The difference between the effects of sophomore perceptions of attendance behavior and the actual average attendance behavior of all other students was this: We found the effects of students' actual behavior (absences, cutting classes) to be consistently negative, but, generally, the amount of loss or gain in achievement is lower. This suggests that although something more than actual student attendance is captured by the student perception of behavior, actual average school attendance does have a negative effect on student achievement.

derstand new material, and the distractions that disorder in the school imposes on the student may all have an effect.

In one of the areas, disciplinary climate, the inconsistent results present something of a puzzle. If the lesser degree of student behavior problems in private schools does make a difference in achievement, then presumably the disciplinary differences between the public and private sectors should as well, because they influence student behavior. The last dependent clause is the key to the puzzle of why disciplinary differences show inconsistent, sometimes negative effects. By statistically controlling student behavior and homework, we controlled on the intervening variables through which the school's disciplinary climate should have its effect. Thus the very paths through which a disciplinary climate can have its principal effect have been excluded from consideration in assessing the effect of the disciplinary climate. To see the true effect of the disciplinary-climate differences between public and private schools, we should examine not only their direct effect, but also their effect through student behavior.

A portion of this is shown in table 6–22 which presents the effect of public-Catholic and public-other private differences in disciplinary climate on the four items of perceived student behavior that were shown as part E in table 6–20, again for a standardized public school sophomore student body. This does not capture the effects of disciplinary climate by the two measures of individual student behavior included in the analysis—that is, homework and attendance—but it does capture the effects by the paths of the four aspects of student behavior as perceived by sophomores.

Table 6–22 shows how much of the differences in perceived absenteeism, class-cutting, student fights, and threatening teachers between the public sector and the two private sectors can be accounted for by differences in disciplinary climate (see table 6–20 for the three items of disciplinary climate), for both sophomores and seniors. These "discipline-related" differences in behavior can be compared to part E of table 6–20, to see what proportion of the difference in behavior is accounted for by these items of disciplinary climate. For example, the total difference between public and Catholic schools in perceived absenteeism is .70, and the difference accounted for by disciplinary climate is .18, or 26 percent of the total. (It is important not to conclude that only this much of the variation in background-standardized attendance is a consequence of the discipline in the school. The three items used as indicators must certainly be only weak indicators of the disciplinary character of the school.)

With this information, it is possible to estimate the effect of the disciplinary

TABLE 6-22

Differences Between Private and Public Schools in Levels of Behavior
Problems Due to Differences in Levels of Disciplinary Climate and
Achievement Through Effects on Behavior Problems (Student Background
Statistically Controlled): Spring 1980

	Effects of Disciplinary Climate Differences:	
	Catholic-Public	Other Private-Public
Sophomores		
Effects On:		
Mean perceived absenteeism	.18	.13
Mean perceived cutting class	.29	.16
Mean perceived student fights	.15	.14
Mean perceived threaten teachers	.14	.11
Seniors		
Effects On:		
Mean perceived absenteeism	.17	.13
Mean perceived cutting class	.19	.14
Mean perceived student fights	.14	.14
Mean perceived threaten teachers	.13	.10

	Effects Through Behavior Problems in Achievement					
	Catholic			Other Private		
	Read-ing	Vocab-ulary	Mathe-matics	Read-ing	Vocab-ulary	Mathe-matics
Effects for						
Sophomores	.13	.07	.25	.10	.07	.22
Seniors	.06	−.01	.13	.06	.04	.16

Summary of Educational Outcomes

climate through four aspects of school-level student behavior. This is shown in the lower half of the table. In nearly all cases, the positive effects of disciplinary climate through student behavior outweigh the negative direct effects shown in table 6–21. Thus, through the aspects of behavior shown in table 6–22, the disciplinary-climate differences between the public and private sectors lead to greater achievement in the private sectors, though the imperfections of measurement have very likely masked part of the effects.

This chapter has examined two kinds of outcomes in public and private schools: cognitive outcomes, as measured by standardized test scores in reading, vocabulary, and mathematics; and plans for after high school, primarily plans for further education. These questions were addressed: How do outcomes in the sectors differ? Are the differences in outcome due to differences in schools; and, What are the mechanisms leading to different achievement levels?

In answering these questions for the case of the other private schools, the distinction between the available sample of students and schools in the other private sector and the actual population of other private schools and students must be kept in mind. The results found for the sample of other private schools may very well not be generalizable to the population of such schools because of the small sample size, the heterogeneity of that population, and the sampling problems discussed in chapter 1. With this important point in mind, we may turn to these questions.

The answer to the first question is that achievement in both the sophomore and senior years is somewhat higher in Catholic schools and in other private schools than it is in public schools. Achievement in the high-performance private schools is considerably higher than that in the high-performance public schools, but both are higher than in either of the private sectors.

The differences between sectors in educational expectations and aspirations are similar to the differences in achievement. The sectors are ordered in the same way, with public school students having the lowest educational aspirations and those in the high-performance private schools having the highest aspirations. For the other postsecondary activity, employment, the order is reversed. Among seniors who planned to work full time after graduation, a higher proportion in the public schools already had a job lined up. This suggests that the greater vocational resources and opportunities in the public schools, as shown in chapter 4, lead to a better connection with the world of employment for those students who are going into the full-time labor force.

The second question, which attempted to separate effects of private schools on achievement and aspirations from selection into private schools, is examined in several ways. In the examination of effects on achievement, statistical controls on family background are introduced, in order to control on those background characteristics that are most related to achievement. The achievement differences between the private sectors and the public sector are reduced (more for other private schools than for Catholic schools), but differences remain. Then there is an examination of imputed growth from the sophomore to the senior year. Learning rates were calculated under three different sets of assumptions. Examining these ranges of estimated rates shows that under all assumptions, growth in vocabulary and mathematics achievement is greater in both private sectors than in the public sector; but for the Catholic-public sector comparison in reading, the different estimates are in conflict.

In addition, there is a major difference in homogeneity of achievement between Catholic schools on the one hand and public and other private schools on the other. Students of parents with different educational backgrounds achieve at more nearly comparable levels in the Catholic schools than in the public schools, while the achievement levels are even more divergent in other private schools than in the public schools. And comparison of blacks and Hispanics in Catholic and public schools (controlling on parental income and education) reveals that as sophomores these minority students achieve at a level closer to that of non-Hispanic whites in Catholic schools than in public schools; the achievement gap between minorities and non-Hispanic whites as seniors decreases slightly in Catholic schools, while it increases slightly in public schools. Altogether, the evidence is strong that the Catholic schools function much closer to the American ideal of the "common school," educating children from different backgrounds alike, than do the public schools.

Turning to educational aspirations, the question arises whether the private-public difference is wholly due to selection or is in part due to effects of the sector. Statistical controls on family background leave a difference, with students in Catholic schools showing especially high aspirations. No differential sophomore-senior growth is found, except for lower growth in Catholic schools. This result is suspect, however, because of a ceiling effect due to the higher level of aspirations among Catholic school sophomores. An analysis that uses retrospective reports of seniors and sophomores in earlier years about expectations of attending college confirms this, through evidence that the proportion planning to attend college increases more in the Catholic sector than in the public sector, while the background-standardized proportion planning to attend college in the sixth grade was (according to retrospective accounts) nearly the same in all sectors. Again, the Catholic schools show much greater homogeneity than do other schools in the educational aspirations among students from different parental education backgrounds.

The third question is a question about what differences between public and private schools are responsible for the additional achievement that occurs in the private schools. The answer to this is only partial, because the investigation covered only selected differences. But the partial answer is fairly clear.

There are at least two important ways in which private schools produce higher achievement outcomes than public schools. First, given the same type of student (that is, with background standardized), private schools create higher rates of engagement in academic activities. School attendance is better, students do more homework, and students generally take more rigorous subjects (for instance, more advanced mathematics). The indication is that more extensive academic demands are made in the private schools, leading to more advanced courses and thus to greater achievement. This is a somewhat obvious conclusion, and the statistical evidence supports it. Second, student behavior in a school has strong and consistent effects on student achievement. Apart from mathematics coursework for seniors, the greatest differences in achievement between private and public schools are accounted for by school-level behavior variables (that is, the incidence of fights, students threatening teachers, and so forth). The disciplinary climate of a school, such as the effectiveness and fairness of discipline and teacher interest, affect achievement at least in part through their effect on these school-level behavior variables.

Although these answers are only partial in that additional school factors may also explain the different outcomes in the sectors, they strongly suggest that school functioning makes a difference in achievement outcomes for the average student. And private schools of both sectors appear to function better in the areas that contribute to achievement.

7

Conclusion

IN chapter 1 of this book, we examined a number of premises underlying policies that would increase the role of private schools and a number underlying policies that would decrease their role. Perhaps the best way to conclude is to review those premises, to see just which premises this report has provided evidence on, and what can be concluded from the evidence about each premise. In addition, other results were found along the way, some of which provide additional information that bears upon the overall policy questions. In reviewing these results, it should be kept in mind that the principal comparison about which there can be some assurance that the samples represent that population is the public-Catholic comparison. The other private school sample, as discussed earlier, is both small, relative to the large and heterogeneous set of non-Catholic private schools, and possibly nonrepresentative of this heterogenous set of schools.

Premises Underlying Policies That Would Increase the Role of Private Schools

Private Schools Produce Better Cognitive Outcomes Than Do Public Schools (chapter 6). The evidence from chapter 6 is that private schools do produce better cognitive outcomes than public schools. When family background factors that predict achievement are controlled, students in both Catholic and other private schools are shown to achieve at a higher level than students in public schools. The difference at the sophomore level, which was greater for Catholic schools than for other private schools, ranged from about a fifth of the sophomore-senior gain to about two-thirds the size of that gain (that is, from a little less than half a year's difference to something more than one year's difference). This evidence is subject to a caveat: Despite extensive statistical controls on parental background, there may very well be other unmeasured factors in the self-selection into the private sector that are associated with higher achievement.

When we examined gains for the sophomore to the senior year in the three sectors, the difficulties were sufficiently great that we estimated a range of learning rates, two estimates having probable upward biases and bias favoring the public sector, and one having probable downward biases and biases favoring the private sectors. For mathematics and vocabulary learning rates, both private sectors showed higher rates over the whole range of estimates than did the public schools. For reading comprehension, the same was true for the other private schools, but the evidence was mixed for the Catholic-public comparison, one estimate showing lower Catholic rates, one showing higher Catholic rates, and one showing equivalent rates.

A caveat to all these results is shown by the high-performance public and private schools. Performance was much higher in both of these sets of schools than in any of the three sectors, although these schools could not be separately studied in the extended analysis of chapter 6 because of the ceiling effects in achievement scores and the way the sample was drawn.

Private Schools Provide Better Character and Personality Development Than Do Public Schools (chapter 5). Little evidence on character and personality development was provided in this report. However, students in other private schools show both higher levels of self-esteem and sense of fate control than sophomores and higher gains from the sophomore to senior year than students in public or Catholic schools. The inference that there is greater growth on these dimensions in other private schools is strengthened by the fact that students in high-performance private schools showed even higher levels as sophomores and similarly high sophomore-senior gains, while students in high-performance public schools did not, despite the fact that the parental backgrounds of students in the latter schools are higher than those in other private schools.

Private Schools Provide a Safer, More Disciplined, and More Ordered

Conclusion

Environment Than Do Public Schools (chapter 5). The evidence is strong that this premise is true. The greatest difference found in any aspect of school functioning between public and private schools was in the degree of discipline and order in the schools (chapter 5, pages 97–115). The Catholic and other private schools appear somewhat different in their discipline and behavior profiles, with students in other private schools reporting more absences and class-cutting but also more homework, fewer fights among students, and greater teacher interest in students. However, in all these respects, both sectors showed greater discipline and order than the public schools.

Private Schools are More Successful in Creating an Interest in Learning Than Are Public Schools (chapter 5). There is little evidence to confirm or disconfirm this premise. The sectors differ only slightly in student responses to the two direct questions concerning interest in school, and there is not much to be inferred from indirect evidence presented in the report.

Private Schools Encourage Interest in Higher Education and Lead More of Their Students to Attend College Than Do Public Schools With Comparable Students (chapter 6). The evidence on this premise is toward a positive answer, but it is not extremely strong evidence. There is some evidence (table 6–15) that although students from comparable backgrounds in Catholic high schools had the same aspirations for attending college when they were in the sixth grade, their aspirations have increased more than those in public schools.

Private Schools are Smaller and Thus Bring About Greater Degrees of Participation in Sports and Other Activities Than Do Public Schools (chapter 5). The evidence suggests that this premise is true for other private schools, but not for Catholic schools (though Catholic school students report highest school spirit, and other private school students, lowest). The fact that Catholic schools are smaller in size than public schools does not result in increased participation in extracurricular activities.

Private Schools Have Smaller Class Size, and Thus Allow Teachers and Students to Have Greater Contact (chapter 4). The other private schools have sharply lower student-teacher ratios than the public schools, while the Catholic schools have slightly higher ratios. There are fewer than half the students per teacher in other private schools than in public or Catholic schools (table 4–3). No direct evidence on contact between students and teachers is presented.

Private Schools are More Efficient Than Public Schools, Accomplishing Their Task at a Lower Cost. The report contains no evidence on this premise.

Premises Underlying Policies That Would Decrease the Role of
Private Schools

*Private Schools Are Socially Divisive Along Income Lines, Skimming
the Students From Higher Income Backgrounds, and Segregating Them
into Elite Schools (chapter 3).* The evidence on this premise works in two
directions. First, among the three major sectors, the other private schools
contain students from somewhat higher income backgrounds and the
Catholic schools contain students from slightly higher income backgrounds than the public schools. The differences are primarily at the
highest and lowest income levels, with all three sectors having a majority
of students in a broad middle-income category ranging from $12,000 to
$38,000 a year, and similar proportions at different levels within this
range. Second, the internal segregation by income within each sector goes
in the opposite direction, with the public sector showing slightly higher
income segregation than either the Catholic or other private sectors. However, income segregation is not high within any sector. The end result of
these two forces acting in opposite directions is that U.S. schools as a
whole show slightly greater segregation by income than would be the case
if private school students of differing income levels were absorbed into
the public schools in the same way that public school students of differing
income levels are currently distributed among schools.

*Private Schools Are Divisive Along Religious Lines, Segregating Dif-
ferent Religious Groups Into Different Schools (chapter 3).* The evidence
is strong that this is true. Besides the 30 percent of private schools that are
Catholic, enrolling 66 percent of all private school students, 25 percent of
private schools, enrolling 12 percent of private school students, are affiliated with other religious denominations. Examining religious segregation
solely in the Catholic/non-Catholic categories, the report shows that the
great majority of Catholics are in public schools, but that over 90 percent
of the students in Catholic schools are Catholic. Within each sector, the
Catholic/non-Catholic segregation is least in the Catholic schools themselves, greatest in the other private schools. The overall impact of the
between-sector segregation and the differing segregation within sectors is,
as might be expected, that schools in the United States are more segregated along Catholic/non-Catholic lines than they would be if private school
students were absorbed into the public schools.

*Private Schools Are Divisive Along Racial Lines, In Two Ways: They
Contain Few Blacks or Other Minorities, and Thus Segregate Whites in
Private Schools From Blacks in Public Schools; and the Private Sector*

Conclusion

Itself is More Racially Segregated Than the Public Sector (chapter 3). The evidence shows that the first of these premises is true with respect to blacks but not with respect to Hispanics and that the second is not true with respect to blacks or Hispanics. The end result with respect to Hispanics and blacks is that the segregation of U.S. schools is little different from what it would be if there were no private schools.

Catholic schools enroll about half as high a proportion of blacks as the public schools, and other private schools, only about a quarter as high a proportion. Internally, however, the other private sector is least racially segregated and the public sector by far the most segregated. The end result of these two opposing forces, between-sector and within-sector, is that the segregation of black and white students in U.S. schools is no greater and no less than it would be if there were no private schools, and their students were absorbed into the public sector, distributed among schools as public sector black and white students are now distributed.

Private Schools Do Not Provide the Educational Range That Public Schools Do, Particularly in Vocational and Other Nontraditional Courses or Programs (chapter 4). The evidence on this premise is that it is correct. Schools in both the Catholic and other private sectors provide primarily academic programs and have few vocational or technical courses. Even in academic areas, however, some of the smaller schools in the other private sector have a limited range of subjects, as evidenced by the fact that 44 percent of students in the other private sector are in schools with no third-year foreign language courses. The lesser educational range of the private sector is also shown by the more comprehensive character of the high-performance public schools compared to the high-performance private schools.

Private Schools Have a Narrower Range of Extracurricular Activities, and Thus Deprive Their Students of Participation in School Activities Outside the Classroom (chapter 5). This premise is almost the direct opposite of the sixth premise on the other side, so the answer is the same as was given there. Students in Catholic and public schools show about the same amount of participation in extracurricular activities, while students in other private schools show more, and participation is higher for seniors than for sophomores. Thus this premise is not correct.

Private Schools are Unhealthily Competitive, and Thus Public Schools Provide a Healthier Affective Development (chapter 5). The report provides no direct evidence on this premise.

Facilitating the Use of Private Schools Aids Whites More Than Blacks and Those Better Off Financially at the Expense of Those Worse Off; In addition, It Increases Racial and Economic Segregation (chapter 3).

183

An examination of the predicted effect of a marginal income increment for all income groups shows that this would lead to a marginal increase in the proportion of blacks and Hispanics in the private sector.

The evidence indicates that facilitating use of private schools through a change of the sort just described would not increase segregation along racial or economic lines but would decrease it (though the evidence indicates that religious segregation would increase). Such policies would bring more blacks, Hispanics, and students from lower income backgrounds into the private schools, thus reducing the between-sector segregation, and these students would be moving from a sector of high racial segregation to a sector of low racial segregation, as well as from a sector slightly higher in economic segregation to one slightly lower.

No evidence is presented in the effects of a tuition tax credit or school voucher. However, several effects can be inferred from this hypothetical experiment.

1. The overall numbers of students shifting to the private sector would probably be far greater than the minuscule numbers predicted to shift with an income increase, because the credit or grant is contingent on attendance at private school.
2. So long as the proportion of the white student population which was enrolled in the private sector was higher than the proportion of blacks, as is likely with any policy, whites would benefit more financially than would blacks. It is likely that such a policy would lead to a higher proportion of Hispanics than non-Hispanic whites in the private sector (predominantly Catholic schools), because of their already high enrollment rate, and the greater increases in enrollment with income than for non-Hispanic whites. Hispanics would benefit more than non-Hispanic whites.
3. Considering only educational benefits rather than financial benefits means considering only new entrants into the private sector. The evidence from the marginal-income-increment hypothetical experiment does not allow inferences as to whether, for tuition tax credit or voucher policies, this new entrant population would have a higher proportion of blacks than in the population as a whole or a lower proportion. Without a substantial increase in the number of non-Catholic private schools, it is likely that the proportion of Hispanics in the new entrant population would be higher than that in the population as a whole.

Conclusion

Additional Results Relevant to the Policy Question of Facilitating or Constraining Use of Public Schools

1. The increase in probability of enrollment of blacks and Hispanics with increase in income is higher than that of whites. Comparing Catholics with Catholics and non-Catholics with non-Catholics shows that blacks have the highest absolute rate of enrollment in Catholic schools, at low as well as high income levels and among both Catholics and non-Catholics, while Hispanics have the lowest rate. In other private schools, black enrollment is low at all income levels except the very highest.
2. Catholic schools more nearly approximate the "common school" ideal of American education than do public schools, in that the achievement levels of students from different parental educational backgrounds, of black and white students, and of Hispanic and non-Hispanic white students are more nearly alike in Catholic schools than in public schools. In addition, the educational aspirations of students from different parental educational backgrounds are more alike in Catholic than in public schools.
3. Important factors in bringing about higher scholastic achievement in private schools than in public schools are the greater academic demands and more ordered environment in the private schools. The evidence shows not only that the sectors differ greatly in these respects, but also that within the public schools students who are better disciplined and are in schools with more ordered environments achieve more highly.

It may or may not be useful to attempt to sum up the overall implications for the premises underlying policy arguments to facilitate or constrain the use of private schools. Of the premises examined here, some on each side are confirmed and some on each side are disconfirmed. It is hard, however, to avoid the overall conclusion that the factual premises underlying policies that would facilitate use of private schools are much better supported on the whole than those underlying policies that would constrain their use. Or, to put it another way, the constraints imposed on schools in the public sector (and there is no evidence that those constraints are financial compared with the private sector) seem to impair their functioning as educational institutions without providing the more egalitarian outcomes that are one of the goals of public schooling.

Epilogue

I T IS useful to examine the broader implications of the results of this research. For the report is focused on specific policy questions concerning private schools, yet the results have implications both for the way that schools function and for the organization of education generally. In this epilogue, we will examine some of the major results of the research which do appear to have broader implications.

Implications for Achievement in High School

THE SCHOOL CHARACTERISTICS THAT BRING HIGHER ACHIEVEMENT

When study of the effects of school characteristics on achievement began on a broad scale in the 1960s, those characteristics that were most studied were the traditional ones described in the prologue: per pupil expenditures as an overall measure of resources, laboratory facilities, libraries, recency of textbooks, and breadth of course offerings. Those characteristics showed little or no consistent relation to achievement. The characteristics of schools that are currently found to be related to achievement, in this study and others (see, for example, Rutter et al., 1979), are of a different sort. They are attributes of the school's functioning, sometimes called "process" variables in educational circles. The two broad areas of process variables found in this study to be related to achievement are academic demands and discipline (chapter 6).

These two areas of academic demands and discipline are closely related, both in the functioning of the school and in the measures used in this study. The amount of homework done is an indicator of academic demands; yet homework requires the use and acceptance of teacher authority, if it is to be done. Attendance at school and attendance at classes while in school stem from maintenance of disciplinary standards; yet it is only a prerequisite to the meeting of academic demands. It is similar with behavior standards within the school. Thus, achievement and discipline are intimately intertwined, and it is no accident that in the sectors (and presumably in the schools within a sector) where one is high, the other is high as well. In the Catholic sector and in the schools of the other private sector in our sample, the academic demands as measured by the homework done and the advanced mathematics courses taken by students from comparable family backgrounds (table 6–20), or as measured in the number of standard academic courses taken (tables 5–1, 5–2, 5–3), are greater than in the public sector. Some part of the latter is of course due to the taking of vocational courses by some public school students. But as table 5–4 shows, there remains in the private sector a substantially greater proportion of seniors, among those who expect to finish four years of college, who have taken selected mathematics courses, science courses, and foreign languages in schools where these courses are offered (table 5–4). Further research would be valuable in separating the differences in demands due to vocational programs from those due merely to course proliferation and watering down of the curriculum in nonvocational courses.

Similarly, in the Catholic sector and in the schools from the other private sector, disciplinary standards in every area measured are higher, and discipline problems, as measured by absenteeism, cutting classes, threats to teachers, and fights among students, all for students from comparable backgrounds, are lower than in the public schools (table 6–20).

The demonstration, in the latter part of chapter 6, that in public sector schools where these academic demands and disciplinary standards are higher, the achievement in verbal and mathematical skills is also higher indicates that the effects of these aspects of school functioning is not merely a private sector phenomenon. According to our results, this relationship holds true to at least as great an extent in the public sector as in the private sector.[1]

Sources of the Lower Academic and Disciplinary Demands

In many respects, the private-public comparison merely serves as a way of identifying some of these factors affecting achievement in schools. This study has not shown how it is or why it is that the academic and disciplinary demands are at the level they are found to be in the average public school. Nevertheless, it is useful to point to some of the changes that have occurred in American education, and in the society as a whole, which seem likely to have contributed to reduced academic demands and looser disciplinary standards.

First, we should point out that the data of this study do not show that academic demands and disciplinary standards in the public high schools have become lower in recent years. We believe, however, that there is sufficient external evidence that this is so. Extensive investigation of the decline in SAT scores show that a substantial part of the decline is real, and not merely a change in the composition of the test-taking group.[2] And some of the evidence indicates that the change is at least as pronounced among high-performing students as among lower-performing students. Secondly, grade inflation and the substitution of pass-fail for traditional grading systems, which began in the universities in the 1960s and moved to the high schools in the 1970s, is a matter of common knowledge. The proliferation of undemanding courses with socioemotional focus and in a broadened definition of what counts as an "English" course is also generally known. In discipline and behavior, surveys have shown that principals regard the problems as having grown worse,[3] and in recent Gallup public opinion polls, both parents and students report that they regard discipline problems as the most important problem in schools. Thus, although we present no evidence of recent changes in these two areas, there seems little question that both academic and disciplinary demands in high school have slackened during the 1970s.[4]

[1] Table 6–21 shows that in the public sector, the achievement of students in the schools that are similar to private schools in their academic and disciplinary demands differs from the achievement of comparable students in an average public sector school in terms of academic and disciplinary demands more than the standardized private sector achievement differs from the average achievement in the public sector, in seven of the twelve comparisons.

[2] See, for example, Jencks, 1978.

[3] See Coleman and Kelly, 1976, chapter 5.

[4] See Toby, 1980.

Epilogue

It seems likely that there is no single cause for these changes. One important source was the youth movement, which, beginning in the 1960s and continuing well into the 1970s in the high schools, exercised a strong pressure toward a student-defined curriculum, with an emphasis on "relevant" courses and a de-emphasis traditional courses, and toward liberalized grading. A part of this was transmitted downward from the colleges by more flexible entrance requirements. The removal by many colleges of a foreign language requirement for admission is probably the clearest example, for it is in high school foreign language courses that enrollment has dropped most precipitously.

Growing out of the antiauthority aspects of the youth movement has been the increase in student rights, reinforced by legal decisions in the 1970s. The growth of student rights constitutes a fundamental change in the relation of the school to the student, which had been that of trustee for parental authority. This has been replaced by a relation in which the student in a high school is regarded as having full civil rights (in particular, the right of due process), undiminished by the student's status as a minor. The institution of due process rights for students, and the general reduction in the school's authority over the student, means that public schools are not only constrained in the exercise of authority, they are also increasingly involved in litigation brought on behalf of the student.

Another important change has been the emphasis on equal opportunity and the general growth of an egalitarian ethic. This emphasis, which has been in part, but not wholly, due to the integration of blacks into the mainstream of American education, and which properly takes the form of increased efforts to improve the achievement of disadvantaged students, has sometimes taken the form of easier courses, systems of grading that obliterated distinctions in achievement, and reduction of standards. Some of these changes have, in part, been reinforced by judicial rulings in desegregation cases, acting to insure that minorities were not discriminated against, but failing to maintain the distinction between discrimination on the basis of race and discrimination on the basis of performance.

Other sources of the changes have been reductions in school authority due to federal policies that impose various requirements on school authorities (such as Public Law 94–142, on education of handicapped children, which concerns not only physically handicapped children, but also reduces school discretion in coping with emotionally disturbed children). These federal policies, in the same way as the establishment of full civil rights for students, increasingly narrow the range of discretion of the principal and teacher, and change the balance of power within the school. As a consequence, a student who is violent toward other students or teachers has less fear of apprehension and punishment. As in the case of crime generally, this reduced authority of the schools, to the point where violators need not fear punishment, does not favor the interests of the students, but sacrifices their interests to those of the violators. In particular, the interests of minorities in increasing their achievement in school and gaining full equality have been harmed by this reduced scope of authority, because it is they who are most likely to be exposed to an undisciplined environment. Ironically, the protection of individual student rights and the attendant reduction in school authority has sometimes meant loss of the right to an orderly environment in which to learn.

Finally, while some of the changes we have described may be reversed, one is likely not to. The family structure and authority has clearly weakened in recent years, a weakening that appears most consequential for high school youth. Apart from the increased level of divorce, there appears to be a reduced interest on the part of parents in regarding their adolescent children as full members of their family subject to their attention and authority, and a reduced willingness on the part of adolescents to being subject to family constraints and obligations.[5] The fundamental causes of this change are not clear, but one likely source is that with a reduction in the number of children and an increase in the number of years of active adult life (through increases in longevity), parents now have less reason to regard "raising a family" as the central focus of their adult life. Childrearing has come to be merely a phase in an adult's life, a phase which begins late and ends early, allowing the adult to resume the leisure activities enjoyed before the child or children were born. With such an orientation, it is to be expected that parents will be eager for the children to be effectively autonomous as early as possible.

These changes in parental attitude are manifested not only in the behavior of parents; they can be seen in changed norms about the proper role of a parent, as well as in legal changes. The development of due process at school to replace the old principle of *in loco parentis* and the reduction of voting age to eighteen both reflect, in part, the increased willingness of parents to relinquish authority over and responsibility for their adolescent children. The great increase in the portion of high school youth who work part-time for pay (earning money to be used in pursuit of independent leisure activities, not as a contribution to family income) is among the host of indicators of this change in attitudes of parents.

This change, although least well documented in its relation to changes in the functioning of the high school, has potentially the most dramatic

---

[5] For a discussion of parental negligence as it affects achievement of middle-class students, see Levine, 1980.

and serious consequences. For if studies of school achievement have shown one thing, it is the importance of the family. And school achievement is only one element in the process of becoming adult; the family's contributions to other elements are even more important. If an early withdrawal of family attention, interest, and involvement is to become the fate of an increasing fraction of our youth, it can be expected to have especially serious consequences.

Implications for the Organization of Education

A second set of implications of this report concern the organization of American education, both in the public-private division and in the organization of the public sector itself. In the remaining part of this epilogue, we will discuss some of these implications.

LEVELS OF ACHIEVEMENT IN PUBLIC AND PRIVATE SCHOOLS

The achievement difference attributable to greater effectiveness of the private schools, as shown in chapter 6, has been the result of this study most fully commented on, as well as the result most hotly disputed. The controversy over the methods used and the result itself is addressed in the addendum. Here, we take the result as given (our confidence in it increased by the further analyses carried out after the report was released— also reported in the addendum), and raise the question: Why the greater effectiveness?

First, it is useful to see the size of the estimated differences in some perspective. The size of these differences is approximately one grade level. The variation among students within any sector, or even within a school, is far greater than the differences between sector averages. For example, the estimated effect of a Catholic or other private school in increasing mathematics achievement, as shown in table 6–7, would move a child at the 50th percentile up only 6 or 7 percentile points.[6] Individual differences loom much larger than differential effects of schools; and this discrepancy is especially large when we compare only the average sector effects.

An economist might expect effects of about this size, that is, expecting the average private school to be only marginally more effective than the

[6] This is the percentile gain equivalent to a gain of about a sixth of a standard deviation.

average public school, even if all parents were able to accurately judge a school's effectiveness and used only this criterion in deciding whether to send their child to a private school or a public school. A private school that survives in the market will balance off the extra burdens it imposes on students and parents (burdens of work for students and of money and parental discipline for parents) against the benefits in achievement that these burdens bring. And both parents and students will ordinarily opt for a set of burdens that bring the student only somewhat higher than his public school counterpart, seeing additional benefits beyond that as not worth the additional costs. If the private school were competing against schools in the public sector that imposed much more work on students than do public schools in America and achieved considerably higher results, as evidence indicates Japanese schools do (Coleman, 1975), then the private school that competed successfully with such public schools would do so by imposing a much heavier set of burdens on students and parents. All this is to say that within a given sociocultural system, achievement in a private school will not show an extraordinary divergence from achievement in the public schools, which constitute the benchmark in that society—since additional achievement is brought about only at a cost.[7]

While an economist might expect only marginal differences in effectiveness of public and private schools, others might see it as obvious that private schools would be more effective: parents pay for a private school because they believe it increases the achievement of their children. Yet we should remember that not long ago it was equally "obvious" to some persons that Catholic schools provided an inferior education. Thus the result is not at all a trivial one.

The section on factors affecting achievement outcomes in chapter 6 gives some initial insight into the differences between public and private schools which contribute to the achievement differences. These can be broadly divided into two areas: academic demands and discipline. For these are not only major differences between the public and private sectors; as stated earlier, the schools within the public sector that impose the greater academic demands (such as greater homework) and stronger discipline (such as better attendance) bring about greater achievement than does the average public school with comparable students.

This leads naturally to the question of why the private schools make greater academic demands and have more effective discipline. In part,

[7]Even the marginal amount of difference predicted in this way would not necessarily hold if the private school is chosen on other grounds, such as religious grounds. Parents might be willing to accept lower achievement to insure that their children received religious instruction. Perhaps the best example would be in self-contained religious communities such as the Amish.

the difference is due to the lesser constraints under which the private schools operate. They can more easily discipline, suspend, or expel students without concern about legal suits from parents (a matter which is of serious concern to some public school principals); and they can more frequently depend on parents to reinforce the demands they make on students. These lesser constraints on the private sector are often offered to excuse any lesser effectiveness of the public sector. They can, however, serve instead to pose the question of whether some of the constraints within the public sector might not be reduced. In the prologue, a number of different modes of organization were described that involve more choice by parents and students and more leverage for the school to make demands and exercise authority. These include specialized high schools, magnet schools, alternative schools, and open choice among schools within or across school district lines. While this book has not examined the differential functioning of such schools, the results suggest the importance of examining these alternatives to assignment strictly by residence or assignment on racial grounds.[8]

It is important to note, however, that the principal mode of parental choice of school in the public sector, that is choosing a school by choice of residence, does not provide school staff with leverage to make greater demands or exercise greater authority. A suburban school principal with middle-class students whose parents have chosen to live there because the school is "good" cannot exercise the authority of either a principal in the private sector or a principal of a magnet or specialized school entered by choice in the public sector, for the student cannot choose another school without change of residence. In an era when school authority was accepted by middle-class students and reinforced by middle-class parents, this burden of conforming to the strict assignment was borne by students. At present, when this acceptance of school authority is no longer automatic, the burden is borne by the schools, in accommodating to levels of motivation and behavior by students that they would once have regarded as unacceptable.

One mode of accommodation to these lower levels of motivation has been, as described earlier, grade inflation. Another has been the proliferation of courses that instead of imposing an academic discipline and rigor of thought, aim to increase motivation through "relevance," or are sufficiently undemanding that students pass through them without great effort. For two reasons, private schools have not exhibited the same course

[8]The data set used in this analysis, High School and Beyond, does allow some examination of this sort, because there is some variability of school organization within the public sector, and that variability is reflected in the sample.

proliferation that is found in public schools. One reason is the greater demands private schools can impose because students and schools are not assigned to each other, but are together by choice; another is the smaller size and lesser resources of these schools. The result is greater concentration on courses that, unlike the new courses which have sprung up in the 1970s, continue to require effort and lead to acquisition of the skills and knowledge students will need in later life.

EQUALITY OF EDUCATIONAL OPPORTUNITY: THE CATHOLIC SCHOOL
AND THE PUBLIC SCHOOL

A major issue in the concern about growth in private schools has stemmed from the belief that private schools exacerbate inequality of opportunity. Certainly there are factors which point in that direction: Private school parents have higher incomes than the average (figure 3–5), and private schools have considerably smaller proportions of minorities than do public schools (table 3–1). Furthermore, the role of some elite preparatory schools in educating the children of the economic and political elite is well known.

However, there are three results from this study, one in chapter 3 and two in chapter 6, which indicate that a portion of this concern is misplaced, and that one might well say that—as compared to the Catholic schools—the public schools exacerbate inequality of educational opportunity. The result from chapter 3 is that blacks and whites are less segregated within Catholic schools than are blacks and whites in public schools. Note that this does not mean that Catholic schools make a positive contribution to school integration, because they have only about half as high a proportion of black students as do the public schools, and the overall impact depends on both the within-sector segregation and the between-sector segregation, which in this case work in opposite directions.[9] In the case of Anglo-Hispanic segregation, Catholic schools have about the same proportion of Hispanics as do the public schools, and they are somewhat more integrated than the public schools, though not by a great amount. However, the most important difference between Catholic and public schools that is relevant to equality of educational opportunity was noted in chapter 6, in the study of achievement patterns. The result, very simply, is that achievement difference between students from advantaged backgrounds and those from disadvantaged backgrounds are considerably

[9] It is important to recognize these two aspects—some commentators on the report have paid attention only to the internal segregation components; and at least one pair of investigators has also failed to attend to the distinction. See Page and Keith, 1981.

less in Catholic schools than in public schools. Table 6–9 shows that this is true in comparing the predicted achievement in each sector for students with well-educated and poorly-educated parents, white and black students, and Anglo and Hispanic students, in each case controlling on other aspects of the students' backgrounds. And in expectations for higher education, there are similarly smaller differences between children from advantaged and disadvantaged backgrounds in the Catholic schools compared to public schools.

The set of other private schools in our sample shows even slightly more variability for students of parents with high and low education than do the public schools, so that it appears that the inequalities of achievement in this sector are as great as, or greater than, in the public sector.[10] Generalizations about the other private schools are limited because of the small size and diversity of the sample of other private schools; but it is that very diversity which is evident in the variability of scores for students with different backgrounds. Thus although generalization about the other private sector should be made cautiously, the analysis suggests that in the achievement differences among students from different backgrounds, and in expectations for further education, students in the other private schools exhibit high differences as do public school students, in contrast to students in Catholic schools.

In addition to the evidence that students from different backgrounds achieve at more nearly the same level in Catholic schools than in public (or other private) schools, there is also evidence that this difference in inequality grows over time (table 6–9). In seven of nine comparisons in the public sector, seniors from advantaged and disadvantaged backgrounds are further apart than sophomores; in six of nine comparisons in the Catholic sector, seniors from the different backgrounds are closer together than sophomores. Yet because of the greater dropout rate in the public sector, one would expect the public school seniors to show more apparant convergence than Catholic school seniors if nothing changed at the individual level. Thus it appears that there is a tendency toward con-

---

[10] It is possible to imagine selection processes that would produce the results found in the Catholic sector: If the selection into the Catholic sector were such that especially high-performing students from low educational backgrounds, or especially low-performing students from high educational backgrounds, or both, were selected into the Catholic schools, then that would give the results found. The fact that the opposite result holds in the other private sector (i.e. there is a greater background-related achievement difference than in the public sector) indicates that the differential selection process into Catholic and the other private sectors would have to be in exactly the opposite directions if these results were due to differential selection. Thus, it seems unlikely that differential selection can account for the results. Also, the sophomore-senior differences discussed later in the text are consistent with the interpretation that the effect is due to less divergences in amount learned among students in the Catholic sector.

vergence over time among students from different backgrounds in the Catholic schools, and a tendency toward divergence in the public schools.[11]

THE COMMON SCHOOL, AND ITS DEMISE IN AMERICAN PUBLIC EDUCATION

These comparisons between the Catholic and public sectors in the degree of segregation and inequalities of achievement (with schools from the other private sector showing results like those in the public sector) suggest a closer look at the usual assumption that the public schools constitute the "common school" which acts in egalitarian directions, while the private school must be inegalitarian. The premise underlying this assumption is that public schools enroll everyone from a community in the same school, without selection based on achievement, elite status, family income, or on other grounds. Yet, in recent years that premise has come increasingly to be violated, as the "community" has increased in size and parents have increasingly selected a school within the public sector by choice of residence.

In effect, the growth in personal transportation since World War II, which contributed to the extensive growth of suburban areas and the flight of middle-class whites from large central cities, has led to a highly stratified public school system in urban areas. The result has few resemblances to the common school ideal of American education, an ideal which led to the growth of the comprehensive high school serving students from all backgrounds and destined for all occupations. Outside metropolitan areas, the myth is still a reality, in that the common or comprehensive school continues to serve students from all backgrounds and destinations in the [near] vicinity. Even this is, in part, a fiction, because the families living in these areas are themselves self-selected, far from a cross section of the population.

This stratification has in effect produced a "public" school system which not only no longer integrates the various segments of the population of students, but appears no more egalitarian than private education, and considerably less egalitarian in outcome than the major portion of the private sector in America—the Catholic schools. The attempts at bussing to overcome racial segregation constitute one attempt to overcome these

---

[11] The difference between public and Catholic schools in these trends is statistically significant at probability less than .05. The separate convergence and divergence statements, however, can be made with less confidence, because of the small number of senior-sophomore comparisons (nine in each case).

segregating processes within the public sector; but the general unpopularity of this policy, greatest among whites, but true also for Hispanics and blacks, indicates the difficulty of attempting to reinstate by law the constraints that were once imposed by nature.

Where then does that leave the idea and ideal of education as an equalizing and integrative force in society? Certainly it dictates abandoning the myth of the system of public education as a set of "common schools," each available to all and each attended by a broad cross section of American children. It dictates abandonment of the myth of public schools as integrative and equalizing, while private schools are segregative and unequalizing. Most important, it indicates that the principles of organization of education for the future in America must recognize a technological and ecological reality that is far different from that on which the principles currently in use were based. It may mean a more pluralistic and flexible definition of "community," one which need not be based on locus of residence; and it must certainly mean a set of principles in which the opportunity to choose a school is less dependent on income and race than occurs at present, whether that choice occurs within the public sector or between the public and private sectors. Finally, to be successful, it can hardly mean an arbitrary restriction of choice for those whose resources make choice possible, but must mean an expansion of choice for those without such resources.

Addendum

SINCE the report that the body of this book is based on was made public in April, 1981, there has been some controversy surrounding it. The controversy has focused on a number of questions:

1. Have we demonstrated a private-school effect on achievement?
2. Are there alternative ways to test for a private-school effect?
3. Are the conclusions concerning the effect of private schools on racial segregation the same for all regions?
4. What is the proper role of social research in relation to social policy?

In this addendum, we examine each of these four questions, in the above order.

Have We Demonstrated a Private-School Effect?

Whether or not we have demonstrated a private-school effect involves two methodological issues. Regarding the first methodological issue, there are two general approaches taken in the criticisms. One is to say that if only the correct selection variables had been taken into account, the private schools would show no greater cognitive achievement, perhaps even less, than the public schools. It is useful to address this criticism first. The most common objection has been that Catholic and other private schools appear more successful merely because better students are selected to attend them. Specifically, this issue arises in considering the student's program: academic, general, or vocational. In effect, the critics assume that selection of program is exogenous to the set of school policy variables, while we assume it is endogenous, affected by school policy.

Not only does the criticism assume that program of study is exogenous to the system of school policy, it assumes also that it exerts an effect both on selection of a private school and on achievement over and above the effect of the parental background variables and even over and above the effect of parental expectations for the child's education. Another way of putting this assumption is that being in a vocational or general program of study is assumed to be an indicator (over and above family background and parental aspirations for the child's education) of low potential for academic achievement, potential that is prior to and independent of school policy.

This assumption would imply that school program should be statistically controlled when examining the school effect; our assumption implies that to statistically control a program is to statistically control one of the very paths through which school policy has its effects. In this view, public schools place students into general or vocational programs when they would be kept in academic programs in Catholic or other private schools.

The evidence appears to us strong that this latter assumption is the correct one. First, if being in an academic program is taken as a dependent variable with all seventeen background variables controlled, there is a strong effect in the sophomore year of being in a Catholic or other private school.[1] Even more important, the same analysis in the senior year shows stronger Catholic and other private effects in the direction of academic program. This indicates that apart from the causes of the relationship at the sophomore level, its increased strength at the senior level can hardly be attributed to selection, but must almost certainly be a consequence of policy differences in the public and private schools in assigning the same kinds of students to academic, general, or vocational programs—not only at the beginning of high school, but also as high school proceeds.

[1] This was done using a makeshift statistical procedure, a dichotomous dependent variable in a regression equation. Although this procedure results in heteroscedasticity, and a maximum likelihood estimate of parameters in a logistic model would have been preferable, the lack of need for more than approximate results made such a usage unnecessary.

Addendum

Finally, this assumption is consistent with work of Alexander and McDill (1976), as well as others, which suggests that more than family background and student ability is involved in high school program assignment or selection.

The near absence of vocational programs in private schools, in our view, is based largely on two points: first, the more traditional educational philosophy in the majority of private schools; and second, the greater cost of vocational programs than of academic programs, combined with the absence of state or federal funds for vocational education in the private sector. It is probably the case that for large numbers of Catholic high schools, a higher proportion of graduates have, historically, gone into skilled trades than did graduates of public schools. But despite this, Catholic schools have seldom had vocational programs, in the past or present.

The second kind of selection-bias criticism that has been made about the finding of a private-school effect has been more fully methodological, a criticism of the ordinary least squares regression analysis we carried out. On this point, the critics are at least in part correct: The analysis, the results of which are given in table 6–7 (showing an effect of roughly one grade level of the private sector schools) is not quite at the state of the art. There are more statistically sophisticated methods designed to eliminate selection bias. But in fact, the field is in disarray on this issue, as exhibited by differences among the critics, some of whom are themselves innovators in this area. Some suggest that the problem is merely one of measurement errors in the independent variables measuring family background, and if we had used a technique like LISREL, designed to overcome the effects of measurement errors, the problem would have been eliminated, and the estimates of school effect would be unbiased (see Campbell, 1981). A second position is that it is necessary to have a measure of at least one variable that affects selection into private schools but not achievement to use as an instrumental variable, and that if this is done, something like two-stage least squares, but with the first stage a probit analysis having selection into a private school as a dependent variable, will be sufficient to eliminate selection bias (see Goldberger, 1982). A third position is that neither of these techniques [nor others, such as that of Heckman (1979) which depends upon the joint distribution of correlated errors in the two equations, rather than solely on instrumental variables] can be assured of eliminating selection bias, because both assume there is no misspecification. Both depend on correct model specification—that is, on use of the right variables (see Cronbach, 1981, Murnane, 1981). In our judgment, the third of these is correct, because any method of correction for selection bias depends upon an assumption that the model is correctly specified—and it is precisely the fact that one does not know exactly the factors that determine selection which creates the largest portion of the problem in the first place. At the same time, if one were to hold to this position consistently, it prevents any statistical analysis in the absence of random assignment to treatments, or something approximating it. Later in this addendum, we pursue other methods of analysis.

Some further points should be made here. It is not true that any biases in our analysis must favor private schools. We have included among the seventeen background factors introduced to control for selection bias seven which are not clearly prior to and unaffected by the child's experience in private school (the two most important of which are the mother's and the father's educational aspirations for the child). If these are affected by the child's achievement in school, then this introduces a bias against finding a private-school effect when one exists. In addition, the basic cognitive skills covered by the tests give less latitude for effects of the greater academic coursework in the private schools than would tests more closely linked to the high school curriculum.

There is no wholly satisfactory way of distinguishing selection from effect in the absence of randomized assignment. For that reason, we chose to address the question of effect by several strategies. In chapter 6, we estimated achievement in public and private schools with statistical controls for all measured background factors which might also affect achievement and be related to the student's educational sector. The method, however, is subject to at least three kinds of difficulties. Two of these would ordinarily lead to attributing to effect of the sector some achievement differences actually due to selection. The other kind of difficulty would ordinarily lead to attributing to selection some achievement differences actually due to differential sector effects. Two of the three may be illustrated by the path diagram in figure X–1(a), and the third, by the path diagram in figure X–1(b).

In figure X–1(a) if there are effects as shown by lines 1, 2, and 3, then the method properly estimates the sector effects. If, however, there are other background factors, not included in the equation, labeled (A) in the diagram, and if there are nonzero effects represented by broken lines 4 and 5, then some achievement differences due to selection into the private sector are mistaken for sector effects. However, the closer to 1.0 the correlation (represented by line 6) between measured and unmeasured background factors, the smaller the error, reducing to zero if the correlation is 1.0.

Still in figure X–1(a), there may be intermediate factors represented by (B), that are *affected* by school sector, and in turn affect achievement.

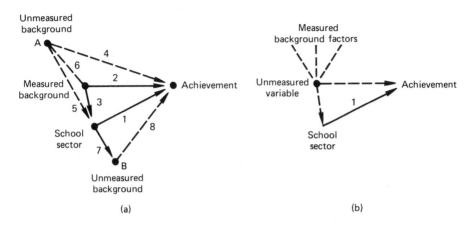

FIGURE X–1
Unmeasured Background and Achievement Models

These intermediate factors include such things as parental interactions and expectations that are responsive to school performance and school demands. If these intermediate factors *are* included in the equation, then some achievement differences due to sector effect—and operating through these factors (B)—are mistakenly attributed to selection.

The third kind of difficulty is shown by figure X–1(b). If the same equation is used as in figure X–1(a), but instead of lines 1, 2, and 3 being true effects, there are unmeasured variables of which the measured background factors are only imperfect indicators, then some differences due to selection will be mistakenly attributed to sector effect.

In the presence of these problems, our strategy consisted of the following:

1. Including as many background factors as possible, so that in figure X–1(a), the possibility of variables like those labeled (A)—that is, with effects 4 and 5 but with a small relation to measured background—is reduced. Also, if figure X–1(b) is the correct specification, the inclusion of many factors, if they are together perfect indicators of the unmeasured variable, will eliminate any difference between the true sector effect and the measured sector effect.
2. Including in the equation some intermediate factors (represented by (B) in figure X–1(a)), so that any tendency toward overestimates of sector effects due to unmeasured factors (A), or toward the paths shown in figure X–1(b), is counterbalanced by a tendency toward underestimates due to inclusion of factors (B).

Given the uncertainties about selection bias, our strategy in the report was not to let the inferences depend on one grand analysis which purported to eliminate all selection bias, but to carry out other kinds of analysis that could provide partially independent information about the differential effect of being in a Catholic school, or other private school, or public school. Thus, the second kind of analysis we carried out to examine this question made use of the sophomore and senior cohorts, estimating growth rates under three different sets of assumptions. Clearly, assumptions are necessary in doing this, but given these assumptions, this second mode of analysis shows greater growth rates in both Catholic and other private sectors than in the public sector. The two modes of analysis would lead to minor differences in inference, but the inference of greater learning in the private sector would remain unchanged.

Another method of analysis was quite different. Beginning with those characteristics of schools and student bodies which we found in chapter 5 to be strongly related to school sector, we found that component of each of these factors (such as homework, absences, and disciplinary climate in the school) which remains when differences in family background are statistically controlled. The remaining differences can be regarded as due to differences in school policy;[2] and the question can be asked within the public school sector: What are the differences in achievement in the public sector (statistically controlling on family background) when those characteristics (homework, absenteeism, disciplinary climate, and student behavior) are as different from those in the average public school as can be attributed to policy differences between public and private schools? In short, if there is a differential effect of public and private schools, and if it does operate through the policies explicitly introduced in the analysis, then one should find somewhat the same effect in public schools with those policies.

The results of the analysis, given in table 6–21, are wholly consistent with the inference of higher achievement in private schools due, at least in part, to the policy differences explicitly introduced in the analysis. For even if there is selection bias remaining in the estimation of a private-

[2]Or, to reinforcing effects of the whole set of family backgrounds in the school. This elimination of effects of the student's own background means that there remain two kinds of possible differential effects of the school: direct effects of school policies, or effects of the backgrounds of other students, which are different in the average private and public school. For example, statistically controlling on a child's own family background shows that there remain differences in the amount of homework an average public school sophomore would do, and the amount that a background-comparable Catholic school sophomore does. But this difference can either be due to differences in school policy or to systematic differences in family backgrounds of other students in the school (which if they lead to greater homework, presumably might have an effect of inducing greater homework for the student in question as well). In principle, these two kinds of private-school effects can be separated, and in fact, they are partly separated in table 6–21, though this is not discussed there. See text for further discussion.

school effect after the background characteristics are statistically controlled, it seems hardly likely that there is the same or greater degree of selection bias associated with the school policies in question, wholly within the public sector. Yet the estimated effects of public schools where these policies are in effect are all positive, and in reading and mathematics are greater than the previously estimated private school effects.

There are two additional implications of this last form of analysis. One is implications about the functioning of schools generally, whether in the public or private sector, and how this functioning affects achievement. This analysis is especially important for its implications about public school policy, a point to which we will return. A second implication concerns the different paths through which private schools have a differential effect on achievement. Because these different kinds of school effects have different implications for policy and different research implications, it is valuable to explicitly distinguish those different effects here. Although the discussion will be in terms of effects of private school policy, the points are applicable to school policy in general, as will become evident. And the analyses on which the discussion is based are in fact carried out wholly in schools in the public sector. Throughout, it will be useful to refer to figure X–2, which shows the different kinds of effects diagrammatically.

Figure X–2 describes the possible ways that school sector may affect the achievement outcome of students. Our focus in the last section of chapter 6 has been on school policies. The graph indicates, first, how school policies can affect achievement. School policies, such as level of homework, curriculum, and disciplinary practices, indirectly affect a student's achievement by influencing that student's behavior (see path 10). This is

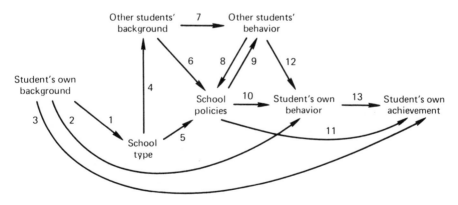

FIGURE X–2
General Model of Student Achievement

the most straightforward path. In addition, those policies directly affect student achievement (illustrated by path 11) and include such factors as teachers' skill or commitment. School policies can also affect a given student's achievement through their impact on other students' behavior (via path 9). That is, the same policies that increase one student's homework or decrease that student's absence or disorderly behavior can be intensified through the medium of other students' behavior (illustrated by the sequence of paths 9 and 12). This report suggests that these school policies vary between sectors, (particularly in the public and other private sector), as well as within sectors, and are indeed related to student achievement.

There is, however, another path through which school type and school policies affect achievement: through the background and behavior of other students (see sequences 4–7–12–13 and 4–6–9–12–13). With a given level of tuition, coupled with a given income distribution, and specific policies of student selection, the school type "determines" the distribution of other students in the school. These background variables greatly affect the other students' behavior in the school (path 7) and may directly affect school policies (path 6), which in turn affect student behavior (paths 9 and 10). Other students' behavior can affect a given student's achievement in either of two ways: through their direct effect on that student's behavior (path 12) (for example, a hard-working and committed student body will ordinarily generate commitment among its incoming members); or through school policies (path 8). A disobedient or truant student population can impede academic and disciplinary policies to the point that the demands are relaxed and the policies accommodated to the students' behavior. This is one aspect of the change that many schools underwent during student protests of the late 1960s and early 1970s.

If private schools were available to a larger segment of the population, then the effect of this alternative path, from school type to other students' background (path 4) becomes important to the question of whether achievement will be increased. In part, what is at issue in disagreements about the effects on achievement of making private schools available to a broader range of students lies in implicit beliefs about the relative importance of paths 4, 6, 7, 8, and 12 compared to 5, 9, 10, and 11. If the principal effect of the school type on achievement is through the sequence 4–7–12–13, or 4–7–8–10–12–13, or 4–6–10–13, then such broadening of availability would have little impact on achievement because the policy change would disrupt path 4. If a large component of the effect is through paths 5, 9, 10, and 11, then such increased access to private education should not dilute the school's impact on achievement. Furthermore, if the effects are through 9, 10, and 11, then any change that resulted in the appropriate changes in school policies, whether or not it had anything to do with private schools, would be effective in increasing achievement. Thus, where such things as curriculum and disciplinary policies have effects on student behavior and achievement that are independent of school type and student background, we can institute changes in any school that would affect achievement. It is for this reason that the results in this chapter are as relevant to public schools as they are to private schools.

It is useful to review, in light of this path diagram, just what our analysis in chapter 6 is designed to do in separating the different type of effects. Tables 5–7 and 5–9 and figure 5–1 showed the combined effects of path 5 from school type to school policies, and 4–7–8—that is, from school type through background through student behavior to policies. Similarly, tables 5–10, 5–13, and 5–14, and figure 5–2 show the combined effects of school policies to student behavior, and 4–7, 4–6–8 (and 4–7–12) from school type through student backgrounds to student behavior.

Table 6–20 is designed to separate [panel (D)] the part of school type effect on school policies (called disciplinary climate chapter 6) that operates through path 5 and eliminates that part which operates by paths 4–6 or 4–7–8. That was done by statistically adjusting the policy differences between public and Catholic or between public and other private for differences in student background. The values shown in part (D) of table 6–20 are estimates of the amount of school policy (that is, "disciplinary climate") difference due to school type directly through path 5.[3]

Similarly, panels A, B, and C in table 6–20 are estimates of the effect of school type on the student's own behavior through school policies (paths 5–10 and 5–9–12) uncontaminated by the path 1–2—that is, by the student's own background. For example, the difference in homework done by sophomores in Catholic schools and sophomores in public schools is 1.9 hours per week; .8 hours of this is accounted for by differences in family background, and 1.1 remains as the estimated differences due to policy differences between the two sectors. Figure X–2 shows, however, that there is another uncontrolled path through which the observed difference due to school type might operate: path 4, and from there via path 7 or 6. What should be controlled in order for the values in rows 1, 2, and 3 to reflect only the effects through paths 5–10 and 5–9–12 is not only the student's own background, but also the backgrounds of other students in the school. If that had been done in table 6–20 then the values in these rows would be estimates of the effect of school type via path 5–10 and 5–9–12.

[3]The dependent variables in this analysis are school means of perceived policies, and thus did not differ within school. Consequently, even though the individual's background was statistically controlled, the effect is to control the backgrounds of all students. Thus the effects controlled out in the analysis are those through paths 4–6–12 plus a path (not shown) from student's own background to school policy.

Panel E of table 6–20 is intended to provide estimates of the effect of school type via path 5–9 to other students' behavior, by controlling on other students' backgrounds and thus blocking path 4–7.[4] However, some of the items in this area not only include other students' behavior, but also the student's own. As a consequence, the items in panel E are measures of the effect of school type via both paths 5–10 and 5–9.

Then, table 6–21 is designed to show the direct effects of school types on achievement through the student's behavior (rows 1, 2, 3 in the table; paths 5–10–13), through school policies directly (row 4 in the table; paths 5–11) and through the student body behavior (row 5 in the table; path 5–9–12–13). The last of these is ambiguous. If the measures were indicative of average student behavior in the school, they could then be modified to exclude the student's own behavior and would truly be measures of other students' behavior in the school. Consequently, a regression analysis including the student's own behavior and the other students' behavior, measured in this way, would give the effects of his own behavior on his achievement and the effect of other students' behavior on his achievement. The ways in which the latter might occur are numerous but, perhaps most importantly, behavior in the classroom affects how much the teacher can teach and the level of distraction for any given student.

However, since the components of "student behavior" as measured and used in tables 6–20 and 6–21 are averages of student perceptions about behavior problems in the school, and because for two of these (fights among students and students threatening teachers) there are no measures of the individual's own behavior, the effects shown for "student behavior" in table 6–21 cannot be unambiguously interpreted as effects of *other* students' behavior. Nevertheless, it appears likely that some part of this effect (which is the strongest shown in the table in nine of the twelve analyses) is due to other students' behavior. This would mean that there is a missing path, say path 14, in figure X–2, from other students' behavior directly to the student's achievement.

The upper part of table 6–22 shows the effects of school policies (as measured by "disciplinary climate" differences) on various aspects of student behavior, as indicated by path 9. The lower part shows the effects of those policies on a student's achievement through the student behavior in the school—that is, through both the student's own behavior and that of other students, paths 10 and 12.[5]

[4]Since the dependent variable is at the level of the school in these cases, the student backgrounds controlled in this analysis effectively become the aggregate student background in the school.

[5]The effects of school policies on a student's achievement through his own and other students' behavior (that is, through paths 10–13 and 9–14) cannot be distinguished here. If the methods used had allowed distinguishing the effects on achievement of the students'

Addendum

The analysis as carried out in this chapter does not, of course, allow for distinguishing the sizes of the effects through all the paths shown in figure X-2. It only begins to allow distinguishing qualitatively between the kinds of effects identified by the various paths shown in figure X-2. Most important for purposes of policies vis-à-vis private schools, of course, is the relative importance of the direct effects of school type on school policy (path 5) and the indirect effects which begin with path 4, the effect of school type upon other students' backgrounds. Policies that would affect the social composition of the students attending schools in the private sector would change path 4, but would not change path 5.

Are There Alternative Ways to Test for a Private-School Effect?

The existence of selection into private schools is sufficiently pervasive that one can ask whether it is possible to definitively determine whether there is a differential effect of these schools, and if so, how strong it is. It is true, of course, that there are several possible kinds of private-school effects, as we have indicated earlier. But the overall question is nevertheless a meaningful one. A first answer is that we believe the three types of analyses we have carried out do give a definitive answer, though the size of the effect is not clear. The second and third analyses suggest somewhat larger effects than the first, which, as indicated earlier, average about one grade level.

A second answer, however, is to ask whether there are other or additional types of data that could give very much better results. A common response is that longitudinal data would do so. But it is not clear that this would be true, given that there are background differences between students in public schools and those in private ones. Just as these background differences are related to the level of achievement, they are related to the rate of growth in achievement. (If they were not, their relation to level of achievement would be difficult to explain.) Thus "selection bias" haunts longitudinal studies almost as much as it does cross-sectional studies.

What would be desirable, in the absence of randomized assignment to

---

own behavior and that of the other students (path 13 and missing path 14), then the effect of school policies through other students' behavior and own behavior would simply be in proportion to the sizes of paths 14 and 13. This must be so, since the effect of school policies, a variable that is constant for all students in the school, on a given student's behavior and on the average behavior of all students cannot even in principle be distinguished.

schools, is a baseline level of achievement gains over a given length of time, in the absence of school. The achievement which occurs in the presence of school could then be superimposed upon that baseline. There is research (see Heyns, 1977) which has attempted to examine the effects of schooling per se in this way, using the summer nonschool period to provide the baseline. It appears that this technique, which requires three measurements (for example, Fall, Spring, Fall, or Spring, Fall, Spring) is more broadly applicable—not just to examine the effects of school versus no school, but also to examine the differential effects of different school programs. For if this approach can be used to examine the effects of school per se, resulting in an estimate of the size of those effects, then it should also be useful for examining the differential effects of different school programs.

Another general strategy for an answer to the question is the use of multiple modes of analysis, as carried out in the body of the report. Not much can be said about this strategy in general, for the feasibility of different analyses differs in different circumstances. Nevertheless, the general strategy appears a wise one—using the consistency of partially independent modes of analysis to increase or decrease confidence in the inferences drawn from any one.

Using the data available in this report, additional modes of analysis do exist which will give further information on the specific issue of private school effects. One strategy is to employ a more sophisticated method for correcting for selection bias than was done in table 6–7. Another strategy is to use an alternate method of estimating achievement differences. Since the release of the report, we have pursued both modes of analyses and will discuss our findings here. An analysis using Heckman's (1979) method for correcting for selection bias will be reviewed at the end of this section. As an alternate form of estimating achievement, we have chosen to take the approach mentioned in chapter 6, footnote 5, page 136. This analysis will be discussed first followed by a modification of it designed to test for residual selection bias.

The alternative estimate of school effects, follows a method originally proposed by Donald Campbell. Consider two groups with achievement that would be anticipated equal, say s, in the absence of a differential school effect. Then if private schools are available to the first group, with p_1 choosing a private school, and not to the second, and there is a school effect of size c, the achievement in the first group, averaged over both public schools and private schools, should be $s + p_1c$, while it is only s in the second group. Or more generally, if private schooling is less available to the second group, with only p_2 in the private school, the achievement should be $s + p_2c$ in the second group. The difference, d, between achievement in the two groups is $(p_1 - p_2)c$, and since p_2 and p_1 are known, c may be estimated as $c = d/(p_1 - p_2)$.

Two groups which can be assumed to have equal achievement, other things constant, are Catholics and non-Catholics. Catholics, however, have much greater access to a private school. For Catholics, $p_1 = .195$, and for non-Catholics, $p_2 = .051$, giving a difference of .144. Thus a bias-free estimation of the private (mostly Catholic) school effect is given as $d/.144$.

The problem with this approach is that unless one can be fairly certain that the achievement in the two groups is—in the absence of private school attendance—equal, the method fails. More generally, the method is highly sensitive to small differences in s for group 1 and group 2, so long as the denominator, $p_1 - p_2$, is small.

The difference, d, can be calculated in two different ways: first, simply by the raw difference between Catholics and non-Catholics, and second, by the difference which remains after statistically controlling on variables related to achievement on which Catholics and non-Catholics might differ. The latter is done by a regression analysis on the total sample, using background factors (the seventeen used elsewhere in the report) and an additional dummy variable for Catholic religion.

The six regression analyses (three tests in each of two grades) resulted in regression coefficients which when divided by .144 give the following estimates for c, the effect of attending a Catholic school. (These numbers should be comparable to row 2 of table 6–7) Standard errors are in paren-

	Reading	Vocabulary	Mathematics
Sophomores	.54 (.18)	.73 (.16)	1.59 (.34)
Seniors	−.43 (.20)	.38 (.17)	.42 (.37)

The comparable raw differences when divided by .144 are

	Reading	Vocabulary	Mathematics
Sophomores	1.53	1.96	4.94
Seniors	.63	1.53	3.69

theses. These results indicate much larger effects of Catholic school attendance for sophomores than the analyses in chapter 6 and smaller effects for seniors. The results therefore appear to indicate that the assumption that s (public school achievement) is comparable for Catholics and non-Catholics, even after controlling for possible background differences, is not a valid one—or that the divisor, .144, is sufficiently small as to make the results unstable. However, the evidence they do provide is in the direction of a positive effect of Catholic school on achievement (except for reading, at the senior level).

The issue of selection effects can be addressed more directly using the same general strategy as the previous method, but among Catholics in public schools. Some Catholic students have a Catholic school nearby, making attendance at Catholic schools easy; others do not. Our sample design does not allow distinguishing these two sets of Catholic students, but it does allow distinguishing a subset of those with access. Each of the public schools in our sample can be identified as one with or without a sampled Catholic school in the area (using five digit zip codes). One knows then, that Catholics in public schools in some areas had the opportunity to attend Catholic school, but did not, and constitute the "nonselected" Catholic students in an area. In the remaining public schools, some Catholic students did not have access to a Catholic school but some did (that is, a Catholic school that was in the same area but not in our sample). Catholic students in these remaining public schools should be higher achieving by the amount of the selection bias. Adjusting the average achievement by use of the statistical controls will give a difference attributable to a selection bias not controlled in our earlier analysis.

Both the adjusted (using the five-variable background statistical controls used in table 6–9) and unadjusted differences are shown below; they are averaged over the three tests to give a single number at each grade level; and as a further control, the same comparison for non-Catholics (that is, those who are in public schools in the same five-digit zip code area as a sampled Catholic school, and those in public schools not in those areas) is made. The amount of selection bias is the achievement in public schools in those areas without a nearby Catholic school minus achievement in public schools in those areas with a nearby Catholic school. If this difference is zero, it is evidence that all the selection bias has been removed; if it is positive, it is evidence that not all the selection bias has been removed.

	Catholic Students	Non-Catholic Students
Adjusted with Five-Variable		
Background Regression		
Sophomores	−.20	.16
Seniors	.02	.103
Raw Differences		
Sophomores	.21	.26
Seniors	.19	.20

If there is a selection effect, then the Catholic column should be positive, as it is in three of four cases; but the non-Catholic column shows in all cases a positive value that is slightly larger. Thus, non-Catholics are used as a comparison to control for unmeasured characteristics associated with the zip code areas in which the Catholic schools in the sample are located. They show that there is in general lower achievement among non-Catholics in those areas (even after controlling in the regression on family income, mother's and father's education, race, and Hispanic ethnicity) than in zip code areas where there are no sampled Catholic schools. This means that the positive values for three of the four Catholic members, using both raw and adjusted values, do not indicate a selection bias favoring Catholic schools. If anything, it appears that any bias in the main analysis is in the other direction. Therefore, the test using the zipcode areas provides no evidence that there is an unremoved selection bias favoring Catholic school achievement in the analysis of chapter 6.

Another strategy which has been advocated is the use of econometric models designed to eliminate selection bias (Goldberger, 1981).[6] These models have been designed for use in estimating, for example, the effect of a manpower training program on subsequent wages when there is self-selection into the manpower training program. Ordinarily, the necessity for such modeling arises because the dependent variable (for instance, wages) is observed only for the "selected" portion of the population (see Heckman, 1979), introducing bias into regression estimates.

The problem this approach addresses is this: Suppose the correct structure of effects is that shown by paths 1, 2, and 3 in X–1(a). But as shown by path 5 in Figure X–1(a), there may be unmeasured factors which affect entry into a sector and also affect achievement (path 4). To the degree that these factors are not tapped by the measured background variables, then a selection bias occurs. The Heckman technique allows one to estimate this selection bias and adjust for its effect on achievement. In many ways the problem it addresses is simply model misspecification error. Thus, the technique should apply not just to the sector effects, but to any of the independent variables which are affected by variables excluded from the model but related to the dependent variable.

Nevertheless, effects can be estimated and achievement estimates in each section adjusted accordingly. Two equations must be identified for such an analysis: one, a probit equation, which predicts entry into the private (or public) sector; the other, a regression equation which predicts

---

[6] A more appropriate use of the model would be to estimate the effects of various factors on achievement among seniors in 1982 on whom observations as sophomores were made in 1980, but who are not all present in 1982. If no testing of dropouts were to be done in 1982, the method could be used to correct for dropouts when estimating effects of background and school factors on achievement.

the achievement outcome, controlling on the probability of having the observed background characteristic governing selection, into the private (or public) sector.

Two model specifications were used. In both, the sophomore mathematics (full) test was used as the outcome variable. The first model assumes that all the variables which affect achievement directly also affect entry into the private or public sector. Thus, the selectivity bias control in the achievement regression equation captures the nonlinear effects of the set of variables in question on the achievement outcome. For both the probit equation predicting sector entry and regression equation predicting mathematics achievement, all but two of the seventeen variables used earlier were entered into the equation: father's education and father's expectations for college were deleted.[7] Two variables were added to the analysis because of their relationship to entry into the private sector: religious background (Catholic versus non-Catholic) and region (Northeast versus other). The results for this model were not reasonable.[8]

For the second model specification we identified three variables as instrumental—that is, they affect entry into the private or public sector, but do not have a direct effect on achievement: income, religion, and educational expectations in the eighth grade. Each variable captures some major factor thought to contribute to private school entry: parents' financial assets, religious value preferences, and early educational ambitions. The estimates for increments to achievement due to being in a private sector school using this second model of selection and achievement were again greater than the raw increments, a result at odds with our other analyses, which showed that controlling on background factors reduces the raw increments by a half to two thirds or more. The dependence of these results on model specifications and their instability with these data suggest that this potential avenue toward separating selection from a sector effect is not helpful in this particular case.

---

[7] The program available for this analysis required a listwise deletion of cases and only 70 percent of the respondents had usable data on father's education. Sophomore response to item BB039 (father's education) included 8 percent who said they did not live with father, 17 percent who said they did not know, 4 percent multiple punch, and 2 percent who either refused to answer or had missing data.

[8] The results of the first stage, the probit analysis, are shown in appendix table A–7 for both models. The probit analysis showed quite reasonable coefficients; the second stage analysis is where the problems arose.

The estimated increments due to being in a Catholic or other private school were not only positive, they were greater than the raw increments shown in table 6–7 and in fact, put scores for private sectors beyond the test limits.

Addendum

Are the Conclusions Concerning the Effect of Private Schools on Segregation the Same in All Regions?

One objection to the report's results on segregation has been that segregation is properly compared only within a local area. For example, part of the segregation in the public sector results from the fact that blacks and whites are distributed differently over localities and regions of the country. What appears to be a high degree of segregation (.49 in the index for black-white segregation given in the report) is in part due to geographic separation; and this inflation of the measure of segregation is probably greater in the public sector, where the proportion of blacks varies over a greater range from locality to locality than in the private sector.

There is merit to this point. It is not possible, however, to measure the degree of segregation or interracial contact within each locality, because the survey covers only a sample of schools. The closest that it is possible to come to examining what the internal segregation would be in the public sector if it were calculated on a district-by-district basis and averaged over the country is to use published figures from several years ago. Data for 1972, published in 1975, give as the average segregation within districts of the public sector a figure of .29 (Coleman, Kelly, and Moore, 1975:34) There will have been some changes since 1972, though it is difficult to know in which direction, because, on the one hand, some court-ordered desegregation has occurred since that time, and, on the other, there has been continuing resegregation (see Farley, et al., 1980).

This index of average within-district segregation, though not the most desirable for comparison purposes, is the closet available. It suggests that most of the .49 segregation calculated for these data remains as within-district segregation, and thus that the comparison with the within-sector segregation measures in the private sector (some of which are also in part due to geographic separation) may be usefully made, as was done in the report.

EXAMINATION OF SEGREGATION BY REGION

One way to reduce the geographic variability in racial and ethnic distribution is to estimate the effects of the private sector on segregation (between blacks and whites and between Anglos and Hispanics) at a regional level.

The sample of public schools is representative for the nine census regions of the country. However, the Catholic and other private samples were selected to be representative only for the broader division of four regions. Consequently, it is possible to compare for the four regions (East, South, Midwest, and West) the segregation in the public and private sectors, and to examine the overall contribution that the private sector makes to segregation or integregration in each region. For the other private sector, though, there are only twenty-seven schools; and since in this analysis the school is the relevant unit, inferences about regional differences in the other private sector can only be made with extreme uncertainty. Consequently, the following analysis is restricted to comparisons between the public and Catholic sectors, and between these sectors and the regions as wholes.

Table X–1 shows first the proportions of non-Hispanic whites, non-Hispanic blacks, and Hispanics in each of the school sectors in each of the four regions. It is important to note that the standard errors to the proportions, particularly in the Catholic sector are quite large. This means that any interpretations must be done with recognition that a high degree of uncertainty is involved. The comparisons, therefore, in this section must be regarded with some caution.

With these precautions, it is useful to note the following indications from the data:

1. Catholic schools have proportions of Hispanics that are comparable in every region to the proportions in the public schools.
2. In the Midwest and West, the proportions of blacks in the Catholic schools are not greatly different from those in the public schools. In the East, the Catholic schools have less than half the proportion of blacks that the public schools do. In the South, the disparity is much greater, with the Catholic schools having only about a fourth the proportion of blacks as in the public schools.
3. The regional differences in proportion of black and Hispanic children are themselves great, with a much higher proportion of black children in the South than in the East, Midwest, and West.

Turning to the measures of interracial contact (s_{bw} and s_{wb}) and segregation (r_{bw}) shown in table X–2 for blacks and whites, the following generalizations can be drawn:

1. The levels of interracial contact are highest, and the level of segregation the lowest, for secondary schools overall in the South; and among the public schools only, this is true as well. The Catholic schools of the South also show greater interracial contact and less segregation than in the Midwest or West, but slightly less integration than in the East.
2. In three regions, the internal segregation (r_{bw}, which takes as given the proportion of blacks and whites in each sector) is lower in the Catholic sector

TABLE X-1

Percentage Distribution of Whites, Blacks, and
Hispanics in Public and Catholic Schools
by Region[a] Spring 1980

Race-Ethnicity	U.S. Total	Public	Catholic
1. East			
Number (in thousands)	1,539.7	1,319.3	152.8
Percentage	100.0	100.0	100.0
White	80.9	79.4	88.0
Black	11.4	12.5	6.0
Hispanic	5.1	5.4	4.3
Other	2.7	2.8	1.8
2. South			
Number	2,118.3	1,958.0	77.5
Percentage	100.0	100.0	100.0
White	66.8	65.2	79.7
Black	22.9	24.4	6.0
Hispanic	7.9	8.1	10.8
Other	2.3	2.3	3.5
3. Midwest			
Number	1,899.3	1,726.1	152.2
Percentage	100.0	100.0	100.0
White	86.9	86.8	87.4
Black	7.5	7.7	5.1
Hispanic	3.7	3.6	5.4
Other	1.9	1.9	2.1
4. West			
Number	1,195.9	1,097.4	44.8
Percentage	100.0	100.0	100.0
White	72.4	72.3	72.0
Black	5.2	5.1	5.4
Hispanic	12.9	12.7	16.1
Other	9.7	9.9	6.5

NOTE: Details may not add to totals due to rounding. The figures under "U.S. Total" include the students in the non-Catholic private schools.

[a] The four regions used here and in tables X-2 and X-3 are composed of the following U.S. Census regions: (1) "East": New England and Middle Atlantic; (2) "South": South Atlantic, East South Central, and West South Central; (3) "Midwest": East North Central and West North Central; and (4) "West": Mountain and Pacific (see table 2-3 for the states included within these regions).

than the public sector. In the West it is higher. Comparing the public-sector segregation with the regional total shows that in the East, Midwest, and West reabsorption of private sector students into the public sector in exactly the same way that blacks and whites are currently distributed there would

TABLE X–2

Indices of Interracial Contact and
Segregation for Blacks and Whites
in Public and Catholic Schools by
Region: Spring 1980

Measure[a]	U.S. and Regional Totals	Public	Catholic
1. Overall National:			
S_{bw}	.39	.38	.58
S_{wb}	.07	.07	.04
R_{bw}	.49	.49	.31
2. East:			
S_{bw}	.38	.37	.63
S_{wb}	.05	.06	.05
R_{bw}	.52	.54	.22
3. South:			
S_{bw}	.41	.41	.61
S_{wb}	.14	.15	.05
R_{bw}	.38	.37	.24
4. Midwest:			
S_{bw}	.33	.32	.50
S_{wb}	.03	.03	.03
R_{bw}	.62	.64	.42
5. West:			
S_{bw}	.41	.41	.39
S_{wb}	.03	.03	.03
R_{bw}	.43	.44	.46

[a] S_{bw}: The proportion of the average black student's schoolmates who are white.

S_{wb}: The proportion of the average white student's schoolmates who are black.

R_{bw} (mathematically equal to R_{wb}): The degree to which blacks and whites are segregated; ranges from 0 = no segregation to 1 = complete segregation.

increase the segregation in the region as a whole or at least keep it constant. In the South, however, the disparity between the proportions of blacks in public and private sectors more than compensates for the lesser internal segregation in the private sector. Thus, reabsorption of private-sector students in the South into public schools would decrease the black-white segregation.

Table X–3 shows the measures of interethnic contact and segregation for Hispanics and Anglos. The results are similar to those for black-white

Addendum

TABLE X–3

Indices of Interracial Contact and Segregation for Hispanics and Non-Hispanic Whites in Public and Catholic Schools by Region: Spring 1980

Measure[a]	U.S. and Regional Totals	Public	Catholic
1. Overall National:			
S_{hw}	.53	.53	.63
S_{wh}	.05	.05	.05
R_{hw}	.30	.30	.25
2. East:			
S_{hw}	.49	.47	.61
S_{wh}	.03	.03	.03
R_{hw}	.39	.40	.30
3. South:			
S_{hw}	.48	.46	.65
S_{wh}	.06	.06	.09
R_{hw}	.29	.29	.19
4. Midwest:			
S_{hw}	.74	.73	.78
S_{wh}	.03	.03	.05
R_{hw}	.15	.16	.11
5. West:			
S_{hw}	.52	.54	.46
S_{wh}	.09	.10	.10
R_{hw}	.28	.25	.36

[a] S_{hw}: The proportion of the average Hispanic student's schoolmates who are white.

S_{wh}: The proportion of the average white student's schoolmates who are Hispanic.

R_{hw} (mathematically equal to R_{wh}): The degree to which Hispanics and whites are segregated; ranges from 0 = no segregation to 1 = complete segregation.

contact and segregation, with the West for Hispanics replacing the South for blacks. There is a difference, however. In the South, the segregative impact of the private sector is through an underrepresentation of blacks in that sector, not through internal segregation. In the West, the segregative impact of the private sector is not through underrepresentation, but

219

through greater internal segregation between non-Hispanic whites and Hispanics within the private sector. In the other three regions, the internal segregation is less in the private sector, and comparison of r_{hw} in the public sector with the region total shows that the overall contribution of the private sector is toward reduced segregation. In the West, however, the overall contribution is toward increased segregation (.28 compared to .25), and in contrast to all other comparisons, the internal segregation within the private sector is greater than that in the public.

Altogether, these regional comparisons indicate that for both blacks and Hispanics, the private schools in three regions of the country have an overall integrative impact on the system. In the South for blacks, however, and the West for Hispanics, this pattern is reversed, due to the much greater proportion of blacks enrolled, and in the West due to the greater internal segregation between Hispanics and Anglos in the private sector.

These two regional discrepancies suggest what may be a broader principle, for they both occur in the region where the given minority (black in the South, Hispanics in the West) is most numerous. The principle they suggest is that schools in the private sector will be more likely to exert a segregative impact where the proportion minority is greater.

What Is the Proper Role of Social Research in Relation to Social Policy?

Our conception of the role of social policy research grows out of a broader philosophy of policy research in modern society. It is this philosophy of policy research that was responsible for this report; and the general approach of the report, as well as the reasons it has generated controversy, can be better understood by first understanding this philosophical position.

A PHILOSOPHY OF SOCIAL POLICY RESEARCH

There are two fundamentally different schools of thought concerning the role of scientific research (whether social research and social policy, or research in natural science and policy to which that research is relevant). One school of thought sees policy research as a private dialogue between the policy maker and the policy researcher. The policy maker poses the problem and the questions, and the policy researcher acts as adviser to the

220

prince: to answer the questions on the basis of existing scientific knowledge if possible, and if not, to gather the right kind of data and analyze it properly to arrive at a conclusive answer.

This conception is of a clear, orderly process, with the final stage being implementation of the policy researcher's results. The scientific answers are conclusive, sources of controversy are stilled by the conclusiveness of the research results, and rational action based on scientific evidence replaces interest group politics. The other school of thought—the one to which we subscribe—sees policy research as a largely public activity, one in which there is no "policy maker," and in which the policy researcher's role is that of the servant of multiple interests. Interested parties define the issues to which policy research should be addressed; and interested parties are the principal users of the research results. Policy is the resultant of pressures from a multitude of interests, and properly so. The role of policy research is to inform these interests. And the role of publicly-funded policy research is to inform all interests—not just those who happen to be in control of the government apparatus. The proper function of policy research is to make it possible for each of these interested parties to better see the lines along which to pursue its interests. Sometimes this will reduce conflicts, as when research shows that two parties' interests, which previously appeared opposed, in fact lead to the same or similar policies. But often it will increase conflict, by making it possible for interested parties to see how they are harmed by particular policies.

In such a process, research results do not replace interest groups—they are used by interest groups. The result is often disorderly, with conflict, in which the contribution of the policy research to the end result is that of raising the level of discourse which leads to policy: facilitating disposal of false issues, narrowing attention and political conflict to the important issues. The research results cannot specify policy to be implemented; they are only one of a number of inputs into the policy process. And ordinarily, they should be an input which makes that process a more open one, helping to provide a window to the consequences of policy that enables more persons to effectively press for their interests and ideals. This does not of course imply that policy research can provide each interest the results it wants; some interests may be harmed by results of particular research. It is rather to say that these results should be available to all and in full view, and that the very openness of the process will lead to disputes over what the research data really show.

It is this second view of social policy research that has shaped the research that resulted in this report on public and private schools. At various points throughout the research, this philosophy guided the steps that were taken and in the following paragraphs, we describe some of those steps.

Pluralistic Research Design. The use of pluralistic research design implies that the principal questions to be studied within broad policy areas should be determined not by the research investigator, nor by a government official, but by inputs from interested parties. The interested parties in the areas covered by High School and Beyond are the various individuals and organizations who are directly affected by policies at all levels of government in secondary and postsecondary education and by policies related to youth employment. Although these interested parties include government agencies with policy roles in these areas, they are primarily interested parties outside government. Without such pluralism in design, the research design will be largely shaped by a narrow set of interests, either those served by the values of the research investigator or those to which government agencies are currently most responsive. (The dramatic shifts in the latter with the change in federal government administrations in January 1981 should be sufficient evidence that government agencies are not equally attentive to all interests, despite expressed goals of "serving the people.")

This view is at variance with that of many social scientists, who generally believe it should be they, the professionals, who determine what questions are appropriate for study. It is at variance also with that of most federal government officials, whose conception of the appropriate set of interested parties is limited to those federal agencies with policies in this area.[11]

To implement this view, NORC, during the design stage of this research, engaged in a search process for inputs into the research design, beginning at the level of state legislative committee hearings (in Illinois) and congressional committee hearings and involving interviews with an extensive set of interested parties.[12] It may well be that there are other more effective institutions for insuring pluralistic input into policy research (something, for example, patterned after congressional or regulatory agency hearings). The design of such institutions is an important question, but not one we can pursue here.

[11] Evidence for this last is in the fact that when, in the design of research like High School and Beyond, input is sought from outside the agency (that is, through a "user's conference"), the set of persons convened ordinarily consists of officials in various federal agencies who might have use for the data. Even state officials are generally ignored. Exceptions to this parochial view of interested parties may be found in the design of some surveys by the Bureau of the Census, particularly surveys of economic institutions and local governments.

[12] The results are contained in "Pluralistic Policy Research Design," by James Coleman, Virginia Bartot, Noah Lewin-Epstein, and Lorayn Olson, report submitted to NCES, 1979.

Addendum

Pluralistic Access to Data and Its Reports. Pluralistic access implies that no party, neither government agency nor research contractor, should have special rights to the data nor to reports based on analysis of the data. Rather, the data should be freely available and easily accessible to all, ranging from academic investigators to government agencies to interested parties outside government. The necessity of this access lies in the self-corrective mechanism that arises from the conflicting interests. The conflicts among interests will help ensure that any result which is potentially harmful to some interest will be subject to intense scrutiny with full use of the available data.

The intensity of the controversy that was generated by the Public and Private Schools report illustrates this scrutiny. The report, with results that were more favorable to private schools than to public schools, immediately led many whose values or interests were opposed to those results to examine the report's methods carefully, or to introduce data that disagreed with the report's results. (For example, the National Assessment of Educational Progress, carried out under the auspices of the Education Commission of the States, a body generated by the public school systems of the states, immediately released a report based on a preliminary analysis of their data, showing no achievement benefits of private schools.) Such attention is valuable; from it may come more correct assessment of public and private schools, as well as greater insight into educational practice.

The perspective that leads to the view we express here is that the less constrained this competitive process in research, the more nearly correct will be the research results which ultimately have an impact on policy. In the case of the Public and Private Schools report, there were two meetings convened for exactly this purpose, one by the National Institute of Education, on July 21 and 22, 1981 and one by the National Academy of Sciences on July 23, 1981. The convening of these conferences, one of which focused on data from two additional research sources, and one of which focused only on the Public and Private Schools report, exemplify both an open competitive process and the emergence of an institutional structure that may improve the quality of research results. It is not always easy for investigators whose reports are subject to such scrutiny, but such processes are valuable.

Most research investigators profess a belief in free access to data (though some would limit that access to "disinterested academics," excluding interested parties). Yet it is not always easy to obtain data, expeditiously, from researchers, especially if it is likely that one may use it to challenge the investigator's research results. Government agencies, however, are sometimes blatant in their attempts to ensure that data from research they have commissioned not be used in ways that can hurt them. Techniques used to avoid this may include the use of small, compliant research organizations, often wholly dependent on the agency for their existence and seldom associated with a university; they may also include the use of extensive red tape to block access to data by outsiders; and they may include the burying of report results which are inimical to agency interests.[13]

NCES, as a statistical agency, has had a policy, though sometimes executed with considerable deliberation, of making its data bases available to outside parties. For High School and Beyond, NORC proposed to greatly increase this accessibility by maintaining, or creating for NCES to maintain, an on-line data base, making it possible for any researcher with a computer terminal and a codebook to make immediate use of the data. Unfortunately, NCES did not agree to this proposal. However, the data were made available by the somewhat more cumbersome means of data tapes, provided to NCES by NORC in December 1980 and made available by NCES in March 1981. Thus, the tapes containing the data on the basis of which the analyses of this report were prepared are available (we trust with little red tape) from NCES.

Had the data been instantly available via an on-line data base, disagreements with our report's analysis and interpretation of the data could have taken a more direct form, and the issues could have been more quickly resolved. Some of the distortions necessarily introduced by the media when the sequence of report-issuing, critiques, and reanalysis takes place in a time frame of weeks and even months might vanish with such data accessibility. It is unfortunate that this case could not have provided a test of the effects of on-line immediate availability.

Policy Research Analyses Directed to Potential Areas of Policy Conflict. The philosophical position stated earlier holds that policy reserach should be directed to areas of policy conflict, not to more diffuse goals. The implication of this is that the research results are likely to be controversial and disputed, as has been true with this report. The implication also is that the results are more likely to be useful in setting policy than if

[13] The most prominent recent example of the last of these devices was the burying by the Department of Health, Education & Welfare of analyses of the income maintenance experiments in Seattle and Denver which showed large increases in divorce rates and reductions in remarriage rates in the experimental groups. An investigation by GAO cleared HEW of intentionally hiding the results, but attributed the burying of the results (which was effective for several years) to poor administration. It is interesting, however, that the results of this "poor administration" were to promote the results beneficial to the agency's policy interests and hide those inimical to its interests. Institutions insuring free access are necessary to protect against such "poor administration."

224

the research avoided such direct examination of policy-related issues. Yet in the eyes of some social scientists, this leads to "bumper sticker sociology," by which is meant results are of direct use to some interested party and lend themselves to simple slogans.

It is our view that most research relevant to policy will be used by parties interested in that policy area—and there may very well be misuse of the results (although the judgment that a particular use is misuse often depends on the values or interests of the party doing the judging). The process will be disorderly, and there will not be a nice, neat progression toward truth.

To implement the view that policy research should directly address issues of policy concern, the research group at NORC designed four analyses focused directly on areas of policy.[14] The Public-Private report is one of these.

The Extent of Disciplinary or Governmental Filtering Processes. The difference of views about the proximity of policy research goals to policy issues is closely related to different views of the way in which the truth is arrived at through the use of policy research, and the role of other social scientists in filtering and processing research results before they are released to the general public. For example, one social scientist was sufficiently concerned that this report was to be released to the general public without what he regarded as sufficient scientific review that he organized six other social scientists to quickly review the report so that he could distribute their reviews, along with his own, at the April 7 conference at which results from the report were presented publicly. Those six social scientists apparently agreed with this position that more extensive filtering within social science is appropriate. Some were undoubtedly motivated also by opposition to the results of the report, but such motivations are necessarily present.[15]

Our view is that the danger of suppression of results by extensive social science filtering of the results is greater than the danger of confusing the public and discrediting social science due to premature release of insufficiently reviewed results. The values of social scientists opposing a given

---

[14] The other three reports are "Discipline and Order in American High Schools," by Thomas DiPrete, "Youth Employment During High School," by Noah Lewin-Epstein, and "Hispanic Students in United States Schools," by Francois Nielsen and Roberto Fernandez.

[15] The seven social scientists are Donald Campbell, Robert Crain (who organized the set of reviews), Lee Cronbach, Michael Kirst, Robert Klitgard, David Kratwohl, and Richard Murnane. Six of the reviews (excluding that of Cronbach) together with the summary of the report, are published in Educational Research Service School Research Forum, April 1981. The ERS Forum is sponsored by eight national associations of school administrators and school boards.

result, which can exercise a salutary influence in motivating a critical examination of results, can also lead to unwarranted suppression of results if in the social science filtering process the criticism generated by these values is allowed to block release.

On the other hand, of course, is the fact that once released and reported in the mass media, research results, even if later scientifically discredited, have a life of their own. There is often more news content in an initial announcement of results than in subsequent correction. What is obviously necessary is the creation of institutions which would have little likelihood of suppressing research results but would reduce the distortions introduced by the mass media. However, the design of appropriate institutions is not a topic we can pursue here.

Values and Objectivity. There is, according to the philosophical position that has guided this research, no conflict between the recognition that values play a part in research and the assertion that objectivity is possible in social policy research. Values shape the research questions posed, as well as the implications one draws from a particular set of research results. But this does not preclude objectivity in the execution of the research.

It is useful at this point to say something about the initiation of this research. The first author, Coleman, undertook this analysis, rather than focusing on another topic, in part because of a belief that public schools have come, especially in recent years, to function less well than they should, and that this decline in performance would not have come about if more parents had a choice of the elementary and secondary schools their children attend. Thus, we were not surprised by the results showing greater achievement for comparable students in private schools. (Such an initial predisposition must of course be guarded against by especially extensive analysis to insure that results are not in some way brought about by that predisposition.) But neither would we have been greatly surprised by the opposite results. The critics as well, have values; in many cases their values were disturbed by the results we found. These values stem from one or more of a variety of beliefs: belief in separation of church and state, leading to opposition to any aid to religiously operated schools; belief that the private sector introduces an inegalitarian element into American education, and that an increase in the size of that sector, even if entrance to it is made less dependent on income, would increase the inegalitarianism even more (a belief which seems, to us, oblivious to the stratification that has developed in the public schools system); a negative reaction to market processes; positive reaction to the public school as a communal socializing institution (again, in our view, a belief that overlooks the realities of public schools in metropolitan areas); and in some cases, sentiments against religious education.[16]

While all of these values, some competing, may shape the research questions the research questions posed and the presumed policy implications, the empirical results obtained under such circumstances can be objective. Even while all researchers can—and should—search for consistency of results, objectivity is obtainable. But authoritative judgment is rarely, if ever, obtained. Instead, competing views of reality are tested and analyzed thereby sustaining, modifying, or rejecting some views.

---

[16] The last source of motivation we are freer to comment on than if any of us were Catholic or members of other religious groups strongly represented in private education. It is useful also to say that all of us are products of public schools, and that one (Coleman) has children, all of whom spent some years in public schools but all of whom later attended private schools.

APPENDIX A

Statistical References

Calculation of Standard Errors of Estimates

Neither standard errors nor confidence intervals are reported in the crosstabulations of this book. Instead, this section presents information that allows calculation of approximate standard errors for most percentages based on student data.

The general equation of calculating the approximate standard error of a percentage is

$$\text{s.e. } (p) = A \sqrt{p(100-p)/n}$$

where p is the percentage for which the standard error is to be calculated; s.e. (p) is the approximate standard error of p; A is a correction factor, which increases with the departure of the sample from a simple random sample through clustering or other aspects of the sample design; and n is the unweighted number of students in the particular class over which the percentage is calculated. (For example, table 3–1 estimates that 5.8 percent of sophomores in Catholic schools are black. The unweighted number of sophomores in Catholic schools, which is 2,831—see table A–1—is the correct value of n for calculating the standard error of this percentage.[1])

[1] This does not take into account sample size reduction by nonresponse. Throughout the report, nonresponses are excluded from the base on which the percentage is calculated. An approximate reduction of n for nonresponse can be determined from the marginals provided in "High School and Beyond Information for Users, Base Year (1980) Data," available from NCES.

TABLE A-1

Correction Factors and Sample Sizes for Classes on Which Most Percentages From Student Data in Report Are Based

| | U.S. Total | Public | Private | | | High-Performance Schools | |
			Total[a]	Catholic	Other Private	Public[b]	Private[c]
Sophomores							
A (correction factor)	1.614	1.529	2.160	1.942	2.597	1.529	2.597
n (sample size)	30,263	26,448	3,462	2,831	631	370	353
Seniors							
A (correction factor)	1.620	1.509	2.255	2.038	2.689	1.509	2.689
n (sample size)	28,465	24,891	3,248	2,697	551	311	326

[a] The correction factor A for total private is calculated as an average of the Catholic and other private correction factors, weighting the Catholic correction factor by 2 and the other private by 1.

[b] The high performance public correction factor is taken to be the same as that for the public sector as a whole.

[c] The high performance private correction factor is taken to be the same as that for the other private sector.

Statistical References

The values of A and n for classes on which most of the percentages in this report are based are given in table A–1. When percentages are based on different classifications or on subclassifications within each of these classifications, it is appropriate to use the subclass size together with the largest correction factor of those shown in the table that could apply to the subclass.

The equation for calculating standard errors, together with the data shown in table A–1, were used to calculate approximate standard errors for percentages of 50 percent, 10 percent, and 90 percent (the latter two of which have the same standard error). These are given in table A–2.

It should be emphasized that these standard errors are approximations intended merely to provide guidance as to the confidence interval around a percentage estimate, or the chance that a difference between two percentages could be due to sampling error.

For estimation of approximate standard errors for data from the school questionnaires, a conservative estimate can be obtained by assuming A to be the same as for student data, and taking n from the number of schools shown for the relevant class in table A–3; a nonconservative estimate can be obtained by assuming $A = 1$ for all classes of schools.

Calculation of Measures of the Distribution of Students Within Sectors

The measures employed in chapter 3 for describing variations in student mix among schools within a sector will be described here. The measure of interracial contact within a sector is constructed as follows. If we number the schools in the sector $1, \ldots k, \ldots n$, and consider the first school, there is a given proportion of whites in that school. Call this p_{1w}. There is also a certain number of blacks in the school. Call this n_{1b}. Then, for this number of blacks, the proportion of whites in their school is p_{1w}. If we weight this proportion by the number of blacks, and average over all schools, we obtain the desired measure, which we will call s_{bw}, the proportion of white children in the school of the average black child.

$$s_{bw} = \frac{\sum\limits_{k=1}^{n} n_{kb} p_{kw}}{\sum\limits_{k=1}^{n} n_{kb}} \qquad \text{(A–1)}$$

231

TABLE A–2
Approximate Standard Errors for Percentages Based on Principal Classifications Used in Report

Estimated Percentages	U.S. Total	Public	Private			High-Performance Schools	
			Total	Catholic	Other Private	Public	Private
Sophomores							
$p = 50$ percent	0.46	0.47	1.84	1.82	5.17	4.20	6.91
$p = 90$ percent or 10 percent	0.28	0.28	1.10	1.09	3.10	2.52	4.15
Seniors							
$p = 50$ percent	0.48	0.48	1.98	1.96	5.73	4.59	7.45
$p = 90$ percent or 10 percent	0.29	0.29	1.19	1.18	3.44	2.76	4.47

TABLE A–3
Numbers of Students and Schools in Sample for Major Subclasses Used in Report

Case Unit	U.S. Total	Major Sectors			High-Performance Schools	
		Public	Catholic	Private	Public	Private
Total students	58,728 (58,049)[a]	51,339	5,528	1,182	682	679
Sophomores	30,263 (29,910)[a]	26,448	2,831	631	370	353
Seniors	28,465 (28,139)[a]	24,891	2,697	551	311	326
Number of schools	1,015 (1,004)[a]	894	84	27	12	11

[a] Excluding high-performance private schools.

TABLE A–4
Weighted Numbers of Students and Schools in Sample for Major Subclasses Used in Report

Case Unit	U.S. Total	Major Sectors			High-Performance Schools	
		Public	Catholic	Private	Public	Private
Total students	6,852,441 (6,850,525)[a]	6,195,294	429,217	226,014	88,788	1,916
Sophomores	3,787,782 (3,786,775)[a]	3,436,168	228,417	122,190	44,889	1,007
Seniors	3,064,659 (3,063,750)[a]	2,759,126	200,800	103,824	43,899	909
Number of schools	20,316 (20,303)[a]	15,766	1,571	2,966	128	13

[a] Excluding high-performance private schools.

or for groups i and j

$$s_{ij} = \frac{\sum_k n_{ki} p_{kj}}{\sum_k n_{ki}} \qquad (\text{A-2})$$

This measure is affected not only by the degree of segregation between two groups among schools in the sector, but also by the overall proportion of students in each group. If there are few black children in a sector, for example, then whether or not there is the same proportion of blacks in each school, the average white student will have a small proportion of black children in the same school. Because of this, it is valuable to have a measure of just how far from an even distribution across the schools the actual distribution is, that is, a measure that is standardized for the number of whites and blacks in the school type. Such a measure can be constructed, with a value of 0 if there is no segregation between the two groups in question and a value of 1.0 if segregation is complete.

The standardized measure is constructed as follows. Let the proportion of children from group j in the sector be p_j. If the same proportion of children from group j were in each school, then s_{ij} would be equal to p_j. If the children of group j were all in schools by themselves, totally isolated from children of group i, s_{ij} would be 0. Thus a measure of how far s_{ij} is from p_j is $(p_j - s_{ij})/p_j$. This we will call r_{ij}, which may be thought of as a measure of segregation. The formula is

$$r_{ij} = \frac{p_j - s_{ij}}{p_j} \qquad (\text{A-3})$$

It is important that, although the standardized measure is a measure of the segregation of children in one group from those in another, it is the unstandardized measure that measures directly the presence of children from one group in schools attended by children of another group. Thus the proportion of black schoolmates for the average white child may be low, without the measure of segregation being especially high.

In order to compute these measures from the High School and Beyond data, sophomores and seniors are combined to give a more precise estimate. The weighted numbers of students are used, and the proportion of each relevant group in the school is estimated from the weighted numbers in each group. In equation (A-2), n_{ki}, the number of students from group i in school k, is the number weighted by the design weight.

Calculation of Measures of the Distribution of Students
Relative to the Racial or Ethnic Composition of the Local Area
(Table 3–11)

This section describes the measures employed to compare the racial compositions of schools with those of local areas. Interest in such comparisons derives from concern over the accessibility of private education for students of different minority groups. To follow the line of presentation developed with the measures s_{ij} and r_{ij}, we will conceptualize the problems here in terms of an "average student."

The first measure can be seen as addressing a question about the geographic accessibility of "places" in private education for students of different groups. If the average student within a given sector attends a school that is located in an area that has a lower proportion of, say, blacks, than the average student within another sector, then the conclusion would be that the education provided by schools in the former sector tends to be less geographically accessible to blacks than the education provided by schools in the latter sector. Thus, if the schools in a sector are numbered 1, ... k, ... n, and the first school is considered, this school is located in an area that has some proportion of its population that is black. Call this proportion p_{1b}. There are a certain number of students in this school, n_1, and, for this number of students, the proportion of blacks in the local area of their school is p_{1b}. If this student-weighted proportion is averaged over all schools, we obtain the measure, which will be called U_b, the proportion of blacks in the local area of the school attended by the average student:

$$U_b = \frac{\sum_k n_k p_{kb}}{\sum_k n_k} \qquad \text{(A–4)}$$

or for any population group i:

$$U_i = \frac{\sum_k n_k p_{ki}}{\sum_k n_k} \qquad \text{(A–5)}$$

The proportion obtained for each sector can be compared to those of the other sectors in a straightforward fashion.

If geographic accessibility is taken as given, the question arises: How do the actual enrollments in the different sectors compare to the compositions of the areas where their constituent schools are located? If the schools within a given sector enroll numbers of whites, blacks, and Hispanics that are proportional to the numbers of whites, blacks, and Hispanics living in the areas where the schools are located, then schools of this sector reflect exactly the racial-ethnic composition of the areas where they are located. If, however, the average student in a given sector attends a school that has a lower proportion of, say, blacks or Hispanics, then this means that blacks or Hispanics are not attending schools of this sector despite geographic accessibility. Inferences along this line can be obtained by simply comparing the proportion U_i associated with schools in a given sector to the proportion of that sector's enrollment from group i.

Estimating Cognitive Achievement

Tables A–6 through A–19 provide the regression coefficients as well as R^2's for sophomores and seniors in both the public and private sectors used for predicting achievement in each of the tests analyzed on pages 137 through 174 in chapter 6. Means for each of the background variables used in the equation are found in table A–5.

TABLE A–5
Means for Independent Variable Used in Regression Equations Shown in Tables A–6, A–7, A–8, A–9

	Sophomores		Seniors	
	Public	Private	Public	Private
BB101	4.057	4.887	4.265	5.057
BB042	4.103	5.207	4.176	4.995
BB039	4.531	5.913	4.652	5.843
Number siblings	3.000	2.811	3.065	2.922
BB103	6.839	7.585	6.948	7.482
Two-parent household	.773	.851	.778	.843
BB037B	2.022	1.889	1.928	1.771
BB037C	1.773	1.599	1.673	1.529
BB047G	2.228	2.301	2.385	2.485
BB104C	.766	.864	.816	.900
BB104D	.639	.801	.704	.846
BB104G	.733	.856	.785	.888
BB104I	.697	.814	.769	.861
Father's expectation	.510	.726	.537	.733
Mother's expectation	.592	.778	.618	.782
Hispanic	.076	.064	.062	.058
Black	.146	.045	.120	.050
Other private	DNA	.348	DNA	.340
Elite	DNA	.003	DNA	.003

NOTE: DNA—does not apply.

TABLE A-6

Subtest Regression Coefficients, Standard Errors, and Explained Variance (R^2) for Model Including Public School Sophomores

	Reading (8)[a]		Vocabulary (8)[a]		Mathematics (18)[a]	
	b	s.e.	b	s.e.	b	s.e.
Intercept	2.083	.071	2.129	.065	5.628	.136
BB101	−.005	.008	.036	.007	.091	.015
BB042	.060	.007	.072	.006	.090	.013
BB039	.076	.006	.097	.005	.186	.011
Number siblings	−.049	.006	−.062	.005	−.075	.011
BB103	.037	.007	.026	.006	.122	.013
Two-parent household	.051	.031	.021	.028	.238	.059
BB037B	.005	.017	−.046	.015	.015	.032
BB037C	−.105	.016	−.042	.015	−.228	.032
BB104C	.082	.010	.070	.010	.063	.020
BB047G	.248	.036	.113	.033	.263	.069
BB104D	−.006	.029	.056	.027	.257	.056
BB104G	.255	.035	.296	.032	.378	.067
BB104I	.332	.031	.291	.029	.690	.060
Father's expectation	.180	.034	.135	.032	.484	.066
Mother's expectation	.483	.034	.386	.031	1.183	.065
Hispanic	−.704	.046	−.543	.042	−1.624	.088
Black	−.912	.037	−.852	.034	−2.226	.071
R^2	.190		.214		.255	

[a] Numbers in parentheses refer to total number of test items.

TABLE A-7
Subtest Regression Coefficients, Standard Errors, and Explained Variance (R²) for Model Including Private School Sophomores

	Reading (8)[a]		Vocabulary (8)[a]		Mathematics (18)[a]	
	b	s.e.	b	s.e.	b	s.e.
Intercept	2.612	.217	2.829	.203	7.830	.408
BB101	−.057	.021	.053	.020	.060	.040
BB042	.104	.015	.060	.014	.073	.029
BB039	.050	.014	.107	.013	.140	.027
Number siblings	−.084	.018	−.098	.017	−.120	.034
BB103	.032	.019	−.002	.018	.114	.036
Two-parent household	.243	.093	−.091	.087	−.264	.176
BB037B	.012	.045	.023	.042	.069	.085
BB037C	−.210	.045	−.186	.042	−.591	.086
BB047G	.084	.028	.010	.026	.013	.053
BB104C	−.166	.114	−.104	.106	−.564	.214
BB104D	.170	.093	.358	.086	.459	.174
BB104G	.396	.116	.572	.109	.962	.219
BB104I	.446	.094	.253	.088	.516	.177
Father's expectation	.083	.101	.102	.094	.334	.190
Mother's expectation	.512	.105	.398	.098	1.330	.196
Hispanic	−.326	.139	−.322	.121	−1.007	.244
Black	−.107	.157	−.621	.147	−1.177	.296
Other private sector	−.172	.068	−.023	.064	−.018	.128
High-performance schools	.979	.612	1.151	.572	2.504	1.151
R^2	.120		.166		.153	

[a] Numbers in parentheses refer to total number of test items.

TABLE A-8

Subtest Regression Coefficients, Standard Errors, and Explained Variance (R^2) for Model Including Public School Seniors

	Reading (8)[a]		Vocabulary (8)[a]		Mathematics (18)[a]	
	b	s.e.	b	s.e.	b	s.e.
Intercept	2.994	.079	2.882	.072	6.780	.152
BB101	−.008	.009	.034	.008	.068	.017
BB042	.055	.007	.078	.006	.123	.014
BB039	.065	.006	.080	.006	.177	.012
Number siblings	−.043	.007	−.062	.006	−.031	.013
BB103	.021	.008	.014	.007	−.056	.015
Two-parent household	.066	.034	−.068	.031	.113	.066
BB037B	−.020	.019	.002	.017	−.022	.036
BB037C	−.118	.019	−.124	.017	−.269	.037
BB047G	.086	.012	.068	.011	.038	.023
BB104C	.056	.041	.065	.037	−.021	.079
BB104D	.045	.033	.157	.030	.319	.064
BB104G	.371	.039	.322	.035	.473	.075
BB104I	.369	.036	.338	.033	.993	.070
Father's expectation	.301	.038	.288	.035	.859	.073
Mother's expectation	.541	.037	.478	.034	1.372	.072
Hispanic	−1.072	.055	−.796	.050	−1.961	.105
Black	−1.088	.043	−1.052	.040	−2.416	.084
R^2	.196		.236		.264	

[a] Numbers in parentheses refer to total number of test items in subtest.

TABLE A-9
Subtest Regression Coefficients, Standard Errors, and Explained Variance (R^2) for Model Including Private School Seniors

	Reading (8)[a]		Vocabulary (8)[a]		Mathematics (18)[a]	
	b	s.e.	b	s.e.	b	s.e.
Intercept	3.462	.227	3.482	.200	8.607	.422
BB101	-.095	.025	-.054	.022	.023	.047
BB042	.038	.017	.081	.015	.102	.031
BB039	.087	.015	.076	.014	.207	.029
Number siblings	-.035	.018	-.078	.016	-.045	.034
BB103	.019	.021	.037	.018	-.051	.039
Two-parent household	.106	.101	.177	.089	-.342	.187
BB037B	-.114	.050	-.103	.044	-.443	.093
BB037C	.012	.053	-.023	.046	.100	.098
BB047G	.041	.031	.060	.027	-.005	.057
BB104C	-.060	.132	-.114	.116	-.422	.245
BB104D	.039	.106	.142	.094	.427	.198
BB104G	.357	.129	.485	.113	.874	.240
BB104I	.519	.113	.395	.100	.951	.210
Father's expectation	.273	.113	.127	.100	.333	.211
Mother's expectation	.539	.117	.531	.103	2.034	.218
Hispanic	-.359	.146	-.335	.128	-1.135	.271
Black	-.596	.160	-.623	.140	-1.694	.297
Other private sector	.167	.074	-.043	.065	.137	.138
High-performance schools	1.133	.612	1.105	.540	2.591	1.143
R^2	.109		.153		.199	

a Numbers in parentheses refer to total numbers of test items in subtest.

TABLE A–10

Regression Coefficients, Standard Errors, and Explained Variance (R²) for Table 6–9

	Reading (8)[a]		Vocabulary (8)[a]		Mathematics (18)[a]	
	b	s.e.	b	s.e.	b	s.e.
Public Sophomores						
Intercept	2.650	.038	2.482	.034	6.923	.067
BB101	.061	.008	.092	.007	.252	.015
BB042	.094	.007	.102	.006	.165	.013
BB039	.121	.006	.137	.005	.289	.011
Hispanic	−.824	.045	−.659	.045	−1.849	.089
Black	−1.151	.036	−1.073	.034	−2.744	.067
R^2	.128		.162		.184	
Public Seniors						
Intercept	3.554	.042	3.244	.039	7.956	.083
BB101	.063	.008	.093	.008	.232	.016
BB042	.082	.007	.106	.006	.188	.014
BB039	.116	.006	.131	.005	.298	.012
Hispanic	−1.205	.052	−.926	.052	−2.185	.114
Black	−1.329	.041	−1.283	.041	−2.870	.083
R^2	.129		.169		.177	
Catholic Sophomores						
Intercept	3.802	.129	3.722	.121	10.048	.238
BB101	−.034	.024	.022	.023	.019	.044
BB042	.074	.017	.072	.016	.053	.032
BB039	.072	.016	.089	.015	.156	.030
Hispanic	−.506	.141	−.492	.132	−1.556	.258
Black	−.562	.160	−1.023	.150	−1.992	.293
R^2	.036		.065		.052	
Catholic Seniors						
Intercept	4.757	.136	4.747	.120	10.434	.261
BB101	−.042	.026	−.004	.023	.066	.051
BB042	.007	.019	.062	.017	.079	.037
BB039	.087	.019	.077	.015	.210	.033
Hispanic	−.430	.157	−.492	.137	−1.259	.301
Black	−.599	.173	−.816	.152	−1.675	.332
R^2	.021		.046		.055	
Other Private Sophomores						
Intercept	2.207	.300	1.745	.274	5.527	.592
BB101	.101	.052	.240	.047	.489	.103
BB042	.201	.042	.063	.038	.192	.083
BB039	.071	.039	.232	.035	.345	.076
Hispanic	−.536	.409	−.459	.374	−.262	.808
Black	1.055	.589	.515	.541	.375	1.161
R^2	.135		.239		.182	
Other Private Seniors						
Intercept	3.602	.318	3.380	.296	7.740	.607
BB101	.006	.059	.079	.055	.186	.114
BB042	.109	.047	.145	.043	.200	.090
BB039	.174	.044	.147	.041	.459	.086
Hispanic	−.456	.461	−.258	.429	−1.319	.891
Black	−.882	.471	−.522	.438	−2.039	.909
R^2	.142		.180		.238	

[a] Numbers in parentheses refer to number of items in test.

TABLE A-11
Full Test Regression Coefficients, Standard Errors, and Explained Variance (R²) for Model Including All Sophomores

	Reading (19)[a]		Vocabulary (21)[a]		Mathematics (38)[a]	
	b	s.e.	b	s.e.	b	s.e.
Intercept	5.665	.123	6.933	.134	11.506	.235
BB101	.022	.011	.107	.011	.147	.022
BB042	.121	.011	.166	.011	.204	.022
BB039	.175	.011	.222	.011	.357	.022
Number of siblings	−.113	.011	−.180	.011	−.136	.022
BB103	.065	.011	.067	.011	.232	.022
Two-parent household	.143	.056	.052	.056	.346	.101
BB037B	.010	.034	−.039	.034	.008	.056
BB037C	−.226	.034	−.216	.034	−.511	.056
BB047G	.158	.022	.147	.022	.125	.034
BB104C	.402	.067	.300	.067	.337	.123
BB104D	.053	.056	.211	.056	.499	.101
BB104G	.601	.056	.791	.067	.720	.112
BB104I	.736	.056	.815	.056	1.369	.101
Father's expectations	.325	.056	.291	.067	.988	.112
Mother's expectations	1.018	.056	1.083	.067	2.134	.112
Hispanic	−1.516	.078	−1.722	.067	−3.031	.145
Black	−1.847	.067	−2.615	.067	−4.099	.123
Catholic sector	.540	.089	.921	.089	.882	.156
Other private sector	.063	.112	.435	.123	.752	.212
High-performance school	2.690	1.352	3.190	1.463	5.780	2.513
R^2	.239		.302		.282	

[a] Numbers in parentheses refer to total number of test items.

TABLE A-12

Full Test Regression Coefficients, Standard Errors, and Explained Variance (R^2)
for Model Including All Seniors

	Reading (20)[a]		Vocabulary (27)[a]		Mathematics (32)[a]	
	b	s.e.	b	s.e.	b	s.e.
Intercept	7.386	.145	8.921	.186	13.342	.207
BB101	−.019	.021	.007	.021	.096	.021
BB042	.133	.010	.238	.021	.198	.021
BB039	.140	.010	.231	.010	.271	.021
Number siblings	−.095	.010	−.196	.010	−.038	.021
BB103	.034	.010	.039	.021	.075	.021
Two-parent household	.074	.062	−.072	.083	.077	.093
BB037B	−.036	.031	−.071	.041	−.140	.052
BB037C	−.226	.031	−.317	.041	−.347	.052
BB047G	.160	.021	.172	.031	.042	.031
BB104C	.207	.072	.034	.093	−.051	.114
BB104D	.065	.062	.344	.083	.481	.093
BB104G	.921	.072	.989	.093	.625	.104
BB104I	.865	.072	.908	.083	1.582	.093
Father's expectation	.708	.072	.681	.093	1.248	.104
Mother's expectation	1.181	.072	1.329	.083	2.196	.104
Hispanic	−2.253	.083	−2.176	.103	−2.851	.115
Black	−2.307	.103	−2.689	.124	−3.413	.114
Catholic sector	.320	.093	1.146	.124	.640	.135
Other private sector	.776	.134	.991	.165	.961	.186
High-performance schools	2.687	1.437	5.106	1.831	4.752	2.081
R^2	.239		.240		.280	

[a] Numbers in parentheses refer to total number of test items.

TABLE A-13
Regression Coefficients, Standard Errors, and Explained Variance (R²) for Model of Educational Expectations

	Sophomores				Seniors			
	Public		Private		Public		Private	
	b	s.e.	b	s.e.	b	s.e.	b	s.e.
Intercept	.810	.032	1.205	.092	.977	.032	1.366	.088
BB101	.028	.003	.029	.010	.014	.003	.010	.010
BB042	.055	.002	.042	.007	.050	.003	.052	.006
BB039	.067	.003	.065	.006	.065	.002	.055	.006
Number siblings	-.023	.003	-.046	.008	-.018	.003	-.019	.007
BB103	.015	.003	.005	.009	.012	.003	.013	.008
Two-parent household	-.036	.014	-.038	.040	-.071	.014	-.245	.039
BB037B	.002	.008	.028	.019	0	.007	-.024	.019
BB037C	-.015	.007	-.027	.019	-.009	.007	.030	.021
BB047G	.061	.005	.062	.012	.053	.004	.038	.012
BB104C	.012	.016	-.043	.049	-.039	.016	-.048	.051
BB104D	.050	.013	.067	.039	.049	.014	.065	.042
BB104G	.093	.016	.097	.049	.080	.016	.115	.050
BB104I	.059	.014	.145	.040	.122	.015	.130	.044
Father's expectation	.317	.015	.332	.043	.407	.015	.350	.045
Mother's expectation	.577	.015	.510	.045	.588	.015	.569	.046
Hispanic	.059	.021	.067	.055	.046	.022	.331	.056
Black	.231	.016	.391	.068	.312	.017	.311	.062
Other private sector	DNA	DNA	-.142	.030	DNA	DNA	-.006	.029
High-performance schools	DNA	DNA	.184	.260	DNA	DNA	.298	.239
R^2	.364		.309		.391		.331	

TABLE A–14
*Logit Analysis for Table 6-14: Percentage of Seniors
and Sophomores in Public and Private Schools
Indicating Expectations to Attend College at Earlier
Grades: Actual Percentage[a] and Standardized
Percentage:[b] Spring 1980*

(Unweighted and listwise deletion)

At Earlier Grade	Public	Catholic	Other Private
Seniors			
A. Actual percentage:			
At 8th grade	.51	.70	.69
At 9th grade	.55	.75	.72
At 10th grade	.60	.79	.80
At 11th grade	.66	.84	.80
B. Standardized percentage:			
At 8th grade	.49	.60	.57
At 9th grade	.54	.66	.61
At 10th grade	.61	.71	.72
At 11th grade	.70	.80	.75
Sophomores			
C. Actual percentage:			
At 6th grade	.45	.59	.62
At 7th grade	.49	.66	.65
At 8th grade	.56	.77	.74
At 9th grade	.64	.82	.78
D. Standardized percentage:			
At 6th grade	.45	.49	.50
At 7th grade	.49	.56	.53
At 8th grade	.56	.70	.64
At 9th grade	.64	.76	.72

[a] Actual percentage differs from those given in chapter 6 due to the listwise deletion required by the logit program.

[b] Backgrounds are standardized to the average public school sophomore.

TABLE A–15

Differences in Logits[a] for College Expectations,
Standardized to Public School Sophomores, Between
Each Type of Private School and the Public Schools:
Spring 1980

(Based on logit analysis table A–14)

At Earlier Grade	Catholic	Other Private
A. *Seniors*		
At 8th grade	.37	.24
At 9th grade	.50	.29
At 10th grade	.45	.50
At 11th grade	.54	.25
B. *Sophomores*		
At 6th grade	.16	.20
At 7th grade	.20	.16
At 8th grade	.61	.33
At 9th grade	.58	.37
C. *Sophomores and Seniors*		
At 6th grade (sophomores)	.16	.20
At 7th grade (sophomores)	.20	.16
At 8th grade (both)	.49	.29
At 9th grade (both)	.54	.33
At 10th grade (seniors)	.45	.50
At 11th grade (seniors)	.54	.25

[a] See page 155 for discussion of the method used in calculating these differences.

TABLE A-16
Regression Coefficients, Standard Errors, and Explained Variance (R^2) for Five Background Variable Model of Educational Expectations

| | Sophomores | | | | | | Seniors | | | | | |
| | Public | | Catholic | | Other Private | | Public | | Catholic | | Other Private | |
	b	s.e.	b	s.e.	b	s.e.	b	s.e.	b	s.e.	b	s.e.
Intercept	1.083	.018	1.809	.060	1.270	.129	1.287	.019	1.945	.060	1.545	.128
BB101	.071	.003	.053	.012	.101	.022	.055	.042	.042	.011	.041	.023
BB042	.088	.003	.052	.008	.075	.018	.080	.003	.055	.009	.080	.019
BB039	.110	.002	.086	.007	.084	.017	.111	.003	.071	.008	.113	.018
Hispanic	.079	.023	.089	.066	−.045	.175	.041	.025	.341	.068	.435	.184
Black	.205	.017	.352	.075	.743	.251	.302	.019	.446	.075	.148	.188
R^2	.204		.138		.226		.195		.124		.278	

TABLE A–17
Probit Analysis Predicting Sophomore Entry into Private Sector: Coefficients from Two Models

Variable	Model	
	A	B
Intercept	−2.791[a]	−2.858[a]
1. Income	.086[a]	.083[a]
2. Region (Northeast versus others)	.195[a]	.192
3. Catholic religious background	.868[a]	.866[a]
4. Mother's education	.082[a]	.075[a]
5. Number of siblings	−.031[a]	−.027[a]
6. Number rooms in home	.019[a]	.017[a]
7. Eighth grade college plans	DNA	.263[a]
8. Mother worked while child in elementary school	−.037	DNA
9. Mother worked before child in elementary school	.006	DNA
10. Talk with parents	−.019	−.025
11. BB104C	−.035	−.039
12. BB104D	.192[a]	.189
13. BB104G	.159[a]	.146[a]
14. BB104I	−.003	.017
15. Two-parent family	−.110[a]	−.097[a]
16. Mother's school expectations	.369[a]	.268[a]
17. Hispanic	.196[a]	.179[a]
18. Black	.360[a]	.324[a]

[a] Significant at .05 level for two-tail test.

TABLE A–18

Regression Coefficients, Standard Errors, and Explained Variance (R^2) for Models of Public Sophomore Achievement Which Include School Characteristics

Independent Variables [a]	Reading (8)		Vocabulary (8)		Mathematics (18)	
	b	s.e.	b	s.e.	b	s.e.
Intercept	.703	.211	.912	.196	2.447	.395
BB101	−.007	.008	.032	.007	.083	.015
BB042	.044	.007	.056	.006	.055	.013
BB039	.062	.006	.082	.006	.143	.011
Number siblings	−.046	.006	−.060	.006	−.068	.011
BB103	.026	.007	.021	.006	.094	.013
Two-parent household	.019	.031	.001	.029	.133	.057
BB037B	.012	.016	−.041	.015	.045	.031
BB037C	−.099	.016	−.036	.015	−.214	.030
BB047G	.047	.010	.039	.009	−.018	.019
BB104C	.238	.035	.109	.033	.249	.066
BB104D	−.036	.029	.024	.027	.154	.054
BB104G	.225	.034	.264	.032	.323	.064
BB104I	.306	.031	.268	.029	.605	.057
Father's expectation	.113	.033	.315	.031	.288	.063
Mother's expectation	.404	.033	.071	.031	.946	.062
Hispanic	−.653	.045	−.524	.042	−1.475	.084
Black	−.876	.038	−.816	.035	−2.087	.071
BB011C	.686	.029	.686	.026	DNA	DNA
BB011D	DNA	DNA	DNA	DNA	2.073	.052
Homework [b]	.047	.003	.034	.003	.114	.007
BB016	−.060	.009	−.051	.008	−.243	.017
BB059E	−.069	.027	−.056	.025	−.245	.051
MBB053E	.246	.075	.100	.070	.743	.140
MBB053F	−.109	.063	−.199	.058	−.590	.119
MBB053G	−.349	.076	−.014	.071	−.685	.142
MYB019A	.405	.074	.219	.068	.642	.139
MYB019B	−.077	.054	−.230	.050	−.422	.100
MYB019E	.113	.060	.187	.056	.341	.114
MYB019F	.469	.080	.483	.074	1.452	.149
R^2	.226		.248		.333	

[a] The variables prefixed with the letter M are school level means for the individual level variable. The codings for the latter are found in appendix B.

[b] Recoded as actual hours. See appendix B for specific coding structure.

TABLE A-19

Regression Coefficients, Standard Errors, and Explained Variance (R²) for Models of Public Senior Achievement Which Include School Characteristics

Independent Variables[a]	Reading (8)		Vocabulary (8)		Mathematics (18)	
	b	s.e.	b	s.e.	b	s.e.
Intercept	1.806	.243	2.099	.222	3.361	.387
BB101	−.006	.008	.028	.007	.024	.014
BB042	.041	.007	.064	.006	.028	.012
BB039	.050	.006	.063	.005	.040	.011
Number siblings	−.043	.006	−.062	.006	.015	.011
BB103	.014	.007	.010	.007	.021	.014
Two-parent household	.055	.034	−.061	.031	.069	.054
BB037B	−.021	.018	0	.017	.004	.028
BB037C	−.109	.019	−.113	.017	−.141	.030
BB047G	.045	.012	.035	.011	−.023	.018
BB104C	.065	.040	.078	.037	−.056	.063
BB104D	.012	.033	.122	.030	.069	.052
BB104G	.337	.038	.286	.035	.339	.060
BB104I	.319	.036	.297	.033	.437	.057
Father's expectation	.222	.037	.217	.034	.100	.059
Mother's expectation	.427	.037	.373	.034	.312	.059
Hispanic	−1.054	.054	−.802	.049	−1.495	.085
Black	−1.095	.044	−1.066	.040	−2.062	.071
BB011C	.710	.031	.717	.027	DNA	DNA
BB011D	DNA	DNA	DNA	DNA	.895	.054
Advanced math course[b]	DNA	DNA	DNA	DNA	1.495	.017
Homework[c]	.057	.004	.040	.004	.027	.006
BB016	−.035	.011	−.025	.010	−.049	.016
BB059E	−.032	.027	.028	.025	−.082	.044
MBB053E	.336	.083	.240	.076	.064	.133
MBB053F	−.126	.073	−.101	.066	.192	.115
MBB053G	−.256	.082	−.187	.076	−.674	.132
MYB019A	.304	.081	.238	.074	.375	.128
MYB019B	−.067	.059	−.332	.054	−.415	.094
MYB019E	−.028	.066	.191	.060	.382	.105
MYB019F	.378	.094	.256	.085	1.209	.150
R²	.231		.271		.524	

[a] The variables prefixed with the letter M are school level means for the individual level variables. The codings for the latter are found in appendix B.

[b] Number of advanced mathematics courses taken. EB005 in appendix B.

[c] Recoded as actual hours. See appendix B for specific coding structure.

APPENDIX B

Items from the Student and School Questionnaires Used in the Analysis

Coding Procedures Used in This Report

In general, values used in the analysis are the same as given in the High School Beyond Codebook. Exceptions are described below and should be read in conjunction with the section beginning on page 252 through 277 of this appendix.

MISSING VALUES

In the questionnaire (p. 252–277), a star (*) has been placed beside those response categories which were set to missing in the analysis. For example, in BB039 (Father's education), the responses "Do not live with Father" and "Don't know" have been set to missing.

COLLAPSED CATEGORIES

Response categories that were collapsed in the analysis have been bracketed in the variable listing in the questionnaire.

Items from the Questionnaires Used in the Analysis

The values on a limited number of variables were reconstructed:

Coursework taken: For seniors, EB04A—K recoded such that None = 0, 1/2 year = 1, ... More than 3 years = 7. For sophomores, items YB006A—K and items YB009A—K were combined to match the senior coding.

Advanced mathematics courses: EB005A—G responses were recoded where 1 = have taken, 0 = have not taken. Responses then summed across items.

Honors English and Honors Mathematics: BB011C and BB011D recoded where 1 = Yes, 0 = No.

Homework: BB015 recoded to estimate actual hours. No homework assigned or no homework done = 0; Less than 1 hour a week = .5; Between 1 and 3 hours a week = 2; More than 3 hours, less than 5 = 4; Between 5 and 10 hours = 7.5; and More than 10 hours a week = 12.5.

Two-Parent Household: Using BB036—E variable was constructed such that if respondent lived either with own mother or female guardian and with either father or male guardian, then respondent was considered to be living in two-parent household and response value = 1. Otherwise, response value = 0.

Mother's and Father's expectations: Items BB050A and BB050B were used to construct this variable. If response was "go to college," variable was coded 1, otherwise it was coded 0.

Cutting class: BB059E was recoded where True = 1, otherwise coded as 0.

Race: Race considered black (1) if response to BB089 equals black (1) and response to BB090 is not equal to one of Hispanic or Spanish categories.

Ethnicity: Ethnicity is considered Hispanic (1) if response to BB090 is one of the Hispanic or Spanish categories.

Siblings: Items BB096A—E are used to construct sibling variable. Responses are first recoded to None = 0, One = 1, Two = 2, Three = 3, Four = 4, and Five or more = 5. Then these adjusted response values are summed over all items.

Household possessions: BB104C—I are recoded where Have = 1, Otherwise = 0.

Items From the Student Questionnaire[1]

EB004A—K

4. Starting with the beginning of the *tenth* grade and through the end of this school year how much course work will you have taken in each of the following subjects?

   Count only courses that meet at least three times (or three periods) a week. (MARK ONE OVAL FOR EACH LINE)

	None	½ year	1 year	1½ years	2 years	2½ years	3 years	More than 3 years
a. Mathematics	○	○	○	○	○	○	○	○
b. English or literature	○	○	○	○	○	○	○	○
c. French	○	○	○	○	○	○	○	○
d. German	○	○	○	○	○	○	○	○
e. Spanish	○	○	○	○	○	○	○	○
f. History or social studies	○	○	○	○	○	○	○	○
g. Science	○	○	○	○	○	○	○	○
h. Business, office, or sales	○	○	○	○	○	○	○	○
i. Trade and industry	○	○	○	○	○	○	○	○
j. Technical courses	○	○	○	○	○	○	○	○
k. Other vocational courses	○	○	○	○	○	○	○	○

[1] First two letters in variable identification refer to grade of respondents; "EB" refers to seniors (elder), "YB" refers to sophomores (younger), and "BB" refers to items asked of both sophomore and seniors.

Items from the Questionnaires Used in the Analysis

YB006A—K

6. During the tenth grade, including all of this school year, how much course work will you have taken in each of the following subjects? Count only courses that meet at least three times (or three periods) a week. (MARK ONE OVAL FOR EACH LINE)

	None	½ year	1 year	More than 1 year
a. Mathematics	O	O	O	O
b. English or literature	O	O	O	O
c. French	O	O	O	O
d. German	O	O	O	O
e. Spanish	O	O	O	O
f. History or social studies	O	O	O	O
g. Science	O	O	O	O
h. Business, office, or sales	O	O	O	O
i. Trade and industry	O	O	O	O
j. Technical courses	O	O	O	O
k. Other vocational courses	O	O	O	O

YB009A—K

9. During the 11th and 12th grades, how much course work do you plan to take in each of the following subjects? (MARK ONE OVAL FOR EACH LINE)

	None	½ year	1 year	1½ years	2 years	More than 2 years	Don't know yet *
a. Mathematics	O	O	O	O	O	O	O
b. English or literature	O	O	O	O	O	O	O
c. French	O	O	O	O	O	O	O
d. German	O	O	O	O	O	O	O
e. Spanish	O	O	O	O	O	O	O
f. History or social studies	O	O	O	O	O	O	O
g. Science	O	O	O	O	O	O	O
h. Business, office, or sales	O	O	O	O	O	O	O
i. Trade and industry	O	O	O	O	O	O	O
j. Technical courses	O	O	O	O	O	O	O
k. Other vocational courses	O	O	O	O	O	O	O

* For the analysis in this report, this last response has been set to missing.

EB005A—G

5. Which of the following courses have you taken, counting the courses you are taking this semester? (MARK ONE OVAL FOR EACH LINE)

	Yes, have taken	No, have not taken
a. First-year algebra	○	○
b. Second-year algebra	○	○
c. Geometry	○	○
d. Trigonometry	○	○
e. Calculus	○	○
f. Physics	○	○
g. Chemistry	○	○

BB011

13. Have you ever been in any of the following kinds of courses or programs in high school? (MARK ONE OVAL FOR EACH LINE)

	No	Yes
a. Remedial English (sometimes called basic or essential)	○	○
b. Remedial Mathematics (sometimes called basic or essential)	○	○
c. Advanced or honors program in English	○	○
d. Advanced or honors program in Mathematics	○	○

BB015

15. Approximately what is the average amount of time you spend on homework a week? (MARK ONE)

No homework is ever assigned	○
I have homework, but I don't do it	○
Less than 1 hour a week	○
Between 1 and 3 hours a week	○
More than 3 hours, less than 5 hours a week	○
Between 5 and 10 hours a week	○
More than 10 hours a week	○

Items from the Questionnaires Used in the Analysis

BB016

17. Between the beginning of school last fall and Christmas vacation, about how many days were you *absent* from school for any reason, *not counting illness?* (MARK ONE)

None	O
1 or 2 days	O
3 or 4 days	O
5 to 10 days	O
11 to 15 days	O
16 to 20 days	O
21 or more	O

BB017

18. Between the beginning of school last fall and Christmas vacation, about how many days were you *late* to school? (MARK ONE)

None	O
1 or 2 days	O
3 or 4 days	O
5 to 10 days	O
11 to 15 days	O
16 to 20 days	O
21 or more	O

YB019A—F

19. To what extent are the following disciplinary matters problems in your school? (MARK ONE OVAL FOR EACH LINE)

	Often happens	Sometimes happens	Rarely or never happens
Students don't attend school	O	O	O
Students cut classes, even if they attend school	O	O	O
Students talk back to teachers	O	O	O
Students refuse to obey instructions	O	O	O
Students get in fights with each other	O	O	O
Students attack or threaten to attack teachers	O	O	O

255

YB020A—E

20. Listed below are certain rules which some schools have. Please mark those which are enforced in your school. (MARK ALL THAT APPLY)

School grounds closed to students at lunch time	O
Students responsible to the school for property damage	O
Hall passes required	O
"No smoking" rules	O
Rules about student dress	O

BB019

22. Did you do any work for pay last week, not counting work around the house? (MARK ONE)

Yes	O
No	O

BB032B—G, J, L—O AND YB034L

34. Have you participated in any of the following types of activities either in or out of school this year? (MARK ONE OVAL FOR EACH LINE)

	Have not participated	Have participated actively
a. Athletic teams—in or out of school	O	O
b. Cheer leaders, pep club, majorettes	O	O
c. Debating or drama	O	O
d. Band or orchestra	O	O
e. Chorus or dance	O	O
f. Hobby clubs such as photography, model building, hot rod, electronics, crafts	O	O
g. School subject-matter clubs, such as science, history, language, business, art	O	O
h. Vocational education clubs, such as Future Homemakers, Teachers, Farmers of America, DECA, FBLA, or VICA	O	O
i. Youth organizations in the community, such as Scouts, Y, etc.	O	O
j. Church activities, including youth groups	O	O
k. Junior Achievement	O	O
l. Co-op club	O	O

Items from the Questionnaires Used in the Analysis

32. Have you participated in any of the following types of activities either in or out of school this year? (MAKE ONE OVAL FOR EACH LINE)

	Have not participated	Have participated actively (but not as a leader or officer)	Have participated as a leader or officer
a. Varsity athletic teams	O	O	O
b. Other athletic teams—in or out of school	O	O	O
c. Cheer leaders, pep club, majorettes	O	O	O
d. Debating or drama	O	O	O
e. Band or orchestra	O	O	O
f. Chorus or dance	O	O	O
g. Hobby clubs such as photography, model building, hot rod, electronics, crafts	O	O	O
h. Honorary clubs, such as Beta Club or National Honor Society	O	O	O
i. School newspaper, magazine, yearbook, annual	O	O	O
j. School subject-matter clubs, such as science, history, language, business, art	O	O	O
k. Student council, student government, political club	O	O	O
l. Vocational education clubs, such as Future Homemakers, Teachers, Farmers of America, DECA, FBLA, or VICA	O	O	O
m. Youth organizations in the community, such as Scouts, Y, etc.	O	O	O *
n. Church activities, including youth groups	O	O	O *
o. Junior Achievement	O	O	O

* For the analysis in this report, these responses were set to missing.

36. Which of the following people live in the same household with you? (MARK ALL THAT APPLY)

a. I live alone	O
b. Father	O
c. Other male guardian (step-father or foster father)	O
d. Mother	O
e. Other female guardian (step-mother or foster mother)	O
f. Brother(s) and/or sister(s) (including step- or half-)	O
g. Grandparent(s)	O
h. My husband/wife	O
i. My child or my children	O
j. Other relative(s) (children or adults)	O
k. Non-relative(s) (children or adults)	O

BB037A—C

37. Did your mother (stepmother or female guardian) usually work during the following periods of your life? (MARK ONE OVAL FOR EACH LINE)

	Did not work	Worked part-time	Worked full-time	Don't know [*]	Does not apply [*]
a. When you were in high school	O	O	O	O	O
b. When you were in elementary school	O	O	O	O	O
c. Before you went to elementary school	O	O	O	O	O

[*]For the analysis in this report, these responses were set to missing.

BB039

39. What was the highest level of education your father (stepfather or male guardian) completed? (MARK ONE)

Do not live with father (stepfather or male guardian)		O [*]
Less than high school graduation		O
High school graduation only		O
Vocational, trade, or business school after high school	{ Less than two years	O
	Two years or more	O
	{ Less than two years of college	O
	Two or more years of college (including two-year degree)	O
College program	{ Finished college (four- or five-year degree)	O
	Master's degree or equivalent	O
	Ph.D., M.D., or other advanced professional degree	O
Don't know		O [*]

[*]For the analysis in this report, these responses were set to missing.

Items from the Questionnaires Used in the Analysis

42. What was the highest level of education your mother (stepmother or female guardian) completed? (MARK ONE)

Do not live with father (stepfather or male guardian)		○ *
Less than high school graduation		○
High school graduation only		○
Vocational, trade, or business school after high school	{ Less than two years	○
	{ Two years or more	○
	⎧ Less than two years of college	○
	⎪ Two or more years of college (including two-year degree)	○
College program	⎨ Finished college (four- or five-year degree)	○
	⎪ Master's degree or equivalent	○
	⎪ Ph.D., M.D., or other advanced professional degree	○
Don't know	⎩	○ *

* For the analysis in this report, these categories were set to missing.

47. How often do you spend time on the following activities outside of school? (MARK ONE OVAL FOR EACH LINE)

	Rarely or never	Less than once a week	Once or twice a week	Every day or almost every day
g. Talking with your mother or father about personal experiences	○	○	○	○

BB046A—C

46. Are the following statements about your parents true or false? (MARK ONE OVAL FOR EACH LINE)

	True	False	✿ Does not apply
a. My mother (stepmother or female guardian) keeps close track of how well I am doing in school	O	O	O
b. My father (stepfather or male guardian) keeps close track of how well I am doing in school	O	O	O
c. My parents (or guardians) almost always know where I am and what I'm doing	O	O	O

✿ For the analysis in this report, this category was set to missing.

BB048

48. During week days about how many hours per day do you watch TV? (MARK ONE)

Don't watch TV during week	O
Less than 1 hour	O
1 hour or more, less than 2	O
2 hours or more, less than 3	O
3 hours or more, less than 4	O
4 hours or more, less than 5	O
5 or more	O

Items from the Questionnaires Used in the Analysis

BB050A—E

50. What do the following people think you ought to do after high school?
(MARK ONE OVAL FOR EACH LINE)

	Go to college	Get a full-time job	Enter a trade school or an apprenticeship	Enter military service	They don't care	I don't know	Does not apply
a. Your father	O	O	O	O	O	O	O
b. Your mother	O	O	O	O	O	O	O
c. A guidance counselor	O	O	O	O	O	O	O
d. Teachers	O	O	O	O	O	O	O
e. Friends or relatives about your own age	O	O	O	O	O	O	O

BB053E—H

53. Please rate your school on each of the following aspects. (MARK ONE OVAL FOR EACH LINE)

	Poor	Fair	Good	Excellent	Don't know *
e. Teacher interest in students	O	O	O	O	O
f. Effective discipline	O	O	O	O	O
g. Fairness of discipline	O	O	O	O	O
h. School spirit	O	O	O	O	O

*For the analysis in this report, this category was set to missing.

BB058A—L

58. How do you feel about each of the following statements? (MARK ONE OVAL FOR EACH LINE)

	Agree strongly	Agree	Disagree	Disagree strongly	No opinion ✿
a. I take a positive attitude toward myself	O	O	O	O	O
b. Good luck is more important than hard work for success	O	O	O	O	O
c. I feel I am a person of worth, on an equal plane with others	O	O	O	O	O
d. I am able to do things as well as most other people	O	O	O	O	O
e. Every time I try to get ahead, something or somebody stops me	O	O	O	O	O
f. Planning only makes a person unhappy, since plans hardly ever work out anyway	O	O	O	O	O
g. People who accept their condition in life are happier than those who try to change things	O	O	O	O	O
h. On the whole, I am satisfied with myself	O	O	O	O	O
i. What happens to me is my own doing	O	O	O	O	O
j. At times I think I am no good at all	O	O	O	O	O
k. When I make plans, I am almost certain I can make them work	O	O	O	O	O
l. I feel I do not have much to be proud of	O	O	O	O	O

BB057

57. How important is each of the following to you in your life?

	Not important	Somewhat important	Very important
j. Working to correct social and economic inequalities	O	O	O

✿ For the analysis in this report, this category was set to missing.

Items from the Questionnaires Used in the Analysis

BB059A—F

59. Are the following statements about your experiences in school true or false? (MARK ONE OVAL FOR EACH LINE)

	True	False
a. I am satisfied with the way my education is going	O	O
b. I have had disciplinary problems in school during the last year	O	O
c. I am interested in school	O	O
d. I have been suspended or put on probation in school	O	O
e. Every once in a while I cut a class	O	O
f. I don't feel safe at this school	O	O

BB061E

67. Are the following statements about yourself true or false? (MARK ONE OVAL FOR EACH LINE)

	True	False
e. I like to work hard in school	O	O

BB065

69. As things stand now, how far in school do you think you will get? (MARK ONE)

Less than high school graduation		O]
High school graduation only		O]
Vocational, trade, or business school after high school	{ Less than two years	O]
	Two years or more	O
	Less than two years of college	O
	Two or more years of college (including two-year degree)	O]
College program	{ Finish college (four- or five-year degree)	O
	Master's degree or equivalent	O
	Ph.D., M.D., or other advanced professional degree	O]

263

YB072A & B, BB068A & B

72. Did you expect to go to college when you were in the following grades?
(MARK ONE OVAL FOR EACH LINE)

When you were	Yes	No	Was not sure	Hadn't thought about it
a. In the 6th grade?	O	O	O	O
b. In the 7th grade?	O	O	O	O
c. In the 8th grade?	O	O	O	O
d. In the 9th grade?	O	O	O	O

BB068A & B, EB068C & D

68. Did you expect to go to college when you were in the following grades?
(MARK ONE OVAL FOR EACH LINE)

When you were	Yes	No	✿ Was not sure	✿ Hadn't thought about it
a. In the 8th grade?	O	O	O	O
b. In the 9th grade?	O	O	O	O
c. In the 10th grade?	O	O	O	O
d. In the 11th grade?	O	O	O	O

✿ For the analysis in this report, these categories were set to missing.

264

EB073

73. If you plan to work full time after high school, do you have a definite job lined up for you after you leave high school? (MARK ONE)

⎡ Yes, I'll continue in a job I now have	○ ⎤
⎣ Yes, I have a new job lined up	○ ⎦
No, but I've inquired at employment agencies	
or potential employers, looked in	
the newspapers, etc.	○
No, I haven't done anything yet to get a job	○
Do not plan to work full time after	
high school	○ *

* For the analysis in this report, this category was set to missing.

Background information . . .

BB083

83. Sex:
(MARK ONE)

Male	○
Female	○

BB087A—G

87. Do you have any of the following conditions? (MARK ALL THAT APPLY)

a. Specific learning disability	○
b. Visual handicap	○
c. Hard of hearing	○
d. Deafness	○
e. Speech disability	○
f. Orthopedic handicap	○
g. Other health impairment	○

BB088

88. Do you feel that you have a physical condition that limits the kind or amount of work you can do on a job, or affects your chances for more education? (MARK ONE)

No   ◯
Yes   ◯

NOTE: The following four questions pertain to fundamental freedoms of expression. These and other questions will provide helpful information for the interpretation of survey results. If you have any reservations about answering questions 91, 92, 93 and 94, please remember that you may leave them unanswered.

BB091

91. What is your religious background? (MARK ONE)

Baptist	◯
Methodist	◯
Lutheran	◯
Presbyterian	◯
Episcopalian	◯
Other Protestant denomination	◯
Catholic	◯
Other Christian	◯
Jewish	◯
Other religion	◯
None	◯

BB089

90. What is your race? (MARK ONE)

Black	◯
White	◯
American Indian or Alaskan Native	◯
Asian or Pacific Islander	◯
Other	◯

Items from the Questionnaires Used in the Analysis

BB090

91. What is your origin or descent? (If more than one, please mark below the one you consider the *most important* part of your background.) (MARK ONE)

HISPANIC OR SPANISH:
- Mexican, Mexican-American, Chicano ○
- Cuban, Cubano ○
- Puerto Rican, Puertorriqueno or Boricua ○
- Other Latin American, Latino, Hispanic, or Spanish descent ○

NON HISPANIC:
- African:
  - Afro-American ○
  - West Indian or Caribbean ○
- Alaskan Native ○
- American Indian ○
- Asian or Pacific Islander:
  - Chinese ○
  - Filipino ○
  - Indian, Pakastani or other South Asian ○
  - Japanese ○
  - Korean ○
  - Vietnamese ○
  - Other Pacific Islander ○
  - Other Asian ○
- European:
  - English or Welsh ○
  - French ○
  - German ○
  - Greek ○
  - Irish ○
  - Italian ○
  - Polish ○
  - Portuguese ○
  - Russian ○
  - Scottish ○
  - Other European ○
- Canadian (French) ○
- Canadian (Other) ○
- United States only ○

Other (WRITE IN) _____ ○

BB095

96. Did anyone at home read to you when you were young before you started school? (MARK ONE)

Never	○
Less than once a month	○
One to four times a month	○
Several times a week	○
Every day	○
Don't remember	○

BB096A—E

97. How many brothers and sisters do you have in each of the age groups below? Please include step-brothers and step-sisters if they live, or have lived, in your home. (MARK ONE OVAL FOR EACH LINE)

How many brothers and sisters do you have who are ...	None	One	Two	Three	Four	Five or more
a. Three or more years older than you	○	○	○	○	○	○
b. 1–2 years older	○	○	○	○	○	○
c. Same age as you	○	○	○	○	○	○
d. 1–2 years younger	○	○	○	○	○	○
e. Three or more years younger	○	○	○	○	○	○

BB100

99. American families are divided below into three equal groups according to how much money the family makes in a year. Mark the oval for the group which comes closest to the amount of money your family makes in a year. (MARK ONE)

1/3 of American families make: $11,999 or less	○
1/3 of American families make: $12,000 to $19,999	○
1/3 of American families make: $20,000 or more	○

Items from the Questionnaires Used in the Analysis

100. This time families are divided into seven groups according to how much money they make in a year. Mark the oval for the group which comes closest to the amount of money your family makes in a year. (MARK ONE)

$6,999 or less	○
$7,000 to $11,999	○
$12,000 to $15,999	○
$16,000 to $19,999	○
$20,000 to $24,999	○
$25,000 to $37,999	○
$38,000 or more	○

BB103

102. How many rooms are there in your home? Count only the rooms your family lives in. Count the kitchen (if separate) but *not* bathrooms. (MARK ONE).

1	2	3	4	5	6	7	8	9	10 or more
○	○	○	○	○	○	○	○	○	○

BB104A—I

103. Which of the following do you have in your home? (MARK ONE OVAL FOR EACH LINE)

	Have	Do not have
a. A specific place for study	○	○
b. A daily newspaper	○	○
c. Encyclopedia or other reference books	○	○
d. Typewriter	○	○
e. Electric dishwasher	○	○
f. Two or more cars or trucks that run	○	○
g. More than 50 books	○	○
h. A room of your own	○	○
i. Pocket calculator	○	○

BB115

112. Do you plan to go to college at some time in the future? (MARK ONE)

Yes, right after high school	⭕
Yes, after staying out one year	⭕
Yes, after a longer period out of school	⭕
Don't know	⭕
No	⭕

Items From the School Questionnaire

SB002

2. As of October 1, 1980 (or the nearest date for which data are available), what was the total membership of your high school, and what were the memberships in grades 10 and 12? (IF NONE, WRITE "0")

Total high school membership	Grade 10	Grade 12
(A)	(B)	(C)

Items from the Questionnaires Used in the Analysis

SB018

18. Please indicate whether each of the following courses are taught in your school as separate courses. (CIRCLE ONE NUMBER ON EACH LINE)

		Yes	No
a.	Second-year algebra	1	2
b.	Art	3	4
c.	Auto mechanics	1	2
d.	Calculus	3	4
e.	Chemistry	1	2
f.	Drama	3	4
g.	Driver training	1	2
h.	Economics	3	4
i.	Ethnic Studies or Black Studies	1	2
j.	Family Life or Sex Education	3	4
k.	Geometry	1	2
l.	Third-year Spanish	3	4
m.	Third-year German	1	2
n.	Third-year French	3	4
o.	Home Economics	1	2
p.	Physics	3	4
q.	Psychology	1	2
r.	Russian	3	4
s.	Trigonometry	1	2
t.	Wood or machine shop	3	4

SB027

27. Which of these facilities are available at your school? (CIRCLE AS MANY NUMBERS AS APPLY)

a. Indoor lounge for students	1
b. Career information center	2
c. Occupational training center	3
d. Media production facilities	4
e. Remedial reading and/or remedial mathematics laboratory	5
f. Subject area resources center(s) other than central library	1
g. Departmental offices	2
h. Teaching resources center for teachers' use	3
i. Child care or nursery school facility	4
j. Student cafeteria	5

29. Please indicate whether or not your school currently offers each of the following programs to students. (CIRCLE ONE NUMBER ON EACH LINE)

	Offered	Not offered
a. Credit by contract	1	2
b. Travel for credit	3	4
c. Off-campus work experience or occupational training for credit	1	2
d. College Board Advanced Placement Courses	3	4
e. Student exchange program	1	2
f. Alternative school program	3	4
g. Special program for pregnant girls or mothers	1	2
h. Continuation school	3	4
i. Program for the gifted or talented	1	2
j. Bilingual program	3	4

Items from the Questionnaires Used in the Analysis

32. Please indicate whether or not this high school participates or has students who participate in each of the following federally assisted or financed programs. (CIRCLE ONE NUMBER ON EACH LINE)

	School/Students participate(s)	School/Students do(es) not participate
a. Upward Bound	1	2
b. Talent Search	1	2
c. Elementary and Secondary Education Act:		
1. Title I (Education of children of economically disadvantaged)	1	2
2. Title IV-B (Library and learning resources)	1	2
3. Title IV-C (Educational innovation and support)	1	2
4. Title IV-D (Supplementary educational centers and services)	1	2
5. Title VII (Bilingual education)	1	2
6. Title IX (Ethnic heritage studies)	1	2
d. Indian Education Act	1	2
e. Emergency School Aid Act (desegregation assistance)	1	2
f. School Assistance in Federally Affected Areas	1	2
g. Comprehensive Employment and Training Act (CETA)	1	2
h. Vocational Education Act of 1963:		
1. Consumer and Homemaking Education	1	2
2. Vocational Education Basic Programs	1	2
3. Vocational Education for persons with special needs	1	2
4. Cooperative Vocational Education Program	1	2
5. High School Vocational Education Work-Study Program	1	2
i. Junior ROTC	1	2

SB033

33. Please indicate whether or not your school uses each of the following criteria to classify students as handicapped. (CIRCLE ONE NUMBER ON EACH LINE)

	Yes	No
Standard tests for evaluating specific handicaps	1	2
Federal guidelines	1	2
State guidelines	1	2
Judgments and observations of school counselors and teachers	1	2

SB034

34. How many students in your high school are classified as handicapped? (IF NONE, WRITE "0")

Number of handicapped students: _____

Items from the Questionnaires Used in the Analysis

35. How does your high school usually accommodate the following types of handicapped students? (CIRCLE ONE NUMBER ON EACH LINE)

	Attend regular classes only	Attend some special and some regular classes	Attend special classes only	No students with this type of handicap in school
a. Multiple handicapped	1	2	3	4
b. Trainable mentally retarded	1	2	3	4
c. Educable mentally retarded	1	2	3	4
d. Hard of hearing	1	2	3	4
e. Deaf	1	2	3	4
f. Deaf-blind	1	2	3	4
g. Speech impaired	1	2	3	4
h. Visually impaired	1	2	3	4
i. Emotionally disturbed	1	2	3	4
j. Orthopedically impaired	1	2	3	4
k. Other health impaired	1	2	3	4
l. Specific learning disabilities	1	2	3	4

SB039

39. Please indicate the size of your high school's staff in each of the following categories. (ENTER NUMBER OR ZERO ON EACH LINE)

	Number of full-time (or full-time equivalent) personnel
a. Assistant principals and deans	_____
b. Counselors	_____
c. Classroom teachers	_____
d. Curriculum specialists	_____
e. Remedial specialists	_____
f. Librarians/media specialists	_____
g. Psychologists	_____
h. Teaching aides	_____
i. Student teachers	_____
j. Volunteers	_____
k. Contributed services	_____
l. Security guards	_____

SB054

54. Listed below are certain rules which some schools have. Please indicate whether or not each is enforced in your high school. (CIRCLE ONE NUMBER ON EACH LINE)

	Yes	No
a. School grounds closed to students at lunch	1	2
b. Students responsible to the school for property damage	3	4
c. Hall passes required	1	2
d. "No smoking" rules	3	4
e. Rules about student dress	1	2

Items from the Questionnaires Used in the Analysis

56. To what degree is each of these matters a problem in your high school?
(CIRCLE ONE NUMBER ON EACH LINE)

	Serious	Moderate	Minor	Not at all
a. Student absenteeism	1	2	3	4
b. Students' cutting classes	1	2	3	4
c. Parents' lack of interest in students' progress	1	2	3	4
d. Parents' lack of interest in school matters	1	2	3	4
e. Teacher absenteeism	1	2	3	4
f. Teachers' lack of commitment or motivation	1	2	3	4
g. Physical conflicts among students	1	2	3	4
h. Conflicts between students and teachers	1	2	3	4
i. Robbery or theft	1	2	3	4
j. Vandalism of school property	1	2	3	4
k. Student use of drugs or alcohol	1	2	3	4
l. Rape or attempted rape	1	2	3	4
m. Student possession of weapons	1	2	3	4
n. Verbal abuse of teachers	1	2	3	4

REFERENCES

Abramowitz, S., and Stackhouse, E. A. *Private High School Today*. Washington, D.C.: National Institute of Education, 1980.

Alexander, K. L., and McDill, E. C. "Selection and Allocation Within Schools: Some Causes and Consequences of Curriculum Placement." *American Sociological Review* 41 (1976):963–80.

Baumol, W. J., and Bowen, W. G., *Performing Arts: The Economic Dilemma*. Cambridge, Mass.: MIT Press, 1968.

Becker, H. J., McPartland, J. M., and Thomas, G. E. "The Measurement of Segregation: The Dissimilarity Index and Coleman's Segregation Index Compared." Social Statistics Section, paper presented at the Annual Meeting of the American Statistical Association, 1978.

Campbell, D. "Comment on the Draft Report of Public and Private Schools." *School Research Forum* (April 1981):35.

Coleman, J. "Methods and Results in the IEA Studies of Effects of School on Learning." *Review of Educational Research* 45 (Summer 1975):335–86.

Coleman, J. *Longitudinal Data Analysis*. New York: Basic Books, 1981.

Coleman, J., and Kelley, S. *The Urban Predicament*, edited by William Gorham and Nathan Glazer, Washington, D.C., 1976, pp. 231–80.

Coleman, J., Hoffer, T., and Kilgore, S. *Public and Private Schools*. Final report submitted to National Center for Education Statistics, December 1981a.

Coleman, J., Hoffer, T., and Kilgore, S. "Questions and Answers: Our Response." *Harvard Educational Review*, (Fall 1981b):

Coleman, J., Hoffer, T., and Kilgore, S. "A Further Look at Achievement and Segregation in Secondary Schools." *Sociology of Education* (special issue, April 1982).

Coleman, J., Kelley, S., and Moore, J. *Trends in School Segregation: 1968–1973*. Washington: The Urban Institute, 1975.

Coleman, J., Bartot, V., Lewin-Epstein, N., and Olson, L. "Pluralistic Policy Research Design." Report submitted to the National Center of Education Statistics, 1979.

Coleman, J., Campbell, E., et al. *Equality for Educational Opportunity*. U.S. Department of Health, Education, and Welfare, Office of Education. Washington, D.C.: U.S. Government Printing Office, 1966.

Conant, J. B. *The American High School Today*. New York: McGraw-Hill, 1959.

Cortese, C. F., Falk, R. F., and Cohen, F. "Further Considerations on the Methodoligical Analysis of Segregation Indices." *American Sociological Review* 41 (1976):630–637.

Cronbach, L. J. "Rejoinder to Coleman." Paper presented at the Annual Meeting of the American Education Research Association, Los Angeles, April, 1981.

DiPrete, T. "Discipline and Order in American High Schools." Report submitted to the National Center for Education Statistics, 1981.

Draper, N., and Smith, H. *Applied Regression Analysis*. New York: John Wiley, 1966.

Elmore, R. "Follow Through: Decisionmaking in a Large-Scale Social Experiment." Harvard University, 1976.

Erickson, D. A., Nault, R. L., and Cooper, B. "Recent Enrollment Trends in U.S. Nonpublic Schools." In *Declining Enrollments: The Challenge of the Coming Decade*, edited by Susan Ambramowitz and Stuart Rosenfelds, Washington, D.C.: National Institute of Education, 1978.

Farley, R., Richards, T., and Wurdock, C. "School Desegregation and White Flight: An Investigation of Competing Models and Their Discrepant Findings" *Sociology of Education* 53 (July 1980):123–39.

Fienberg, S. *The Analysis of Cross Classified Categorical Data*, Cambridge, Mass.; MIT Press, 1977.

References

Galladay, M. A., and Wulfsburg, R. M. *Condition of Vocational Education*. Washington, D.C.: National Center for Education Statistics, 1980.

Goldberger, A. "The Causal Analysis of Cognitive Outcomes in the Coleman, Hoffer, and Kilgore Report." *Sociology of Education* (April 1982).

Hanushek, E. A. "Teacher Characteristics and Gains in Student Achievement: Estimation Using Micro-Data." *American Economic Review* (May 1971):

Hanushek, E. A. "Throwing Money at Schools." *Journal of Policy Analysis and Management* (Fall 1981):

Hanushek, E. A., and Jackson, J. E. *Statistical Methods for Social Scientists*. New York: Academic Press, 1977.

Heckman, J. J. "Sample Selection Bias as Specification Error." *Econometric* 47 (January 1979):153–62.

Heyns, B. *Summer Learning and the Effects of Schooling*. New York: Academic Press, 1978.

Jencks, C. "What's Behind the Drop in Test Scores?" *Working Papers for a New Society*. Cambridge, Massachusetts: Cambridge Policy Studies Institute, 1978.

Kish, L., and Frankel, M. R. "Inferences From Complex Samples." *Journal of the Royal Statistics Society* Series B (Methodological) 36 (1974):1–37.

Kraushaar, O. F. *American Nonpublic Schools*. Baltimore: The Johns Hopkins University Press, 1972.

Levine, E. M. "The Declining Educational Achievement of Middle Class Students, the Deterioration of Educational and Social Standards, and Parents' Negligence." *Social Spectrum* (1980):17–33.

Lewin-Epstein, N. "Youth Employment During High School." Report submitted to the National Center for Education Statistics, 1981.

Lott, J. R., and Fremling, G. M. *Juvenile Delinquency and Education: An Economic Study*. Los Angeles: International Institute for Economic Research, Westwood Center, 1980.

McLaughlin, D. H., and Wise, L. L. Nonpublic Education of the Nation's Children. "Palo Alto: American Institute for Research" (April). (mimeograph), 1980.

Mort, P. *Principles of School Administration*. New York: McGraw-Hill, 1946.

Murnane, R. J. *The Impact of School Resources on the Learning of Inner-City School Children*. Cambridge, Mass.: Ballinger, 1975.

Murnane, R. J. "Evidence, Analysis and Unanswered Questions." *Harvard Educational Review* 53 (1981):4.

National Assessment of Educational Progress. "Reading and Mathematics Achievement in Public and Private Schools: Is There a Difference?" (mimeograph), 1981.

National Catholic Educational Association. *How to Service Students with Federal Educational Program Benefits*. 1980.

National Catholic Educational Association. *Summary and Evaluation Report*. National Catholic Educational Association, 1980.

National Longitudinal Survey of High School Seniors. Washington, D.C.: U.S. Department of Health, Education, and Welfare, National Center for Education Statistics, 1972.

Nielsen, F., and Fernandez, R. "Hispanic Students in United States High Schools." Report submitted to the National Center for Education Statistics, 1981.

Page, E., and Keith, T. "Effects of U.S. Private Schools: A Technical Analysis of Two Recent Claims." *Educational Researcher* 10 (August 1981):7–17.

Plackett, R. L. and Burman, J. P. "The Design of Optimum Multifactorial Experiments." *Biometrika* 33 (1946): 305–25.

Project Talent. Washington, D.C.: U.S. Department of Health, Education, and Welfare, Office of Education, 1960.

Rivlin, A. M., and Timpane, P. M. *Planned Variation in Education: Should We Give Up or Try Harder?* Washington, D.C.: Brookings, 1975.

Rutter, M., et al. *Fifteen Thousand Hours*. Cambridge Mass.: Harvard University Press, 1979.

Schwartz, J., and Winship, C. "The Welfare Approach to Measuring Inequality." In *Sociological Methodology 1980*, edited by Karl F. Schuessler, San Francisco: Jossey-Bass, 1979.

Taubman, P., ed. *Kinometrics: Determinants of Sociometric Success Within and Between Families*. Amsterdam, New Holland, 1977.

Thomas, G. E., Alexander, K., and Eckland, B. K. "Access to Higher Education: The Importance of Race, Sex, Social Class and Academic Credentials." *School Review* 57 (1979):133–57.

Toby, J. "Crime in American Public Schools." *The Public Interest* (Winter 1980):18–42.

West, E. G. "Education and Crime: A Political Economy of Interdependents." *Character* 1 (1980):5–7.

Zoloth, S. S. "Alternative Measures of School Segregation." *Land Economics* 52 (1976):278–98.

INDEX

Abramowitz, Susan, 23n, 30, 279
Absenteeism, 108, 110, 111; assessment of, 5–14(112); cognitive achievement and, 160–63; questionnaire item on, 255
Academic achievement: self-esteem and, 117; *see also* Cognitive achievement
Academic programs, 200–201
Academic demands, 187–93
Academic subjects: course offerings in, 73–77; coursework in, 90–94
Access: to data and reports, 223–24; to private education, 48–64; to resources, *see* Student access
Achievement, models of, *see* Cognitive Achievement
Advanced degrees: plans for attaining, 131, 132; teachers holding, 80–81
Affective development, policy premise on, 183
Affiliation of schools: day-boarding mix and, 2–8(27); geographical distribution and, 18; selected statistics by, 2–5(24); sex of students served, 2–7(26)
Alcohol use, 110, 111; assessment of, 5–14(113)
Alexander, K. L., 201, 279, 281
Algebra 2, 74; coursework in, 92
Alternative credit programs, 82
Alternative-school programs, 82–83
Amish, 192n
Anglos, *see* Whites
Aspirations, parental, 58–63
Assistant principals, 80
Athletics, participation in, 95, 97
Attendance, 108; cognitive achievement and, 167, 169, 172; good, percentage of students reporting, 5–13(109); problems in, *see* Absenteeism
Attitudes, students', 115–20
Authority, constraints on exercise of, 189–90
Auto mechanics, 77–78

Background of students: cognitive achievement and, 137–51; comparable differences in school functioning for, 167–68; economic, 37–43; means for variables used in regression equations, A–5(235); outcomes of schooling and, 136–59; post-high-school plans and, 151–59; program assignment and, 200–201; questionnaire

items on, 257–60, 266–69; racial and ethnic, 29–37; regression coefficients, standard errors, and explained variance, A–6(236), A–7(237), A–8(238), A–9(239), A–10(240), A–11(241), A–12(242), A–13(243), A–16(246); religious, 43–46; standardized, estimated increments to test scores with, 6–7(138)
Balanced Repeated Replications, 14
Band, participation in, 95
Baptist schools, 24–27, 44
Baptists, 44
Bartot, V., 222n, 279
Baumol, W. J., 70, 279
Becker, H. J., 32n, 279
Behavior, student, 103–15; attendance and, 5–13(109), 108; cognitive achievement and, 160–62, 168–75, 206–8; disciplinary climate and, 6–22(174); involvement in school and, 103–8; problem, 108–15; questionnaire item on, 277
Bilingual programs, 82
Black studies, 77
Blacks, 30–37, 185; in Catholic schools, 9, 49, 51–57, 194; cognitive achievement of, 143–45; economic background of, 41–42; geographic distribution of, 49–51; income levels of, 51–57; increase in income of, 65–71; indices of intergroup contact and segregation, 3–2(33); integration of, 189; parental social status and aspirations of, 58–63; percentage distribution of, 3–1(31), 3–3(35); plans for higher education of, 158, 159; predicted enrollment rates in Catholic schools, 3–16(63); proportion of, in local area, 234–35; regional differences in segregation of, 216–20; underenrollment in private schools of, 48–49, 183
Boarding schools, percentage distribution of, 2–8(27)
Books in home, 139
Bowen, W. G., 70, 279
Burman, J. P., 280
Business courses, 89–91
Busing, 196–97

Cafeterias, student, 83, 84
Calculus, 75; coursework in, 91, 92
California, educational voucher proposal in, 3–4, 123

Index

High School and Beyond survey, *xxi*, *xxvii*, *xxix*, 166*n*, 222; sample design report, 10*n*; for study of blacks and hispanics, 30
Hispanics, 30–37, 185; in Catholic schools, 48, 52–57; coding procedure on, 251; geographic distribution of, 49–51; income levels of, 51–57; increase in income of, 65–71; indices of intergroup contact and segregation of, 3–2(33); outcomes of education for, 138, 143–45; parental social status and aspirations of, 58–63; percentage distribution of, 3–1(31), 3–4(35); plans for higher education of, 158, 159; predicted enrollment rates into Catholic schools, 3–16(63); proportion of, in local area, 234–35; regional differences in segregation of, 216–20; segregation of, 183
History courses, 89, 91
Hobby clubs, 95
Hoffer, T., 36*n*, 279
Home economics, 77–78
Homework, time spent on, 103, 105; average, 5–10(104); coding procedure on, 251; cognitive achievement and, 167, 169–71, 207; questionnaire item on, 254; time spent watching television compared with, 5–11(106)
Honors courses, coding procedure on, 251
Household composition, 139; questionnaire item on, 257
Household possessions, 139; coding procedure on, 251; questionnaire item on, 269

IEA studies, *xxvi*
Income level, family, 39; access to private education and, 51–57; of blacks versus whites, 48; indices of contact and segregation by, 3–6(40); outcomes of schooling and, 138, 143; percentage distribution by, 3–5(38); percentage of private school enrollment by race and, 3–17(67); policy premise on, 182; predicted impact of changes in, 65–71, 184; questionnaire items on, 268–69; social status and aspirations and, 58–63
Inequality, student concern for, 117, 120; percentage distribution of, 5–17(119)
Interest: of students in school, 5–12(107), 103, 105, 108, 181; of teachers in students, 5–9(100), 100–102, 117
Interest groups, 221
Intergroup contact: estimates of, 3–2(33), 32; measurement of, 231–235; regional factors in, 216–20
Internal Revenue Service, 4
Involvement in school, 103–8

Jackson, J. E., 58, 280

Japanese schools, 192
Jencks, C., 188*n*, 280
Jewish schools, *xxviii*, 24–27
Jews, 43
Jobs, post-high-school plans for, 134; percentage distribution of job status, 6–6(135); questionnaire item on, 265

Keith, T., 194*n*, 280
Kelly, S., 32*n*, 188*n*, 215, 279
Kilgore, S., 36*n*, 279
Kirst, Michael, 225*n*
Kish, L., 14, 280
Klitgard, Robert, 225*n*
Kratwohl, 225*n*
Kraushaar, O., 26, 30, 280

Labor, U.S. Department of, 85*n*
Laboratories, remedial, 84
Language courses, *see* Foreign languages
Lateness: cognitive achievement and, 160–63; questionnaire items on, 255
Leadership experience, self-esteem and, 117; learning rates, *see* growth rates
Least squares estimation procedure, 58
Least squares regression analysis, criticism of, 201–9
Levine, E. M., 190*n*, 280
Lewin-Epstein, Noah, 105, 222*n*, 225*n*, 279, 280
Librarians, 79
Library program, federal, 85, 86
LISREL technique, 201
Lott, J. R., 4*n*, 280
Lounges, student, 83, 84
Lutheran schools, *xxviii*, 24–27, 44
Lutherans, 44

McDill, E. C., 201, 279
Machine shop, 77–78
McLaughlin, D. H., 27*n*, 280
McPartland, J. M., 279
Mann, Horace, *xxix*, 48
Mathematics: achievement test scores on, 6–7(138), 6–8(142), 6–21(171), 129, 130; coding procedure for courses in, 251; cognitive growth in, 148, 150–51; course offerings in, 4–1(74), 4–2(75), 74–76; coursework in, 90–92, 187; differences in achievement in, 191, 214–15; discipline problems and scores on, 161–62; remedial, physical facilities for, 84
Measures of distribution, calculation of, 231–33; relative to racial or ethnic composition of local area, 234–35
Media production facilities, 84
Media specialists, 79

285

Index

Policy premises: decreasing role of private schools, 5, 182–84; increasing role of private schools, 4–5, 179–81

Postal Service, U.S., 49

Post-high-school plans, 131–34; background and, 151–59; questionnaire items on, 261, 270; *see also* College plans

Practical courses, 77–78

Pregnant girls, programs for, 82

Private schools: policy issues concerning, 3–7, 178–85; program assignment in, 200; *see also* Catholic schools; other (non-Catholic) private schools

Process variables, 187

Professional staff, ratio of students to, 79

Project Talent, *xxxv, xxvii*, 280

Property damage: enforcement of rules on, 98–99; *see also* Vandalism

Psychology courses, 77

Public Law 94–142, 189

Public schools; academic demands in, 187; cognitive achievement in, 6–7(138), 6–8(142), 6–9(144), 6–11(149), 6–12(150), 6–17(161), 6–18(163), 6–19(165), 6–20(169), 6–21(171), 6–22(174), 124, 127–29, 137, 139–41, 143–44, 146–51, 159–64, 168, 170–75; college expectations in, 6–13(152), 6–14(154), 6–15(156); constraints on exercise of authority in, 189; course offerings in, 4–1(74), 4–2(75), 75–78; coursework in, 5–1(90), 5–2(92), 5–3(93), 5–4(94), 90–94; disciplinary standards of, 5–8(99), 97–103, 120–21; dropout estimation for, 6–10(149); economic background of students in, 3–5(38), 3–6(40), 37–43; equality of educational opportunity in, 194–96; expected educational attainment in, 6–4(132), 6–13(152), 6–16(158); extracurricular activities in, 5–5(96), 5–6(97), 95, 97; federal programs in, 4–6(86), 84–86; geographic distribution of, 18–23; handicapped students in, 3–9(47), 3–10(47), 46–48; high-performance, *see* High-performance schools; job status for seniors in, 6–6(135); mean scores on subtests in, 6–3(126); means and standard deviations for test scores in, 6–1(125), 6–2(125); number and size of, 2–1(17); outcomes of education in, 122–24, 134–36, 175–78; physical facilities of, 4–5(83), 83–84; policy issues concerning, 3–7, 179–85; post-high-school plans in, 131, 152–53, 155–58; program assignment in, 200–201; racial and ethnic background of students in, 3–1(31), 3–2(33), 3–3(35), 3–4(35), 3–11(50), 3–12(53), 29–37; regional aspects of segregation in, X–1(217), X–2(218), X–3(219), 216–20; religious background of students in, 3–7(44), 3–8(45), 43–46; research classification of, 9–10; rule enforcement in, 5–7(98); sample of, 10–14;

special programs in, 4–4(81), 82–83; staffing patterns of, 4–3(79), 78–81; student attitudes in, 5–15(116), 5–16(118), 5–17(119), 115, 117, 120; student behavior in, 5–10(104), 5–11(106), 5–12(107), 5–13(109), 5–14(112–13), 103, 105, 108, 110–11, 115; teacher interest in, 5–9(100); time of entry for college in, 6–5(133)

Puerto Ricans, *see* Hispanics

Quality of school personnel, 80–81

Questionnaire items, 250–77; on absenteeism, 255; on background, 257–60, 266–69; coding procedures for, 250–51; on course offerings, 271; on coursework, 252–54; on discipline, 255–56; on educational expectations, 263–64; on extracurricular activities, 256–57; on federal programs, 273; on functioning of schools, 261; on handicapped students, 265–66, 274–75; on homework, 254; on job plans, 265; on lateness, 255; on post-high-school plans, 261, 270; on rules, 276; on school facilities, 271; on self-concept, 262–63; on size of school, 270; on special programs, 272; on staffing patterns, 276; on student behavior, 277

Racial background of students, 3–1(31), 3–2(33), 3–3(35), 3–4(35), 28–37; discipline and, 100; Census data on, 49; coding procedure on, 251; economic background and, 41–42; by local geographic area, 3–11(50), 234–35; outcomes of education and, 138, 143, 145; plans for higher education and, 158, 159; questionnaire item on, 266; segregation by, 32–37; *see also* Blacks; Whites

Reading: achievement test scores on, 6–7(138), 6–8(142), 6–17(161), 6–18(163), 6–21(171), 129, 130; remedial, 84

Regional indices of interracial contact and segregation, X–2(218), X–3(219)

Regional percentage distribution of students, 2–2(19), 18; by race, X–1(217)

Religious background, 43–46; access and, 48–49; indices of contact and segregation by, 3–8(45); organization of education around, *xxviii, xxix*; percentage distribution of, 3–7(44); and percentage distribution of enrollment in Catholic schools, 55–57; policy premises on, 182; questionnaire item on, 266

Remedial education: physical facilities for, 83, 84; specialists in, 79

Research design, pluralistic, 222–23

Residence, organization of education around, *xxviii, xxix*; segregation through, 29, 37–38, 196–97

Index